Exploring the Geology of the Carolinas

Kevin G. Stewart and Mary-Russell Roberson

Exploring the Geology of the Carolinas

» A FIELD GUIDE TO FAVORITE PLACES FROM CHIMNEY ROCK TO CHARLESTON

THE UNIVERSITY OF NORTH CAROLINA PRESS » CHAPEL HILL

Designed by Heidi Perov
Set in Warnock
Manufactured in the United States of America

Publication of this book was supported by subventions from
Friends of State Parks (http://ncfsp.org) and the Tar Heel Gem
and Mineral Club (http://www.tarheelclub.org).

Unless otherwise noted, the photographs, maps, and diagrams
are by Kevin Stewart.

The paper in this book meets the guidelines for permanence and
durability of the Committee on Production Guidelines for Book
Longevity of the Council on Library Resources.

Library of Congress Cataloging-in-Publication Data
Stewart, Kevin G. (Kevin George)
    Exploring the geology of the Carolinas : a field guide to favorite
    places from Chimney Rock to Charleston / by Kevin G. Stewart,
    Mary-Russell Roberson.
        p. cm.
    Includes bibliographical references and index.
    ISBN 978-0-8078-3077-2 (alk. paper)
    ISBN 978-0-8078-5786-1 (pbk. : alk. paper)
1. Geology—North Carolina—Guidebooks. 2. Geology—South
Carolina—Guidebooks.
I. Roberson, Mary-Russell. II. Title
QE627.5.N8S74 2007
557.56—dc22   2006018985

To Mark and Susannah

    & Carolyn, Maia, and Alex

CONTENTS

A section of plates appears after page 74.

This book is for anyone who has ever wondered:

- Why does Pilot Mountain rise abruptly out of a fairly flat landscape?
- Why do you find so much mica in the mountains but none at the beach?
- Why is Mount Mitchell the tallest mountain east of the Mississippi?
- Why do ocean inlets always seem to be opening, closing, or moving?
- How did Jockey's Ridge get to be so big?
- How were the Appalachians formed?
- What is it about our mountains that makes them such good places to find gems?
- What kind of dinosaur fossils have been found in the Carolinas?
- How have plate tectonics affected the Carolinas?

We will answer all these questions and more in this book, and we will do it in a way that nonscientists can understand. If you're interested in knowing the stories of the geologic events that have shaped the landscape of the Carolinas, this book is for you.

ACKNOWLEDGMENTS

Heartfelt thanks to those who donated their time and expertise to review
the manuscript. We are particularly indebted to Dr. Chris Tacker, curator
of geology at the North Carolina Museum of Natural Sciences, who read
through our manuscript twice and went above and beyond the call of duty
in making an incredible number of insightful suggestions that improved our
book both in content and style. Others who reviewed significant portions
of the manuscript include Andrea Bachl, Catherine Clabby, Tyler Clark,
Jim Hibbard, Don Raleigh, Ruth Roberson, Cheryl Waters-Tormey, and an
anonymous reviewer for UNC Press. Thanks also to park rangers, geologists,
anthropologists, museum curators, botanists, reference librarians, and others who reviewed individual chapters, answered questions, provided information, or helped with photographs, including Ron Anundson, Norman
Beaver, Beth Bilderback, Richard Boyd, Kathryn Boyle, Ryan Boyles, Liz
Butler, Boyd Cathey, Dave Cook, Kelly Cooke, Lisa Coombs, Robin Copp,
Jeff Corbett, Kim Cumber, Randy Daniel, Edward Farr, Lori Fleming, Kenny
Gay, Brian Gomsak, John Graham, Cynthia Gurganus, Duncan Heron, Jack
Horan, Jeff Horton, Mark Johnson, Marti Kane, Miriam Kennard, Rich-
ard Knapp, Jim Knight, Dennis LaPoint, Paula LaPoint, Ida Lynch, Merrill
Lynch, Lindsay Pettus, Bert Pittman, Lynn Richardson, Russell Roberson,
Maria Sadowski, Janell Sauls, James Sorrell, David Southern, Karen Swa-
ger, Dillard Teer, Rich Thompson, Cindy Tripp, Jim Ward, Ken Wright, and
Gene Yogodzinski.

Thanks to dozens of anonymous reference librarians at the Durham Public Library, the North Carolina Collection at the University of North Carolina at Chapel Hill, the UNC Department of Geological Sciences library, the
South Caroliniana Collection at the University of South Carolina in Columbia, Perkins and Lilly libraries at Duke University, the North Carolina
Archives, and the United States Geological Survey.

Boundless thanks to our indexer, Sue Marchman, who made the index to
this book a thing of beauty and utility.

Mary-Russell would particularly like to thank her family and friends for
helping with child care and other domestic duties, engaging in lengthy dis-

cussions about the aptness of one word or another, discussing the pros and cons of various titles, and for answering many, many questions along the lines of "Is 'scarp' a regular word or a geology word? What do you know about plate tectonics? If I said a mineral crystal was platy, would you know what I meant?" She would also like to thank her writing teachers and members of her writing groups and book clubs for many years of stimulating discussion, exceptional insight, rigorous criticism, and sparkling company.

Kevin would like to thank the Chapman family and the Institute of the Arts and Humanities at the University of North Carolina at Chapel Hill for a Chapman Family Fellowship during the writing of this book. The semester spent at the institute was an extraordinary experience, and he is indebted to his fellow Fellows for their insight, encouragement, and sound advice. Many thanks to Stephen Birdsall, Kathryn Burns, Erin Carlston, John Covach, Arturo Escobar, Derek Goldman, Sue Goodman, Beth Grabowski, Shantanu Phukan, Francesca Talenti, Karla Slocum, Ruel Tyson, and Julia Wood.

Kevin would also like to thank all of the UNC-CH graduate students who have contributed to his understanding of Carolina geology: Mark Adams, Josh Borella, Forrest Burton, J. P. Dubé, John Foudy, Lauren Hewitt, Jon Mies, Kara Syvertsen, Charles Trupe, Cheryl Waters-Tormey, and Rod Willard.

Finally, this book could not have been written if not for the work of J. Robert Butler, a professor of geology at UNC who passed away unexpectedly in 1996. This book began as a collaboration between Bob and Mary-Russell, and the chapters on Pilot Mountain and Morrow Mountain were written by them. Kevin was introduced to the fascinating geology of the Carolinas by Bob, and Bob's decades of research provided the foundation for this book, as well as for the work of many other geologists. This book is in memory of Bob.

This book is not intended to be read straight through. We recommend that you read Chapters 1–5 first for a general introduction to some important topics in geology and for an overview of the geologic history of the Carolinas. After that, pick and choose among the field trip chapters as your interests and your travels dictate. Or start right in with the field trips, and refer back to the first five chapters and to the glossary when you need to.

If a favorite spot of yours is not in the table of contents, check the index; it may be discussed in the Nearby Features section of another field trip. When you are planning a visit to a site in this book you might want to get some topographic or trail maps ahead of time (see Additional Resources). Looking at a topographic map can help you pick out interesting landforms, as well as help you locate yourself once you're there.

Even though we want you to pick up rocks to look at them closely, please remember that rock collecting is not allowed in state parks and most other public areas unless you have a special permit. The same goes for plants, archaeological artifacts, and even fulgurites. (Don't know what a fulgurite is? See Chapter 33.)

As you use our book, we hope you will begin to see the Carolinas with new eyes—looking at rocks and landforms with newfound attention and wondering about them, listening for what stories those rocks and landforms can tell you. Knowing a little geology can open up a whole new way of enjoying the outdoors.

Once you begin thinking about the landscape this way, you can begin to notice how often the geologic history of a place lays the foundation for the human history of the place. Morrow Mountain is an archaeological treasure trove because it's composed of a type of rock perfectly suited for making stone tools (see Chapter 19). The nation's first gold rush started in the Carolinas because of an ancient volcanic system that started out on another continent and was later added to North America (see Chapter 17). The Wright brothers chose North Carolina for their flying experiments because that's where they could find a tall soft mountain of sand and lots of wind (see Chapter 33).

As Claude Lévi-Strauss wrote in *Tristes Tropiques*, "Every landscape offers, at first glance, an immense disorder which may be sorted out howsoever we please. We may sketch out the history of its cultivation, plot the accidents of geography which have befallen it, and ponder the ups and downs of history and prehistory: but the most august of investigations is surely that which reveals what came before . . . and in large measure explains all the others" (Claude Lévi-Strauss, *Tristes Tropiques*, trans. John Russell [New York: Atheneum, 1964], 59–60).

We invite you to join us in this "most august of investigations."

The Changing Face of the Carolinas over Geologic Time

When you think of North and South Carolina, what kinds of landscapes come to mind? Sand dunes and wide beaches? Forests and farms? Swamps? Red clay fields? Rolling, green mountains?

All these are present in the Carolinas today, but geologically speaking, "today" is just an instant.

If we could go back in time in the Carolinas, we'd see great rift valleys, shark-filled seas, and soaring mountains. We'd hear and feel volcanoes and violent earthquakes. We'd travel to the South Pole and the equator and countless other places on the globe. While we can't take the trip ourselves, the rocks of the Carolinas have; they contain clues that geologists use to piece together the Carolinas' long and tumultuous geologic history.

Two motors drive geologic change: weather and plate tectonics—the slow but inexorable movement of pieces, or plates, of the earth's outer shell. The plates collide with one other, slide past one another, and pull apart from one another, producing earthquakes, volcanoes, mountains, and ocean basins, and recycling old rocks into new ones deep inside the earth. Landscapes produced by plate tectonics are then sculpted and rearranged by rain, rivers, wind, and glaciers. Water, ice, and plants force their way into cracks in rock, splitting the rock into smaller pieces, which eventually crumble into small grains. Rain and wind tear down broken-up rock, and rivers and glaciers carry the pieces away, depositing them at lower elevations. Rates of erosion vary significantly from place to place, depending on climate, topography, and the nature of the bedrock. Wetter climates tend to break up rocks faster than arid climates because they produce more rain, more rivers, and more vegetation. Huge valley-filling glaciers move more sediment than do trickling streams. Streams racing down steep mountainsides erode more sediment than slow ones on the plains.

The Carolinas have experienced all different kinds of climates and landscapes over millions of years. In fact, before about 330 million years ago, "the Carolinas" weren't even all in one piece—different parts of the states were on different continents and moving in different directions.

To get the picture, let's look at some snapshots of the earth and the Carolinas over geologic time. About seven hundred million years ago, before there were any plants or animals on land, the Carolinas were covered by a thick layer of ice. All the continents were grouped together near the equator, forming a supercontinent called Rodinia. (One might ask how the Carolinas could have been glaciated when they were at the equator. This was a time in earth history that geologists refer to as the "snowball earth," when as a result of a series of climatic and geologic events, most—if not all—of the earth was covered in ice.) As Rodinia broke up, gashes that looked like Africa's Great Rift Valley appeared, some of them on land that would later be part of the Carolinas.

Later, a large island with active volcanoes collided with the Carolinas, pushing up a mountain range. Something similar is happening in the South Pacific today—Australia is colliding with the islands of Irian Jaya–Papua New Guinea and Timor to the north, creating 16,000-foot-high mountains on the islands. When the volcanic island was colliding with the Carolinas—460 million years ago—the seas were full of clams, trilobites, starfish, and armored fish. Primitive plants and arthropods (ancient relatives of modern-day insects and crustaceans) were beginning to colonize the land.

After a later collision, when a continent made of parts of present-day South America and Africa hit the Carolinas, a huge chain of mountains with peaks soaring to 20,000 feet and higher stretched across the Carolinas. These were the fully grown Appalachians. Once again, all the continents were united near the equator. The early Appalachians may have resembled the present-day Andes—high glacier-covered peaks with tropical lower slopes. Insects, amphibians, and primitive reptiles lived on the swampy land; sharks dominated the seas. Mammals did not yet exist; nor did birds, dinosaurs, or flowers.

In the not too distant geologic past—a mere 100 million years ago—dinosaurs roamed the Carolinas. North and South Carolina were near their current locations on the globe, but the Coastal Plain was underwater, and the Piedmont probably was too. A warm climate had melted all the glaciers, causing the sea level to rise. Birds and mammals had evolved, although they would not flourish until the dinosaurs died out. Primates—monkeys, apes, and humans—did not yet exist.

The Carolinas Today

Today, the continents are still moving. We can't see the movement, but using satellite navigation systems, we can measure it at rates of inches per year. The dinosaurs are gone, as are countless other less spectacular species. Humans are by far the most numerous large mammals, at a global population of almost 6.5 billion in 2005.

In the Carolinas, rivers are wearing down the Appalachians, as they have been for millions of years. Water runs downhill, carrying rocks and soil with it, and joins with other water to form streams. When a river enters flatter topography, it slows, dumping some of its load. On reaching the sea, a river gives up all its sediment. In the western Carolinas, then, we have the remnants of a once-great mountain chain, and in the east, thousands of feet of sediments, stripped from those same mountains and laid down in a huge wedge. The wedge of sediments begins not too far east of Raleigh, North Carolina, and Columbia, South Carolina. It gradually increases in thickness, until it is about 10,000 feet thick under Cape Hatteras. Underneath those sediments are the same kinds of rocks found in the rest of the Carolinas—the roots of a great mountain range.

The Three Physiographic Provinces:
Blue Ridge, Piedmont, Coastal Plain

While the Carolinas can be seen as the roots of a single mountain range, they divide neatly into three physiographic provinces: the Blue Ridge, the Piedmont, and the Coastal Plain (Plate 1). "Physiography" refers to the shape of the land; each of our provinces has a distinct topography, and there is a good correspondence between the ruggedness or smoothness of the topography and the underlying geology.

The Blue Ridge Mountains in North and South Carolina are part of the Appalachians, which extend from Alabama to Newfoundland. The Appalachians are at their highest and most rugged in North Carolina, where there are 43 peaks above 6,000 feet. Mount Mitchell, at 6,684 feet, is the highest peak east of South Dakota's Black Hills. In South Carolina, the Blue Ridge reaches elevations of about 3,400 feet.

The Piedmont begins at an abrupt drop in elevation called the Blue Ridge escarpment, which runs from Virginia through South Carolina. The height of the escarpment varies from about 1,000 to 2,000 feet. A good place to experience the Blue Ridge escarpment is driving east on I-40 from the Eastern Continental Divide down to Old Fort, North Carolina. In less than 5 miles, the road loses about 1,500 feet in elevation—one of the steepest stretches of interstate highway in the country.

The Piedmont is an area of gently rolling hills that stretches all the way from New Jersey to Alabama. In northern New Jersey, the Piedmont is only 10 miles wide, but in North Carolina, it is at its widest—150 miles. The Carolina Piedmont reaches elevations of about 1,500 feet at the base of the Blue Ridge escarpment, and gradually declines to between 300 and 600 feet at the border with the Coastal Plain. The western Piedmont is dotted with monadnocks, or isolated hills, made of rocks that are more resistant to erosion than the surrounding rocks. These include Pilot Mountain and the Uwharrie Mountains in North Carolina, and Little Mountain, Glassy Mountain, and Paris Mountain in South Carolina.

The Piedmont ends and the Coastal Plain begins at the Fall Zone, which is the place where you would first encounter waterfalls and rapids if you were traveling upriver from the Coastal Plain, as many early settlers were. The falls are created by a step in the topography as the hard metamorphic and igneous rocks of the Piedmont give way to the soft sedimentary rocks of the Coastal Plain.

The Fall Zone was one of the first areas populated in colonial times, for two reasons. First, the falls and rapids often marked the limit of upstream navigation for boats coming inland. Second, the falls provided power for mills. Washington, D.C., and Richmond, Virginia, are prominent Fall Zone towns. Carolina Fall Zone towns include Raleigh, Roanoke Rapids, Rocky Mount, and Erwin in North Carolina and Columbia, North Augusta, and Cheraw in South Carolina.

The Coastal Plain is the largest province in the Carolinas, covering about 45 percent of North Carolina and about two-thirds of South Carolina. It is overlaid with sediments and sedimentary rocks, which get thicker from west to east. Underneath the sediments are hard metamorphic and igneous rocks similar to those in the Blue Ridge and the Piedmont. In southern North Carolina and northern South Carolina, there is an area of sand and sand dunes called the Sandhills. The Sandhills stand above the rest of the Coastal Plain, with a high point of 740 feet. Elevations in the rest of the Coastal Plain range from sea level to 300 or 400 feet.

Rivers flow wide and slow in the Coastal Plain, dropping sediment along the way. As rivers enter the ocean, they often form large estuaries, where the tide ebbs and flows, and fresh and salt water mix.

Geologic Processes Today

The main geologic processes taking place in the Carolinas today are erosion and deposition. As the rivers continue on their way to the sea, they strip material from the Blue Ridge and add it to the Coastal Plain. The Atlantic Ocean grows wider as the Americas move west and Europe and Africa move east. Sea level is rising, as it has been for the last 10,000 years. Aside from a very occasional earthquake, the Carolinas are geologically quiet. The towering peaks and volcanoes are long gone. Their amazing stories, however, are still being told by the rocks and landforms of present-day North and South Carolina. This book will help you learn how to "read" rocks so you can hear the stories.

How to Read Rocks

Just how do we know that a vast mountain chain towered above the Carolinas? Or that volcanoes erupted near Chapel Hill? Or that the sea once covered Kinston? In all sciences, researchers perform experiments and record the results. Geology is no different: geologists melt rocks, squeeze rocks in hydraulic presses, and run computer simulations. Geologists also measure and monitor the activity of earthquakes, volcanoes, and the earth's tectonic plates. But geology has an added component that not all other sciences do: piecing together events that happened in the past. In a sense, geologists' primary laboratory is nature, and most of their "experiments" have already been run. No human was around millions of years ago to record what happened in a lab notebook. Instead the record is contained in rocks. Geologists have learned to "read" rocks to figure out what processes produced them. Was it movement along a fault? Intense heat and pressure? Slow cooling of liquid rock?

Every rock tells a story, but some rocks speak more clearly than others. Basalt is produced by volcanic eruptions; there's no other way to get it. Sandstone, on the other hand, can form on a beach, along a river, or in a desert. While there are hundreds of different kinds of rocks, like basalt and sandstone, all rocks fall into three main categories: sedimentary, igneous, and metamorphic.

Sedimentary rocks are usually made of bits and pieces of other rocks that are deposited by water or wind. They can also be made of shells or other sediments produced by marine animals or terrestrial or marine plants. You can often recognize a sedimentary rock simply by noticing that there are sediment grains or fossils in it. You might also notice the layers, each layer representing a different episode of deposition.

Igneous rocks form when molten rock cools and solidifies. Molten rock can cool slowly deep underground, or erupt—sometimes explosively—out of a volcano at the earth's surface. When molten rock cools, the minerals crystallize into an interlocking network. Individual mineral crystals may be fairly large—a fraction of an inch to an inch across—or they may be too small to be seen with the naked eye.

Metamorphic rocks form when any kind of rock is subjected to enough heat and pressure to change it, but not enough to melt it. This usually happens deep underground when rocks are forcefully buried by collisions between pieces of the earth's crust called tectonic plates. Metamorphic rocks often have strongly deformed layers, which develop in response to intense pressure.

How to Read Sedimentary Rocks

Sedimentary rocks are formed by the deposition or accumulation of materials at the earth's surface and originate in one of three ways.

Clastic sedimentary rocks form by the accumulation of rock or mineral fragments that have been moved—by wind, water, ice, or landsliding—from one place to another. Some common clastic sedimentary rocks are sandstone (made of sand), conglomerate (made of particles coarser than sand), siltstone (made of particles finer than sand), and shale (made of very fine particles of clay and mud). To estimate the size of the particles in a clastic sedimentary rock, use the following guide: If the individual particles can be distinguished with the naked eye, but are smaller than about a sixteenth of an inch in diameter, the rock is sandstone. If the particles are greater than about a sixteenth of an inch in diameter—whether pebbles, cobbles, or boulders—it's conglomerate. If the particles are not visible to the naked eye, it's either siltstone or shale. To tell the difference between these two kinds of rock, geologists sometimes gently grind a small piece between their back teeth; siltstone feels gritty, shale does not.

Biogenic sedimentary rocks are made of sediments produced by plants and animals. For example, coal is made from plant remains. Limestone is commonly formed by the slow accumulation of the shells of single-celled marine life. Coquina is made from larger sea shells (see Figure 35-2).

Evaporites are formed by the evaporation of salt water. As salt water evaporates, different salts become concentrated to the point that they come out of solution as solids. Halite is an evaporite made of salt (sodium chloride). Gypsum is made of calcium sulfate. Evaporites are rare in the Carolinas, although in some of the sedimentary rocks in the Triassic basins (described in Chapter 21) there are small cube-shaped casts of what were once crystals of halite that have been dissolved away. Other evaporites can be found offshore, buried within the sediments of the continental shelf of the Carolinas. These are large balloon-shaped intrusions of salt called salt domes. They form because salt is less dense than most sedimentary rocks and therefore has a tendency to flow upward and punch its way through the overlying layers. Salt is ductile, meaning it can flow like thick putty, so it rises upward in dome-shaped pillars and blobs.

The place where sediments accumulate is called the environment of deposition. As we mentioned before, sandstone can be formed in more than one environment of deposition, such as a beach, a desert, or a river. Coal, on the other hand, always forms in swamps because the stagnant water in the bottoms of swamps tends to be oxygen poor, keeping the organic debris from oxidizing and disappearing. Coquina usually forms in the ocean. Some sediments are deposited in the same place they were produced, such as reef limestones. Other sediments are carried for miles, by water or wind, before they are deposited. For example, the quartz sand on the beach may have come from granite in the mountains.

Let's say you're looking at an outcrop of sedimentary rock and you want to figure out how it formed. There are several clues that you should look for. If the grains of sediment are big enough to see, take note of their size. If the grains are as large as marbles, then wind could not have carried those grains, but a fast-flowing stream could have. Are the grains all the same size (well sorted), or are they many different sizes (poorly sorted)? Wind tends to carry and deposit grains in a fairly small range of sizes (clay, silt, and fine sand), so wind-blown deposits are well sorted. Beach sands also tend to be well sorted. That's because most rivers travel over areas of low relief right before they dump their sediment into the ocean; they are not traveling fast enough to carry sediment larger than sand. Then, the wave action of the ocean winnows out particles smaller than sand, which are deposited farther offshore. (Not all beach sands in the world are well sorted, however. Where rivers cascade down coastal mountains directly into the ocean, they bring large and small sediments with them.) Sediments deposited by a glacier are never well sorted. Ice picks up everything it comes across, without regard to size, and melting ice dumps sediment in the same haphazard way.

We can also use the shape of the grains to learn something about the origin of a sedimentary rock. Smoothly rounded grains have usually traveled farther from their source than angular grains. That's because when sediment travels a long way, either by water or by wind, it bumps and bounces off the streambed or other particles, causing its corners to round off. In fact, windblown grains typically have a "frosted" surface because of their constant abrasion by neighboring grains.

If you can tell what the grains are made of, that might help you figure out where the sediment is from. The grains, after all, are samples of the original rock that was eroding upstream or upwind. Clastic sedimentary rocks mostly contain common minerals like quartz, feldspar, and clay, which are found just about everywhere. However, small amounts of rarer minerals, such as garnet or kyanite, may help you narrow down possible source areas for the sediment.

Now step back and look at the whole outcrop. Does the rock have any patterns? Is it layered? Sedimentary rocks are usually deposited as horizontal layers called beds, but in some kinds of sandstone, we see bedding that is tilted. For example, think of sand dunes. Dunes migrate because wind blows sand up the back side of the dune, then deposits it on the leeward side of the dune as a sloping pile of sand. The sand accumulates in layers on the leeward face of the dune, and the layers are inclined at angles ranging from 30 to 35 degrees. We can see these inclined layers—called cross-beds—preserved in sedimentary rock (Figure 2-1). Sometimes a rock preserves mud cracks or small ripple marks—just like the ripple marks you've probably seen in sand at a river's edge, at the beach, or on a dune. When you see ripple marks in a rock, you know the sediments were deposited by water or wind. When you see mud cracks in a rock, you know that the sediments were alternately saturated and dried out.

Biogenic sedimentary rocks, such as limestone or coal, usually contain bits of fossilized shells or plants. By looking at the kinds of animals or plants that contributed to making the rock, we can learn the age of the rock, whether or not it formed in the deep sea, at a tropical coral reef, or in a swamp, and what the climate was like at the time the sediments were deposited.

Evaporites, which indicate high rates of evaporation, form almost exclusively in deserts or other arid environments. The salty shores of the Great Salt Lake in Utah are a place where evaporites are being deposited today. The salt domes off the coast of North Carolina rose millions of years ago as flat layers of salt in a deep arid basin, one of many such basins that were formed when the supercontinent Pangea was tearing apart. Later the Atlantic Ocean flooded the area.

FIGURE 2-1. Inclined cross-beds within horizontal beds of sandstone in Utah.

How to Read Igneous Rocks

Igneous rocks form when molten rock cools. Molten rock is called magma when it's underground and lava when it reaches the earth's surface (as in a volcanic eruption). Magma is not everywhere below our feet, contrary to what you might see in movies. The processes that generate molten rock are most commonly found at plate boundaries—the places where pieces of the earth's outer shell are tearing apart, colliding, or sliding past one another. (We'll explore plate tectonics more fully in the next chapter. For now, all you need to know is that the surface of the earth is broken into about a dozen plates that move around very slowly.) Because of this association between molten rock and plate boundaries, much of the information we get from igneous rocks has to do with the way the plates move around. Whereas sedimentary rocks tell us about what was going on at the earth's surface, igneous rocks tell us about what was going on at plate boundaries.

When reading an igneous rock, the first step is to look at the size of the mineral grains in the rock. Large grains—those that are visible to the naked eye—mean the magma cooled slowly. Very small or microscopic grains mean that the molten rock cooled quickly (Figure 2-2). So if you find an

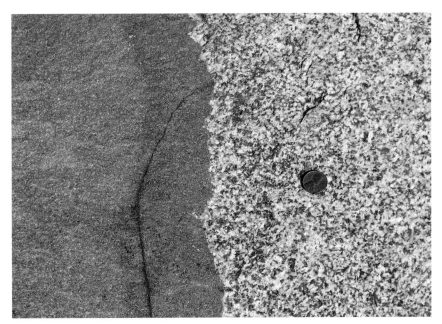

FIGURE 2-2. Fine-grained igneous rock, which cooled quickly, on the left (andesite); it was later intruded by coarse-grained igneous rock, which cooled slowly, on the right (diorite). Photo taken at the Bacon Quarry east of Hillsborough, North Carolina.

igneous rock with large grains, you know the rock cooled deep underground, solidifying gradually over a long period of time—anywhere from thousands to millions of years. These kinds of rocks are called plutonic igneous rocks, after Pluto, the Roman god of the underworld. If you find an igneous rock with very small grains, it probably came to the surface as lava from a volcano and cooled quickly—anywhere from a few seconds to a few days. These kinds of rocks are called volcanic igneous rocks, after Vulcan, the Roman god of fire.

Next, look at the color of the rock. Overall, is it light, dark, or in-between? These colors generally reflect the rock's chemical composition. Light-colored igneous rocks typically have lots of white and pink minerals with smaller amounts of dark minerals; they are rich in silica (a combination of the elements silicon and oxygen). A common silica-rich rock with visible crystals is granite. Granite's visible crystals tell us that the rock cooled slowly underground in a magma chamber. If the magma had cooled quickly, the rock would have hardened before large crystals had time to grow. When similar magma erupts as lava, the resulting rock has small grains and is called rhyolite. Light-colored igneous rocks, such as granite and rhyolite, most commonly form where two plates are coming together and at least one of the plates is a continent.

Dark igneous rocks are made mostly of gray, black, or dark green minerals. They have less silica and more calcium, iron, and magnesium. If the grains are visible, the rock is called gabbro; if the grains are microscopic, it is called basalt. Gabbro forms in underground magma chambers while basalt is hardened lava. Basalt and gabbro form most commonly where plates are pulling apart from one another.

A third class of igneous rock is intermediate in chemical composition between granite and basalt. These rocks either have a salt-and-pepper appearance (visible grains) or are relatively uniform gray (microscopic grains); the salt-and-pepper rock is called diorite (Figure 2-2). The gray rock is called andesite. These rocks commonly form when two plates—one of which is a continent—are coming together.

How to Read Metamorphic Rocks

A metamorphic rock has experienced enough heat and pressure to change the minerals and appearance of the rock, but not enough to melt it. These kinds of conditions exist deep underground.

Metamorphic rocks are full of clues to their origins, and many of these clues are gorgeous—stripes, folds, crenulations, or shapes called augen ("eyes" in German) or boudins ("sausages" in French). Metamorphic rocks can contain gem minerals such as garnets and often have glittery flakes of mica (Plates 2 and 3).

When studying a metamorphic rock outcrop, the first thing you should notice is how extensive the metamorphism is. If it is a narrow band (as narrow as a foot or two) where it is in contact with igneous rock, then it is most likely contact metamorphism. When magma intrudes a preexisting rock, the heat from the magma can cause minerals in the surrounding rock to recrystallize.

If, on the other hand, there is metamorphic rock for miles around, you know something bigger was going on. For example, the vast majority of rocks in the Carolina Piedmont and Blue Ridge are metamorphic. The only way to metamorphose that much rock at once is to push it deep underground. This happens anytime two plates collide, forcing one of the plates below the other. The rock on the down-going plate gradually encounters temperatures and pressures high enough for metamorphism.

Some metamorphic rocks preserve features of the original rock, especially if they have been heated and buried only slightly. In that case, we can use the techniques described above to read the information contained in the original sedimentary or igneous rock. For example, marble (metamorphosed limestone) sometimes contains recognizable fossils. Quartzite (metamorphosed sandstone) sometimes contains cross-beds (see Figure 18-3). Weakly metamorphosed igneous rocks retain their original minerals, although the grains may be a bit rearranged. More commonly, though, metamorphism is intense enough to wipe out the features of the earlier rock. Typical metamorphic rocks in the Carolinas have layers, which in metamorphic rocks we call foliation (Figure 2-3A). These layers are not relic sedimentary bedding; they are a result of elevated temperatures and pressures causing new minerals to grow with a preferred orientation, thus producing the foliation. The foliation is commonly wrinkled or folded as a result of the intense pressure (Figure 2-3B). Rocks undergoing metamorphism are often exposed to temperatures over 1,000°F and pressures of over 150,000 pounds per square inch for millions of years. It's important to remember that metamorphic rocks have not been melted—all the changes they undergo take place in solid rock.

Carolina metamorphic rocks commonly contain mica and garnet (Plate 3). The presence of either of these minerals along with strongly deformed layers tells you the rock is metamorphic. Let's say you find a foliated rock that contains large flakes of mica and crystals of garnet. The large grain size tells you that the rock was heated to a high temperature: high temperatures allow atoms to move more easily in the solid rock, resulting in larger crystals. If you analyze the chemical composition of the garnet and mica in the lab, you can pinpoint quite precisely the maximum temperature that the rock experienced.

Other minerals give you other clues. Sillimanite, which often looks like thin white needles, is present only in rocks that have experienced high temperatures—900°F or more. Kyanite, which has the same chemical formula as sillimanite (Al_2SiO_5), is a beautiful blue or gray mineral and occurs only in rocks that have experienced high pressure, usually over 50,000 pounds per square inch (see Figure 16-2). So, if a rock contains kyanite, you can generally assume that it was once buried quite deeply, 7 miles down or more. Yet another form of Al_2SiO_5 is called andalusite, which is commonly a dark brown blocky mineral that forms under conditions of relatively low pressure and low-to-moderate temperatures (see Figure 20-2). By know-

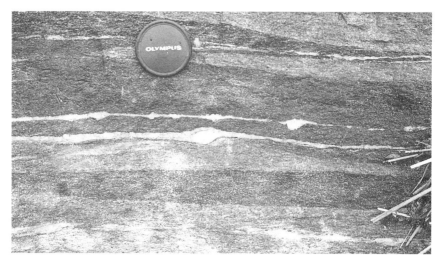

FIGURE 2-3. Foliated metamorphic rock (gneiss). A: Well-developed foliation due to fault movement. B: Folded foliation. Photographs taken in the Blue Ridge Mountains, North Carolina.

ing how hot or how deeply buried a metamorphic rock was, we can learn about conditions far down in the earth and the processes that bring deep rocks to the surface.

Metamorphic rocks usually form at least 5 miles underground. So how do they get back up to the surface? Erosion is the most important way. As mountains rise and erode, once–deeply buried rocks become exposed at the surface of the earth.

How to Tell a Geologic Story

Once you've learned to identify rocks, the next step is to look for the relationships between different kinds of rocks in the field to try to piece together a story about geologic events. For example, when sediments are deposited, younger sediments always are dumped on top of older sediments, so in a stack of sedimentary rocks, the oldest are on the bottom (this is called the principle of superposition). If you see a big quartz vein cutting straight across several different kinds of rock, you'll know the quartz vein formed after the other rocks did, because a quartz vein cannot form in thin air—by definition, it cuts another rock. A body of magma can intrude preexisting rock layers, but sedimentary rocks cannot intrude granite. Using clues like these, you can figure out the relative ages of different rocks and begin to put together a geologic story. An important part of this process is to make sure that the rock outcrops you are looking at are not just loose boulders on the surface, but are in situ (in place)—that is, that they are still connected to the crust.

Sometimes in the field you'll come across puzzling relationships. What if you find older sedimentary rocks on top of younger sedimentary rocks? What if you find a layer of sedimentary rock on top of a body of granite? What if you find a quartz vein that looks like it has been sliced in two and the two halves no longer meet up?

Relationships like these can often be explained by erosion or by faulting. For example, imagine a large body of granite that gets exposed at the earth's surface and the top of it gets eroded away. Then later the area is covered by water and layers of sediment are deposited. The contact between the granite and the sedimentary layers is called an unconformity because it represents a gap in time caused by erosion.

Faulting can put older sedimentary rock on top of younger sedimentary rock or slice quartz veins. Faults are fractures in the earth where two bodies of rock are moving in opposite directions. The three most important kinds of faults in the Carolinas are normal faults, thrust faults, and strike-slip faults (Figure 2-4). Normal faults form when the crust is pulled apart; thrust faults occur when the crust is compressed. Strike-slip faults form when two pieces of crust slide past each other horizontally. In the field, you can work out what type of fault you're looking at by mapping the rock types on either side of the fault and trying to match them up.

Whenever you see rocks in the wrong positions, such as older rocks on

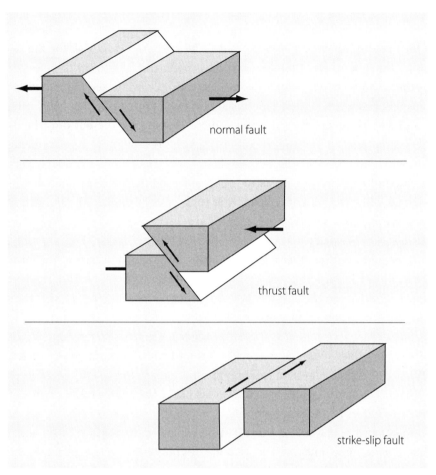

FIGURE 2-4. The three kinds of faults.

top of younger rocks, suspect a fault. Another way to recognize a fault is to look for highly fractured or highly stretched rocks (Figure 2-3A). Highly fractured rocks often indicate a fault in the upper, cooler part of the crust, where rocks grind past one another, breaking and shattering in the process. Stretched rocks often form as a result of faults in the lower, hotter part of the crust, where rocks ooze and stretch like putty.

Faults sometimes contribute to features in the landscape. Rocks that have been ground up in fault zones are more easily eroded than intact rock, so streams tend to form valleys along fault lines. A good example is the series of valleys that correspond to the Brevard fault (see Figure 14-2). Normal faults often produce steep slopes, called fault scarps.

The Carolinas are shot through with faults. Most are inactive, but a few, such as those near Charleston, South Carolina, are still active and capable of producing large earthquakes (see Chapter 36).

The reason we study rocks and the relationships between them is to try to piece together information about how geologic processes work today, and when and where those processes have occurred in the past. Sedimentary rocks give us clues about processes at the earth's surface. Igneous rocks are full of information about what goes on at plate boundaries. Metamorphic rocks contain stories about the conditions that exist miles below our feet. The spatial relationships between rocks in the field tell us about past geologic events. If you find a rock outcrop that contains evidence of a geologic event, and if you are able to discover the age of that rock, then you can add another piece to the puzzle that is geology.

3

Adding to the Body of Geologic Knowledge

Geology, like all science, is a growing and changing body of knowledge. New ideas, new field work, new lab work, and new technologies continue to expand the boundaries of what we know. New data can prove or disprove old ideas or lead to new ideas. Proven ideas are added to the foundation of geologic knowledge; new ideas are tested, leading to more work and more data. Sometimes the pace is steady; sometimes great progress occurs suddenly. Either way, as geologists continue to work in the field and the laboratory, our knowledge grows. Like geology in general, the geologic history of the Carolinas presented in this book contains undeniable facts and controversial new hypotheses and everything in between. (We'll let you know which are which.)

When trying to piece together events of the past, geologists, like crime-scene detectives, look for a "smoking gun" to make a case. Sometimes we find one; sometimes we don't. Usually geologists gather enough evidence to prove a particular explanation to be very likely, often beyond a reasonable doubt. But there are times when simply not enough information is at hand. In that case, several possible hypotheses must be kept in mind until more definitive data become available.

And new data do continue to become available, not just because geologists keep working, but also because new technologies reveal new information, just as DNA analysis can shed new light on an old criminal investigation. Mass spectrometers measure quantities of a particular element down to the picogram (that's one-trillionth of a gram). Scanning electron microscopes and electron microprobes reveal the structure and composition of earth materials as small as a micron (a micron is about 1/100th the thickness of a strand of human hair).

Just as detectives don't get to choose what evidence is present at a crime scene, so geologists must take the earth as it is. Dirt and soil cover the bedrock, as do plants, parking lots, and cities. And, just as in crime-scene investigations, the older the event, the more likely it is that some of the evidence will be missing. Some crimes take a long time to solve because a key piece of evidence is hard to uncover. Geologists often face the same problem. It may take decades of work to arrive at a convincing conclusion.

A great geologic detective story is the discovery of plate tectonics. The realization that the earth's outer shell is broken into large pieces that are constantly (but slowly) moving came about through a series of discoveries over many years. Since the time when accurate maps of the world were first printed, people had noticed that the coastlines of Africa and South America fit together like pieces of a jigsaw puzzle. Geologists documented other patterns that defied easy explanation: Why are the world's volcanoes concentrated in what's known as the Ring of Fire—a narrow zone that rims the Pacific Ocean? Why do the epicenters of deep earthquakes also cluster along the Ring of Fire? Why is there an undersea mountain range that circles almost the entire globe? Why are the Himalayas gaining elevation, while the Appalachians are losing elevation?

The work of many geologists on separate problems eventually led to a comprehensive theory that explained all these patterns and more. In 1928 Kiyoo Wadati of the Central Meteorological Observatory of Japan noticed a zone of deep earthquakes beneath Japan. In 1954 Hugo Benioff of the California Institute of Technology proposed that deep earthquakes beneath active volcanoes and growing mountains were caused by rock sinking deep into the earth at those places. In 1962 Harry Hess of Princeton University suggested that the submarine mountain ranges, or midocean ridges, were places where new oceanic crust was being created and spreading out. Then, in 1968, the work of these geologists and many more was synthesized into an overarching theory by Bryan Isacks, Jack Oliver, and Lynn Sykes of Lamont Geological Observatory at Columbia University. They called their new model "global tectonics," and it essentially describes our modern understanding of plate tectonics: the outer shell of the earth is composed of about a dozen rigid fragments called plates, which move apart, come together, and slide past one another (Figure 3-1).

Plates can be made of continental crust or oceanic crust or, most often, a combination of the two. Practically speaking, the main difference between the two kinds of crust is density: continental crust is less dense and thus floats higher than oceanic crust. (What is the crust floating on? The mantle, the layer of dense rock underneath the crust.) Continental crust is made of many different kinds of rocks, while oceanic crust is virtually all basalt and gabbro. Different sorts of geologic processes take place at the three differ-

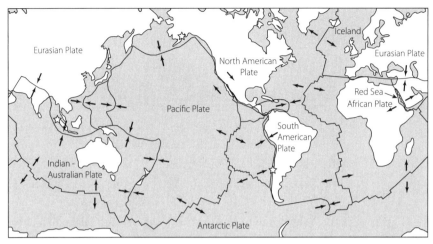

FIGURE 3-1. The earth's major tectonic plates. The arrows show relative motion at plate boundaries. The stars show the locations of the three largest earthquakes on record.

ent types of plate boundaries: divergent (moving apart), convergent (coming together), and transform (sliding past) (Figure 3-2).

Divergent plate boundaries most commonly originate in continental crust. As one plate breaks in two, rocks from the mantle "well up" into the widening crack. The rocks that are welling up are not molten, but rather a flowing solid. They do melt, however, when they meet the lower pressures near the earth's surface, and after cooling and solidifying, they become new oceanic crust. As oceanic crust accumulates in the crack, one continental plate becomes two. Eventually, sea water floods the dense, low-elevation oceanic crust. That's why most divergent plate boundaries are now found in the middle of oceans, such as the Mid-Atlantic Ridge, which separates the North American plate from the Eurasian plate. An active divergent plate boundary can be seen on land where the Mid-Atlantic Ridge emerges in Iceland. The Red Sea is a geologically young "ocean" created by the divergent plate boundary that is pushing apart the Arabian Peninsula and northeastern Africa (Figure 3-1). The Great Rift Valley in East Africa is likely to evolve into a divergent plate boundary. A string of lakes including Lake Tanganyika and Lake Malawi traces the path of the Great Rift Valley in the vicinity of the western border of Tanzania. The rifting of the crust and the generation of magma mean that divergent plate boundaries are commonly associated with earthquakes and active volcanoes.

At convergent plate boundaries, two plates come together. If one of

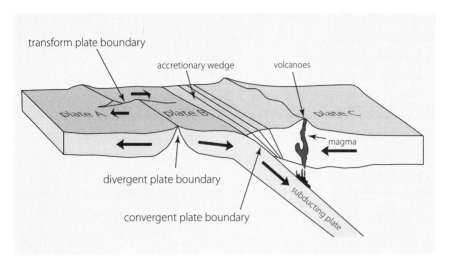

FIGURE 3-2. The three kinds of plate boundaries. In this diagram plates A and B are separated by both a divergent and transform plate boundary. Plates B and C are separated by a convergent plate boundary. Accretionary wedges develop along convergent plate boundaries as rocks and sediments are scraped off the subducting plate.

the plates is oceanic crust, which is denser than continental crust, it will sink—subduct—under the other plate. The movement of the plates scraping together during subduction creates earthquakes. The most powerful earthquakes that have ever been measured occurred at convergent plate boundaries, including the December 26, 2004, earthquake in Sumatra (magnitude 9.0), the 1964 earthquake in Alaska (magnitude 9.2), and the 1960 earthquake in Chile (magnitude 9.5) (Figure 3-1). Convergent plate boundaries are also the sites of some of the most active volcanoes on earth. When an oceanic plate sinks into the mantle, water trapped in the rocks and sediments of the plate is liberated. When this water mixes with overlying hot mantle rocks, the mantle rocks melt, because water lowers the melting point of rock. The molten rock rises to the surface and erupts from volcanoes (Figure 3-2).

If both plates at a convergent boundary are continental, neither plate is likely to subduct because they are too buoyant (in some cases, a small amount of continental crust will subduct, but buoyancy prevents it from going far). The plates collide, and the convergence eventually ceases. These continental collisions produce the largest mountain ranges on earth, such as the Himalayas. The Carolinas have experienced continental collisions in their geologic past.

When two plates simply slide past one another, this is called a transform plate boundary. The San Andreas fault in California is an example: here, the western edge of California is sliding northward. Transform plate boundaries can generate large, damaging earthquakes, but they typically do not produce many volcanoes. When there is a bend in the fault, transform plate boundaries can stimulate the building of mountain ranges, such as the San Gabriel Mountains north of Los Angeles, but these mountain ranges are much smaller than those produced by continental collisions.

From the beginning, plate tectonics was a successful theory because it tied together disparate pieces of information, enabled geologists to make successful predictions, and explained long-observed patterns, such as the following:

- Earthquakes and volcanoes are concentrated at the edges between plates because that is where plates grind against one another, separate, and are recycled into the mantle.
- Submarine mountain ranges are places where upwelling mantle comes to the surface, generating new oceanic crust and pushing plates away from one another.
- The Himalayas are growing because the Indian-Australian plate is colliding with the Eurasian plate, pushing the bedrock of Asia higher and higher.
- The Appalachians are shrinking because the collision that produced them is long over and the mountains are eroding.
- The jigsaw-puzzle fit of the continents is no illusion— South America and Africa used to be stitched together.

The new theory explained so many patterns so well that Isacks, Oliver, and Sykes could express considerable confidence in their pathbreaking paper:

Few scientific papers are completely objective and impartial; this one is not. It clearly favors the new global tectonics. . . . In the final section, however, we report an earnest effort to uncover reliable information from the field of seismology that might provide a case against the new global tectonics. There appears to be no such evidence. This does not mean, however, that many of the data could not be explained equally well by other hypotheses (although probably not so well by any other single hypothesis) or that further development or modification of the new global tectonics will not be required to explain some of the observations of seismology. It merely means that, at present, in the field of seismology, there cannot readily be found a major obstacle to the new global tectonics. (Bryan Isacks, Jack Oliver, and Lynn Sykes, "Seismology and the New Global Tectonics," *Journal of Geophysical Research* 73 (1968): 5855–99)

Even though there were no major obstacles to the new theory, there was no smoking gun—that is, measurable plate movement. Plates move at about the same speed that fingernails grow, and scientists in the 1960s and 1970s didn't have a reliable way to measure such slow movement. That changed during the 1990s with the development of the Global Positioning System. GPS is a constellation of satellites that were launched to provide a means of accurate navigation for the U.S. military; it can measure locations to within a fraction of an inch. During the last decade, geologists have deployed these instruments around the globe and have discovered that the plates are in fact moving in the directions and at the rates predicted. Plate tectonics has now been conclusively proven.

The development of this overarching theory of geology is an example of what Thomas Kuhn, a noted philosopher and historian of science at MIT, called a "paradigm shift." A paradigm shift occurs when a new theory brings together a wide range of information into a cohesive whole, providing a new unified framework with which to understand and interpret both old and new data. There were several other paradigm shifts in twentieth-century science, including Einstein's theory of relativity in the early part of the century and the development of molecular biology in the 1950s. True paradigm shifts in science are rare, and we may not see another for a long time.

Examples of smaller-scale geologic detective stories abound in the Carolinas. Running nearly north-south through the middle of the Carolinas is a belt of igneous and weakly metamorphosed volcanic and sedimentary rocks called the Carolina terrane ("terrane" refers to an area containing the same or similar bedrock throughout that shares the same or similar geologic history). Most of these rocks are about 500 to 600 million years old. Their chemical composition shows that they were created when two plates were coming together at a convergent plate boundary. If we look farther west in the Carolinas, we find sedimentary rocks of a similar age that were deposited on a passive margin, which is the edge of a continent that is not a plate boundary (the east coast of North America today is a passive margin). Clearly, the margin of the Carolinas could not have been a place where there was a passive margin and a convergent boundary at the same time, so how could this be explained?

One key piece of evidence came from fossils. At the dawn of the Cambrian period, the earth's oceans teemed with trilobites, ancient relatives of crabs and lobsters (Figure 3-3). Paleontologists (geologists who study fossils) have identified at least nine different species of Cambrian trilobites in the rocks of the Carolina terrane. These trilobite species never lived off the coast of this continent; they lived in the waters off the coast of an ancient continent called Gondwana, which consisted of parts of South America and Africa. This showed that the rocks of the Carolina terrane were not "native" to North America but started out on a different continent. Because the Carolina terrane originated as part of a different continent and was added to North America later, geologists refer to it as an "exotic" terrane.

So our mystery is solved. Millions of years ago when the ancient North America had a passive margin, the rocks of the Carolina terrane were part of a convergent plate boundary in Gondwana. During a later collision, these rocks were added on to North America—putting passive margin rocks and convergent rocks of a similar age right next to each other.

Other Carolina mysteries are not yet solved. In 1992 Rod Willard, a graduate student working with Bob Butler and Kevin Stewart at the University of North Carolina in Chapel Hill, discovered near Bakersville, North Carolina, a block of metamorphic rock made almost entirely of red garnet and a green mineral called omphacite. Mark Adams, another UNC graduate student, analyzed the chemical composition of the rock and its minerals and determined that it was eclogite—a piece of oceanic crust that sank into the earth's mantle to a depth of at least 30 miles and then came back up to the surface. Stewart, Adams, and another graduate student named Chuck Trupe went looking for more eclogite and found a body near Bakersville that is about a half a mile long and 1,000 feet thick, making it the largest known body of eclogite in North America. It's unusual to find this rock at the earth's surface because it is so dense; it almost always sinks into the mantle at subduction zones and is recycled into the mantle. Somehow, the Bakersville eclogite made its way back to the earth's surface. Is there a fault nearby that might have removed material above the eclogite? Did some

FIGURE 3-3. A fossil trilobite (*Phacops* sp.) from the Devonian period. (In the collection of the North Carolina Museum of Natural Sciences.)

mechanism cause intense erosion that eventually exposed it? Did the dense eclogite somehow "hitch a ride" up with low-density crustal rocks? Stewart and his students are continuing to analyze the eclogite and nearby rocks to try to answer these questions.

The answers could have broad implications because eclogite plays an important role in how plates move. As the basaltic oceanic crust sinks into the mantle at subduction zones, it eventually becomes dense eclogite, and because eclogite is denser than the surrounding mantle, a positive feedback is set up—eclogite pulls the plate down causing more crust to become eclogite. The conversion of oceanic crust to eclogite is an important—perhaps the most important—driving mechanism of subduction and, by extension, of plate tectonics as a whole. The midocean ridge in the southern Pacific Ocean is spreading much faster than the Mid-Atlantic Ridge, and this is because the Pacific is rimmed by subduction zones. Not only is oceanic crust being generated at the South Pacific ridge, but the plates are also being actively pulled away from the ridge by the eclogite-driven subduction.

As the work on the Bakersville eclogite proceeds, thousands of geologists around the world are working on other pieces of the global geology puzzle. Day by day, small and large discoveries come together, bringing into sharper focus the present-day workings of the earth and the geologic events that occurred in the distant past. Plate tectonics continues to work well as an overarching theory by which to understand and evaluate new findings.

And yet, as is always the case in science, much remains to be revealed and explained. Most of the earth's geology has not been mapped in detail. Our knowledge of what is one mile below our feet is a fraction of our knowledge of things millions of miles above our heads in the cosmos. It is the body of knowledge yet to be discovered that motivates geologists to keep searching for new clues in rocks.

And if you're not a geologist? You can make discoveries too. Look around and you might find an interesting mineral along a hiking trail, weird shapes carved in the bed of a neighborhood stream, wind-blown patterns in beach sand, or a remarkable rock outcrop along the highway. Even if you're not a geologist, you can notice the character and shape of the land around you and try to come up with logical explanations for what you see—and that is the heart of geology.

4

Geologic Time

Each year, on average, the Himalayas rise a little less than half an inch. In the same time, the Appalachians shrink, on account of erosion, less than a hair's breadth, and the earth's tectonic plates move an inch or two. Although large earthquakes and landslides can produce much bigger changes almost instantaneously, over time the average rates are very slow. Clearly it takes millions and millions of years to open an ocean like the Atlantic (200 million years, actually), or to raise a mountain range like the Alps. For humans, whose personal experience rarely exceeds 100 years, the idea of 1,000,000 (1 million) or 1,000,000,000 (1 billion) years is almost unfathomable. Yet if we are to understand the geologic history of the Carolinas—or the earth—we must find a way to comprehend these enormous spans of time.

In talking about geologic time, we can use a vocabulary of numbers or the vocabulary of the geologic time scale, which consists of named periods in earth history. The names are analogous to terms concerning human history such as the "Great Depression," the "Stone Age," the "Antebellum era," or the "Renaissance." They have to do with a range of time, not a specific year. By using geologic periods (or the longer "eras" and shorter "epochs"), we can think about geologic time without getting hung up on incomprehensibly large numbers, just as we can think about the Renaissance without knowing exactly when it began or ended.

When geologists first developed the geologic time scale (Figure 4-1), there were no reliable ways of assigning dates to any of the periods, so they tied their definitions to the fossil record and the sedimentary rocks that contained the fossils. The Cambrian, for example, marks the beginning of an explosion of many different types of animal life. The Devonian was a time of a remarkable number and diversity of fishes. The boundary between the Cretaceous and the Tertiary marks the extinction of an estimated 70 percent of the earth's species, including all of the dinosaurs.

Geologists could easily figure out the relative ages of fossils by noting where in a stack of sedimentary rocks they occurred. Younger sediments

GEOLOGIC TIME SCALE

Eon	Era	Period	Epoch	Years (in millions)
Phanerozoic	Cenozoic	Quaternary	Holocene	
			Pleistocene	0.01
				1.8
		Tertiary	Pliocene	
			Miocene	
			Oligocene	
			Eocene	
			Paleocene	
				65
	Mesozoic	Cretaceous		
		Jurassic		
		Triassic		opening of Atlantic Ocean
				248
	Paleozoic	Permian		
		Pennsylvanian		Alleghanian orogeny
		Mississippian		
		Devonian		Acadian orogeny
		Silurian		
		Ordovician		Taconic orogeny
		Cambrian		
				543
Precambrian	Proterozoic			opening of Iapetus Ocean
				Grenville orogeny
				2,500
	Archean			
				3,800
	Hadean			
				4,500

FIGURE 4-1. The geologic time scale.

are always deposited on top of older sediments, so organisms at the top must be younger than those at the bottom. This is called the principle of superposition.

Eventually, scientists came up with ways of measuring the age of rocks by using naturally occurring radioactive elements. When certain minerals crystallize, they incorporate elements that are radioactive. Radioactive elements decay over time into nonradioactive elements. We can determine the age of a mineral by measuring the amount of the radioactive element and the amount of the nonradioactive product and then using the known decay rate to get the age. Finding the age of a rock this way is called radiometric dating. Such measurements are made in sophisticated geochronology laboratories, like the one at the University of North Carolina at Chapel Hill. In fact, many of the ages used in constructing the chronology of geologic events in the Carolinas were measured in the UNC lab.

Radiometric dating provides numbers that we can assign to the time of geologic events, and as with any laboratory measurement, there is some uncertainty associated with the numbers. When radiometric ages are reported, if they have been done by a reputable laboratory, they will always include an estimate of the uncertainty, something like 135 ± 2 million years. What this typically means is that there is a 95 percent chance that the age is between 133 and 137 million years. To avoid tedium, we will not report the uncertainties associated with the absolute ages that we discuss in this book, but in general they are quite small, usually less than 1 or 2 percent.

Once geologists could get absolute ages of rocks, numbers could be added to the time scale. For example, the Cretaceous-Tertiary boundary occurred 65 million years ago. Ages could also be assigned to particular events: all the continental plates came together to form the supercontinent Pangea 300 million years ago.

This is where we get into numbers that are completely outside our intuition. Is something that occurred 125,000 years ago geologically ancient? If a geologic event takes 10 million years, is that slow or fast? Just how long is a million years anyway? The problem when dealing with geologic time is that the numbers are too big. We can imagine how many 10 or 20 or even 1,000 might be, but a billion is beyond our imagination. The numbers are too big because the unit is wrong: a single year is simply too small. It's like describing the distance between Chapel Hill and Durham, North Carolina, as 600,000 inches. We all have a good feel for how long a few inches are, but it's hard to imagine 600,000 of them. Is that a walkable distance? Bikeable? Would you need to drive? Take a plane? Fortunately, we have a larger unit—a mile—for measuring distance. So if we describe the distance between Chapel Hill and Durham as 10 miles, we are now dealing with a number that is easy to understand.

Let's do the same with geologic time. Instead of making a year our basic unit of time, let's use a "million-year," that is, 1 million years. Describing geologic time using this much larger unit means we no longer have to deal with so many digits. Think of 20 million years as 20 units of geologic time, not 20,000,000 years. Now that we have switched to appropriate units, we can start to get an intuitive feel for whether something is geologically ancient or recent.

The age of the earth, based on analysis of meteorites, is 4,540 million years. The oldest rocks found on earth so far are from Canada and are 4,030 million years old, although a single crystal of the mineral zircon from a rock in Australia has been dated at 4,400 million years. The age of the earth is as ancient as we can get when describing earth's history. One can draw an analogy between the span of geologic time and the span of recorded human history, which is about 5,000 years. Think of both as starting about 5,000 "time units" ago ("years" for human history, "million-years" for geologic history). Something that is 3,000 years old in human history feels quite ancient; so should a geologic event that is 3,000 million years old.

The Renaissance was about 500 years ago, quite a long time in the past, but not unfathomably long ago. We have a good record of what society was like at that time, but not a complete record. We should imagine the earth at 500 million years ago as similarly ancient. Globally, we have a good rock record from that time—not complete, but good enough to give us an idea of what the earth was like and what kinds of life existed.

Ten million years may seem a very long stretch of time, but it's analogous to only 10 years in human history. Something that occurred 100,000 years ago, put in terms of our million-year units, happened only 0.1 million years ago, the same as 0.1 years (about 35 days) in human history. So, when we describe an event in the Carolinas that took place 0.1 million years ago, keep in mind that, geologically speaking, it's very recent.

5

The Geologic History of the Carolinas

Exciting geologic events happen at the edge of plates. Edges are where plates collide with each other, or grind past one another, or tear apart. Edges are where volcanoes erupt, new mountains rise, and the earth quakes. While these events can occur midplate—for example, Hawaii's volcanoes or Charleston's 1886 earthquake—they are significantly more common at the edges.

Just because a piece of land is on an edge today doesn't mean it will be on an edge forever. Tectonic plates not only move around; they also change shape. New crust creeps out at midocean ridges, spreading in both directions away from the ridge. Old crust is consumed where one plate dives ("subducts") under another and the subducted plate gets recycled into the mantle.

Although the Carolinas are at the edge of a continent, they are in the middle of a plate—the North American plate. The eastern edge of the North American plate is out in the Atlantic Ocean, at the Mid-Atlantic Ridge, where new oceanic crust is being created; the western edge is the west coast of the United States, where there are volcanoes and earthquakes (see Figure 3-1).

The Carolinas have been on the edge of a plate more than once in their rich geologic history. During the past 1,000 million years, the Carolinas have been caught up in a series of violent edge events: a continental collision, followed by continental rifting (tearing apart), followed by a series of three collisions that resulted in the assembly of the supercontinent Pangea. When Pangea began to rip apart 220 million years ago, the continental margin of the Carolinas was right at the divergent plate boundary where new oceanic crust was filling the growing gap between the Americas and Africa. Since then, the Carolinas have been riding a tectonic conveyer belt west, as new crust created in the middle of the Atlantic Ocean pushes the plate west and adds mass to the plate. Now the Carolinas are more than 2,000 miles away from the edge, and all is fairly quiet here, geologically speaking.

But the violent past is preserved in the rocks of the Carolinas, albeit not in a very orderly fashion. All the smashing and ripping of continents left behind many clues—clues that are mixed up, stretched, folded, diced, distorted, and dismembered. Gathering this evidence and piecing it together is a full-time job for many geologists.

You will sometimes see the geology of the Carolinas discussed in terms of "belts," such as the Carolina Slate Belt, the Eastern Slate Belt, the Charlotte Belt, and so on. That is because when geologists were first looking at the geology of the Carolinas, they noticed that rocks of a similar age and origin tend to occur in belts tens of miles wide and running roughly northeast-southwest. While the belt terminology is useful in grouping together similar rocks, we now know much more about the origin of the rocks, and much of this terminology has become obsolete. Most of the belts now have different names and are called "terranes" in recognition of the fact that they originated as parts of other continents and were later added onto this continent (Plates 4 and 5).

The Oldest Rocks in the Carolinas

So far, the oldest geologic evidence that has been discovered in the Carolinas are rocks that are about 1,800 million years old (1.8 billion years old). Anything older than that has been metamorphosed beyond recognition or recycled into newer rock. The 1,800-million-year-old rocks are located in scattered outcrops near Roan Mountain in the western Blue Ridge Mountains near the Tennessee state line. Some of these rocks are metamorphosed igneous rocks, and others are metamorphosed sediments. (In this case, the age of 1,800 million years refers to the age of the original igneous and sedimentary rocks before they were metamorphosed.) Both igneous and metamorphic activity take place at plate boundaries, so we know these ancient rocks originated at a plate boundary. What is mysterious is that no other rocks in the Carolinas are even close to being this old. The surrounding rocks are at least 600 million years younger. So how did these ancient rocks get here? One hypothesis is that this crust was once part of another continent and was stuck onto North America during a continental collision. As we get more data on the rocks, though, our interpretation may change.

The Grenville Orogeny and the Assembly of Rodinia

The first episode in the geologic history of the Carolinas for which we have abundant evidence is the Middle Proterozoic, from about 900 to 1,200 million years ago. During this time, the rocks of western North Carolina were deformed in a massive continental collision, known as the Grenville orogeny. "Orogeny" is the term we use for a mountain-forming event; the word was coined before geologists knew that most mountain-forming events are caused by continental collisions. The Grenville collision came about as plates of continental crust assembled into a single supercontinent called Rodinia (Figure 5-1). The piece of crust that would become the Carolinas was jammed against crust that would become part of South America. This collision crumpled and thickened the crust, burying the rocks of the Carolinas under high mountains. The mountains in the Carolinas at this time were probably more than 20,000 feet high (based on the fact that similar modern-day collisions produce mountains this high) and were part of a mountain range that extended for thousands of miles, from Canada down through eastern North America, through South America, around Antarctica, and through southern Australia. In all of these places we can find rocks of the same kinds and the same ages as we find in the Blue Ridge of western North Carolina, and the intense regional metamorphism we find in all of these places is characteristic of continental collisions. By matching up rocks of the same kinds and ages around the world, we can reconstruct what Rodinia might have looked like.

Rodinia Breaks Apart

Following the Grenville orogeny, from about 750 million years ago until about 680 million years ago, Rodinia began to break apart, or rift. The stretched and broken crust formed rift valleys, also called rift basins. They are long, deep valleys that form perpendicular to the forces that are pulling a continent apart. These valleys may have looked like the Olduvai Gorge in Tanzania in East Africa, but with no vegetation—plants had not yet appeared on earth. Rivers eventually filled these valleys with sediment. You can see these rift-valley sediments preserved in the rocks at Grandfather Mountain (discussed in Chapter 9) and in the Smoky Mountains. Basaltic magma came piping up through the widening cracks, cutting through both the rift sediments and the metamorphic and igneous crust.

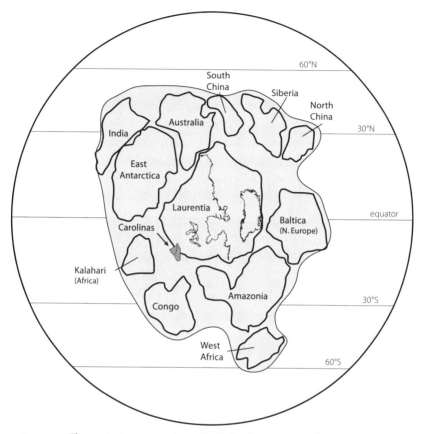

FIGURE 5-1. The ancient supercontinent Rodinia, about 1,000 million years ago. Later, the African terranes and Amazonia would combine to form the core of Gondwana.

The resulting basaltic rocks are present over a wide area in western North Carolina and are very common near Bakersville, North Carolina. Huge quantities of granitic magma were also injected into the crust. The granitic rocks can be found in many places in western North Carolina, including Beech Mountain. This so-called bimodal volcanism (producing both basalt and granite) is characteristic of rifted continental crust. As the hot, mantle-derived basalt intrudes into the continental crust, the continental crust partially melts, making granitic magma.

For some as yet unknown reason, the initial phase of Rodinian breakup ultimately failed and did not produce an ocean—we cannot find any evidence of beach or marine sediments from this phase. Beginning about 620 million years ago, a second pulse of bimodal magmatism began, and the rifting of Rodinia resumed. This time it worked.

As the ancient continent of Rodinia broke apart, a new ocean, the Iape-tus, lapped on the shores of the Carolinas. Ancient beach sands from this time are preserved in several places scattered around the Carolinas, such as the band of rocks at the top of Pilot Mountain (see Chapter 18) and the cliffs at Linville Falls (see Chapter 10). Parts of the crust we now call the Coastal Plain and the Piedmont were not yet incorporated into the Caro-linas; they would arrive much later through plate movement. A midocean ridge churned out oceanic crust in the middle of the Iapetus, slowly wid-ening the gulf between the two main parts of Rodinia—Laurentia, which would much later become North America, and Gondwana, which would become South America and Africa. As the gulf widened, the Carolinas were pushed away from the edge by new crust and became geologically quiet.

During the rifting of Rodinia, from about 700 to 600 million years ago, the earth's climate was rapidly alternating between complete glaciation (called "snowball earth") and greenhouse warming. There is glacial sedi-ment from this time exposed near Valle Crucis, North Carolina. (Unfortu-nately, it's covered in poison ivy and alongside a curvy, busy road.)

The Taconic Orogeny: The Piedmont Terrane Collides

The quiet period following complete rifting of Rodinia lasted for about 100 million years. Then, about 500 million years ago, things started to get excit-ing again. New subduction zones formed in the Iapetus Ocean, and Lau-rentia and Gondwana started moving back toward each other.

Offshore from Laurentia was a sliver of crust. It's not clear if this piece of crust had rifted away from Laurentia or from Gondwana, although there is a growing body of evidence that it was once part of Laurentia. Oceanic crust began to subduct under this crustal fragment, which caused a line of active volcanoes to erupt on it. The Iapetus Ocean now had an active con-vergent plate boundary, and the crustal fragment was moving toward the Carolinas. As the sliver of crust advanced, it scraped off ocean floor sedi-ments and pieces of basaltic oceanic crust. A process of this sort produces what we call an accretionary wedge; it's a lot like what happens when a bulldozer's blade scrapes up dirt and debris (see Figure 3-2).

Eventually, about 460 million years ago, the piece of crust collided with Laurentia (Figure 5-2). The edge of Laurentia was shoved down beneath the overriding accretionary wedge and the crustal fragment, and the wedge and the fragment became a permanent part of the Carolinas. Today we call this accreted crust the Piedmont terrane (Plate 4). (Note that its boundaries are not the same as those of the Piedmont physiographic province.) Because of its uncertain origins (in Gondwana or Laurentia), it's called a "suspect" terrane. The force of the collision, known as the Taconic orogeny, pushed up the ancestral Appalachians. The high peaks of these mountains were likely as high as the Alps—15,000 feet or more. During this time the mountains of the Carolinas resembled a high coastal mountain range, like the Fairweather Range in Alaska, but without the glaciers. Laurentia was still in the Southern Hemisphere, traveling north.

Geologists have found solid evidence of the Taconic orogeny all up and down the length of the modern-day Appalachians.

The Mysterious Acadian Orogeny: Did It Happen Here?

The mountains began eroding, and the Iapetus Ocean continued to close as Gondwana and Laurentia approached each other. Between Gondwana and Laurentia there was a series of crustal fragments that had broken off the outer edge of Gondwana. These fragments were the remnants of ancient volcanoes that had erupted above a subduction zone along the edge of Gondwana much earlier, between about 500 and 600 million years ago. Before Gondwana collided with Laurentia, one of these fragments hit Laurentia, sometime between 450 and 350 million years ago (Figure 5-3).

The Gondwanan fragment is actually an amalgamation of several terranes. Geologists commonly refer to these terranes as peri-Gondwanan terranes to indicate that they originated along the margin of Gondwana. In this book, we will call them the Gondwanan terranes (Plate 4). Each terrane records a slightly different geologic history, and most are separated from each other by faults; they were most likely all stitched together some time before they were added to Laurentia (Plate 5). It's not clear exactly when, where, or how the Gondwanan terranes hit Laurentia or if there was an orogeny associated with the collision. In fact, this issue is one of the most controversial topics among Carolina geologists today. Perhaps in the next decade or so, the problem will be solved as more field and laboratory work provide a clearer picture of the event. In the northern Appalachians, in New England and Canada, there is solid evidence for a collision of a Gondwanan fragment between about 420 and 370 million years ago, and the resulting mountain-building event is called the Acadian orogeny. But

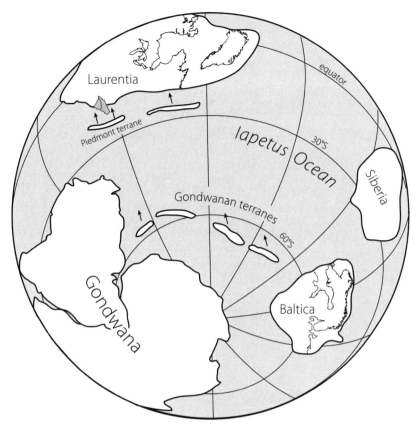

FIGURE 5-2. The Piedmont terrane about to collide with Laurentia, causing the Taconic orogeny 460 million years ago. Notice that crustal fragments called Gondwanan terranes have broken off of Gondwana and are moving toward Laurentia. (Baltica is an ancient continent that consisted of most of northern Europe, including Sweden and Norway.)

in the Carolinas, some of the necessary pieces of evidence are conspicuously missing.

A major mountain-building event produces several characteristic features. The thickened crust of the mountains causes metamorphism in the deeply buried rocks, so we typically see metamorphic rocks of the same age as the orogeny. If the crust is thick enough, the deepest rocks will get hot and melt, so we frequently see igneous rocks as well. We would expect to find thrust faults, again of the same age as the orogeny, because thrust faults are the primary mechanism by which crust gets thicker while forming mountains. And lastly, high mountains shed huge piles of sediments as they erode, producing what we call a clastic wedge. All these features are

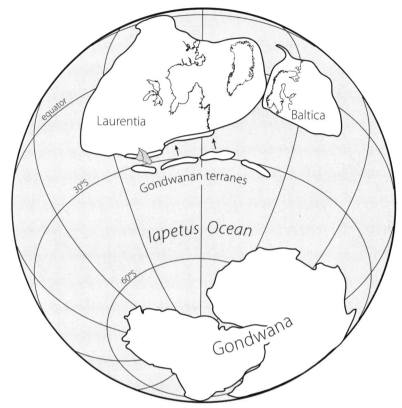

FIGURE 5-3. The Gondwanan terranes approaching Laurentia, between 450 and 350 million years ago. The Gondwanan terranes that are now exposed in the Carolinas are an amalgamation of terranes that were assembled sometime before their collision with Laurentia.

present for the Acadian orogeny in the northern Appalachians, but they are either missing or not clearly evident in the Carolinas.

First of all, there is definitely no clastic wedge of an Acadian age here. Some scattered, localized metamorphic rocks in the Blue Ridge Mountains and the Piedmont of North Carolina can be dated to between about 400 and 360 million years ago. There are also some igneous rocks near Spruce Pine, North Carolina, and in the South Mountains near Morganton, North Carolina, that are about 370 to 380 million years old. However, there are no proven Acadian thrust faults in the Carolinas, although some geologists have proposed that several of the thrust faults in the Piedmont are in fact Acadian. Future work should clarify the true ages of these faults. So far, the only well-dated fault that falls within the Acadian age range is a strike-slip fault that runs through the middle of the Blue Ridge Mountains. The rocks to the east of the fault, which provide the sparse evidence of an Acadian orogeny, appear to have been transported south. It may be that these rocks were involved in the Acadian orogeny in the central and northern Appalachians and were later moved southward away from the clastic wedge.

So the possibilities are that the Gondwanan terranes collided with Laurentia farther north (somewhere in the region of modern-day Canada and New England) and then later traveled down to the Carolinas via a strikeslip fault; that the Gondwanan terranes collided here but did not produce an orogeny, perhaps because the collision was at an angle rather than head on; or that the Gondwanan terranes collided here and did produce an orogeny, for which some of the evidence has not yet been found.

In any case, a fragment of Gondwana did collide with some part of Laurentia between 450 and 350 million years ago, and it is in the Carolinas now.

The Alleghanian Orogeny: Laurentia and Gondwana Collide

Gondwana itself collided with Laurentia about 330 million years ago. This huge continental collision pushed up the Appalachians along great thrust faults, producing a towering mountain range that ran from present-day Alabama to New England. Geologists have estimated the height of these mountains using a technique based on the mechanical behavior of rock in a continental collision. This work shows that the mountains achieved an average elevation equal to the modern-day Andes, and some peaks may have reached Himalayan-scale heights of 26,000 feet or more. This collision, the Alleghanian orogeny, was the last great upheaval of the crust of the Carolinas. Almost everywhere we look in the Carolinas, we can find evidence for this major mountain-building event. Stone Mountain and Mount Airy granite (both discussed in Chapter 12) in North Carolina are two of the large igneous bodies that were created during the collision. The Nutbush Creek fault, which runs through Raleigh, is an Alleghanian strike-slip fault. You can see an exposure of the Nutbush Creek fault behind the grocery store on Glenwood Avenue at Oberlin Road. This fault occurred deep underground where rock behaves like putty, so the rock today preserves the highly stretched texture characteristic of ductile fault zones.

When the Alleghanian orogeny was complete, most of the earth's continental landmass was assembled into a supercontinent called Pangea (Figure 5-4).

Pangea Breaks Apart

Beginning in the Triassic period, about 220 million years ago, Pangea began rifting. As happened when Rodinia started to break up 750 million years ago, the crust cracked and sank as it stretched apart. Rift basins formed up and down what is now the east coast of North America, as well as along the west coast of Africa. The rift basins are aligned approximately parallel to the coastline and are bounded on one or both sides by faults. Some of the basins continued growing to form the Atlantic Ocean. From the Triassic to the present day, about 4,000 miles of oceanic crust have been created between Africa and the Carolinas by the active divergent plate boundary in the middle of the Atlantic Ocean.

The other Triassic basins stopped growing, and they were eventually filled with sediment. Basaltic magma shot through the sediments, producing sheets of igneous rocks, called dikes and sills. Dikes are injected across the layers of rocks, while sills are injected parallel to the layers. These igneous rocks, called diabase, have a composition that is the same as basalt or gabbro; the grain size is intermediate between the two. Although they crystallized underground, like gabbro, they are finer grained because they were intruded at shallow levels in the crust and cooled relatively quickly. North Carolina has two major Triassic basins: the Deep River basin and the Dan River basin (see Figure 21-2 and Plate 4). There is also a small Triassic basin to the west of these that straddles the line between Davie County and Yadkin County. The Deep River basin is divided into three subbasins: the Durham, the Sanford, and the Wadesboro basins. (See Chapter 21 for more information about Triassic basins and about the Durham basin in particular.) South Carolina does not have any exposed Triassic basins (except for the southernmost tip of the Deep River basin), but geologists have used magnetic and seismic mapping to find basins underneath the veneer of Coastal Plain sediments. Drill-hole data have confirmed the locations.

Floods and Ice

For most of the Mesozoic and Cenozoic eras, the Carolinas have been undergoing quiet but continuous geologic change. Erosion has been whittling down the Appalachians into the rounded mountains we see today. Rivers have piled the eroded materials on the Coastal Plain and in the sea, forming sandy beaches, offshore barrier islands, and a sediment-draped conti-

FIGURE 5-4. The supercontinent Pangea, 300 million years ago.

nental shelf. Sea level has risen and fallen dramatically, driven by changes in the earth's climate. During periodic ice ages, a large part of the world's ocean water is tied up in extensive glaciers, causing sea level to drop. When the ice melts, the water rises, flooding low shorelines.

About 90 million years ago, during the Cretaceous period, sea level was the highest it has been in at least the past 600 million years. Every glacier and both polar ice caps had melted. Warm temperatures caused ocean waters to expand, raising sea level even further. At its maximum, sea level was about 800 feet higher than it is today. If North Carolina were to experience a similar flooding today, the shoreline would run from Winston-Salem to Charlotte to Spartanburg.

This huge rise in sea level may have contributed to the formation of the Blue Ridge escarpment. This steep change in elevation from the Piedmont to the Blue Ridge is one of the most noticeable features of the landscape of the Carolinas, in places exceeding 2,000 feet. The origin of the escarpment has been a long-standing question in Carolina geology. Some have proposed that the escarpment was formed by a structural feature like a fault; others have proposed that it is primarily a result of erosion. The most likely answer turns out to include both processes. When continents rift apart, the thinned, buoyant crust at the rifted edge springs up and recovers some of the elevation it lost during thinning. In addition, the rising hot mantle beneath the newly formed divergent plate boundary heats the crust, further lowering its density and causing it to be even more buoyant. These two processes create what is known as a rift-flank uplift. Rift-flank uplifts are long elevated ridges that run along the edges of rifted continents. When North America and Africa split apart 220 million years ago, there would have been a rift-flank uplift that developed along the east coast of North America, and it's likely that the Blue Ridge escarpment is the erosional remnant of just such an uplift. The North American rift-flank uplift would have been at least 100 miles east of the current Blue Ridge escarpment at the time of its formation; so if this hypothesis is correct, the escarpment was eroded back that distance over the past 200 million years. Waves crashing against a rocky shoreline are among the most effective agents of erosion, and no doubt the 800-foot rise in sea level about 90 million years ago played a major role in the erosional retreat of the rift-flank uplift and the formation of the Blue Ridge escarpment.

Right now, the earth is still warming up after the last ice age, which peaked only 18,000 years ago. Sea level in the Carolinas is rising and is about midway between the lowest and highest points of the past 90 million years or so. There is evidence in the Coastal Plain of several ancient shorelines formed when sea level was higher than it is now, but lower than in the Cretaceous. The Orangeburg scarp (see Figure 32-2) is the ancient shoreline of a 270-foot rise in sea level that occurred about 2 million years ago. The Suffolk scarp records a 20-foot rise in sea level that happened only 125,000 years ago. Shorelines from times of low sea level are, of course, now underwater, and as the earth's climate continues to warm, much of our Coastal Plain will be submerged and eventually buried with a veneer of fresh sediment.

As sea level rises, the barrier islands off our shores respond to the change by migrating landward. Barrier islands are nothing but piles of sand; wind and water move the sand from the ocean side to the sound side through inlets and, during storms, right over the top of islands. This geologic process causes great frustration for people because roads get sanded over and beach houses tumble into the surf, but the land on barrier islands is inevitably unstable as sea level changes.

The Future

Although the eastern edge of our continent has been a passive margin for the past 200 million years or so, it won't be that way forever. Sooner or later all oceanic crust cools to a point where it is too dense to float on the mantle anymore. (There is very little oceanic crust on earth older than about 200 million years, whereas continental crust is so buoyant it can last for billions of years before being eroded or partially subducted.) When oceanic crust begins to sink, the sinking becomes the engine for a new convergent plate boundary. The oceanic crust off the coast of the Carolinas is more than 200 million years old and will likely start to sink into the mantle in the not-too-distant geologic future, perhaps in the next 10 to 20 million years. Once this process starts and the crust under the Atlantic Ocean begins to subduct beneath the Carolinas, our coast will change from a passive to an active margin. Earthquakes, volcanoes, and a brand-new mountain range will leave their mark on the land once more.

Field Trips

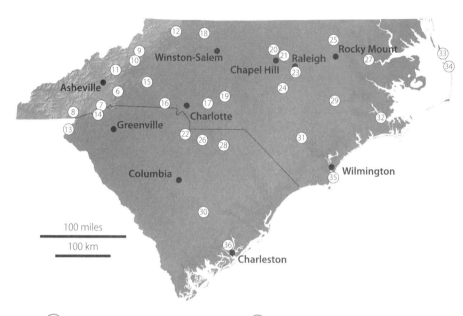

⑥	Chimney Rock	㉒	Landsford Canal
⑦	DuPont Forest	㉓	N.C. Museum of Natural Sciences
⑧	Whiteside Mountain	㉔	Raven Rock
⑨	Grandfather Mountain	㉕	Medoc Mountain
⑩	Linville Falls	㉖	Forty Acre Rock
⑪	Mount Mitchell	㉗	Roanoke River
⑫	Stone Mountain	㉘	Sugarloaf Mountain
⑬	Woodall Shoals	㉙	Cliffs of the Neuse
⑭	Caesars Head	㉚	Santee State Park
⑮	South Mountains	㉛	Jones Lake
⑯	Crowders Mountain	㉜	Flanner Beach
⑰	Reed Gold Mine	㉝	Jockey's Ridge
⑱	Pilot Mountain	㉞	Oregon Inlet
⑲	Morrow Mountain	㉟	Carolina Beach
⑳	Occoneechee Mountain	㊱	Dorchester
㉑	Durham Triassic Basin		*Numbers correspond to chapter numbers.*

The Blue Ridge

6

Chimney Rock Park
Stretched, Folded, Cracked, and Faulted

Chimney Rock Park offers good views of several different kinds of rock deformation all in one place. You will see folds that formed miles underground under conditions of great heat and pressure, now exposed in hard rock at the earth's surface. You will see a fault along which rock layers moved 10 miles or more. And you will see large blocks of rock that have recently fallen off cliffs.

The Skyline-Cliff Trail Loop is the best place to see all these things. You can reach the trail by taking a 30-second elevator ride to the top of the mountain or by walking up a lot of stairs. The Skyline-Cliff Trail Loop is only a mile and a half; but it is quite strenuous in sections and includes many stairs, so be sure to allow plenty of time if you want to tackle it.

Before you take the elevator or the stairs, stand in the parking lot and notice the bare steep cliffs on the sides of Chimney Rock Mountain. Above the cliffs, the mountain has gentler slopes that are covered in vegetation. When you see sharp contrasts on the surface of the earth, like steep bare slopes underneath gentler vegetated slopes, it's a clue that there may be sharp contrasts in the bedrock underneath. As we'll see, this is the case here.

When you get off the elevator and head for the Chimney itself, you are walking on top of the steep, bare cliffs. The rock is coarse grained (individual mineral grains are visible to the naked eye) and rich in the minerals quartz, feldspar, and mica. The strong layering tells you the rock is metamorphic. This type of coarse-grained metamorphic rock is called gneiss, and this particular rock is known as the Henderson gneiss (named for Henderson County, North Carolina). The Henderson gneiss is a metamorphosed granite that covers hundreds of square miles in western North Carolina and South Carolina.

The structure called the Chimney was created when erosion took place

FIGURE 6-1. Cliffs of Henderson gneiss along the Cliff Trail.

along a zone of vertical fractures in the rock, creating a space between this block of Henderson gneiss and the rest. From the top of Chimney Rock, look to the north across the valley of the Rocky Broad River toward Round Top Mountain. There you will see the same sort of pattern that you saw looking at Chimney Rock Mountain from the parking lot: on the side of the mountain there are prominent light-colored cliffs, and above them are forested slopes that are not as steep.

Beginning on the Skyline portion of the trail, at both Opera Box and Exclamation Point, start looking for interesting textures in the gneiss. You will see thin layers of smeared-out minerals and also boudins, which are stretched layers that pinch and swell, looking like strings of sausages. Both features are typical of a "shear zone," which is the deformed area on either side of a fault. This clues you in to the fact that a fault probably has played a role in the juxtaposition of the cliff-making gneiss and the rock above it.

Above Exclamation Point, the trail becomes more vegetated as you leave the Henderson gneiss and enter the mountain's gentler slopes. Here is a good place to start looking for outcrops to see what kind of rock this part of the mountain is made of. The first outcrop is in a bank on the left side of the trail soon after Exclamation Point, near where the trail comes to a boardwalk. The outcrop looks completely different than the rock you've seen so far. It is very dark and resembles wet driftwood. You can also see that the rock layers have been folded (Figure 6-2). This particular outcrop is very weathered, so it's hard to get a good look at the minerals in the rock. However, if you could see a fresh surface, you'd find layers of schist, which is a medium-grained mica-rich rock, and amphibolite, which is a dark-colored metamorphic rock that is rich in the mineral amphibole. These rocks are part of what is known as the Poor Mountain Formation. The schist and amphibolite weather more readily than the gneiss, which is why this part of the mountain is more vegetated and the slopes are gentler.

A little bit farther along, the trail descends and you can see the sharp contact between the Poor Mountain Formation and the Henderson gneiss. This contact is actually a thrust fault, along which a huge sheet of Poor Mountain Formation rocks has been thrust up and over the Henderson gneiss. When you look at Chimney Rock Mountain or Round Top and see the line between the steep bare cliffs and the more vegetated, gentler slopes, you're looking at the thrust fault, which is called the Sugarloaf Mountain fault.

The granite that formed the Henderson gneiss originated as a magma

FIGURE 6-2. Folded amphibolite of the Poor Mountain Formation along the Skyline-Cliff Loop Trail.

chamber beneath a line of volcanoes, and the rock crystallized sometime between 490 and 445 million years ago (it has been difficult finding minerals in this rock that give precise ages). At the time, Laurentia (which would later become North America) and Gondwana (which contained parts of South America and Africa) were moving toward each other on a collision course. The magma chambers and volcanoes were located on a fragment of crust called the Piedmont terrane that lay between the two continents. The Piedmont terrane collided with Laurentia before Gondwana did, in an event called the Taconic orogeny.

The schist and amphibolite of the Poor Mountain Formation began as sediments (the schist) and basaltic lava flows (the amphibolite) in shallow ocean waters between Laurentia and the Piedmont terrane sometime before or during the Taconic orogeny. The sediments and basalt were pushed up onto Laurentia when the Piedmont terrane collided.

Millions of years after the Piedmont terrane collided with Laurentia, a part of Gondwana rifted off and collided with Laurentia. When tectonic plates collide, the crust gets squeezed and shortened. There are several ways for the crust to accommodate the shortening. One way is for some of the crust to get folded, just like a sheet of paper folds when you squash it

FIGURE 6-3. The sheared and folded Henderson gneiss at Inspiration Point. Notice the boudins in the white (felsic) layer.

between your hands. Another way is for the crust to break into blocks that get pushed up over adjacent blocks. For an analogy, imagine how playing cards ride up on top of one another when you sweep them together into a stack. The contact along which a block of crust gets pushed up over another block of crust is called a thrust fault (see Figure 2-4). That's what separates the Poor Mountain Formation from the underlying Henderson gneiss—the Sugarloaf Mountain thrust fault. Plate collisions not only shorten the crust; they thicken it, too. So during this collision, the rocks were deeply buried and metamorphosed (although they may have experienced some metamorphism during the earlier Taconic orogeny as well). The Sugarloaf Mountain fault continues for 60 miles into South Carolina. The rocks along the fault have probably been moved more than 10 miles.

The Skyline Trail continues to the top of Hickory Nut Falls, where Falls Creek tumbles down 404 feet of rock. Falls Creek has cut down through the more easily eroded Poor Mountain Formation to the top of the Henderson gneiss.

After viewing the falls, head back to the Chimney the way you came or via the Cliff Trail. (Portions of the movie *The Last of the Mohicans* were filmed along the Cliff Trail and at Hickory Nut Falls.) If you take the Cliff

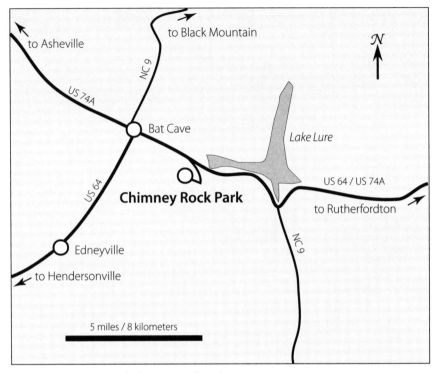

FIGURE 6-4. Location of Chimney Rock Park.

Trail, you'll soon come to Inspiration Point. It may have been named for the view, but for geologists the rock itself is inspirational. Look for layers, tight folds, and veins of light-colored quartz and feldspar in the Henderson gneiss (Figure 6-3).

All the way back along the Cliff Trail, notice how unweathered the cliff surfaces are. That's because large pieces of the cliff break off often enough to keep the surfaces fresh. Water works its way into cracks in the cliff and expands when it freezes, pushing the rock apart. Tree roots grow into the wet cracks and pry the rock farther apart. Eventually, pieces of rock break off and tumble down, pulled by gravity. At Chimney Rock Park, some of these rocks form miniature "caves," like Wildcat Trap, the Subway, and the Grotto.

Chimney Rock Park reminds us that rock, though it seems everlasting and unyielding, is in fact ever changing. Miles below the surface, rock gets hot enough to ooze like putty. Under high temperature and pressure, minerals recrystallize into layers, which are then twisted into folds. These features are not exposed at the surface until millions of years later, when all the overlying rock has eroded away. By then the folded rocks are cold and hard, but they help us imagine how ductile the rock must have been at one time. Nearer the surface, faults sometimes move inches or feet instantaneously, causing earthquakes. Other faults creep along imperceptibly, a fraction of an inch per year. In either case, the rocks along a fault record the strain by changes in texture. And right at the earth's surface, rocks break to pieces under the constant assault from water, weather, plants, and gravity.

We don't usually see the processes by which rocks are broken up, folded, or faulted because such changes happen very slowly, very quickly, or deep underground. But evidence of rock deformation is all around you, particularly if you happen to be in Chimney Rock Park.

Location and Access

Chimney Rock Park is a private park that charges an admission fee. There is no camping. It is about 25 miles southeast of Asheville, near the intersection of US 64 and US 74. The Cliff Trail is closed late fall through early spring because ice makes the trail too dangerous for walking.

In 2006 Chimney Rock Park was put on the market, and the North Carolina Division of Parks and Recreation expressed an interest in purchasing the land for a state park. As this book was going to press, Chimney Rock remained unsold.

7

DuPont State Forest
Waterfalls Galore

If you like waterfalls, you'll love DuPont State Forest. The Little River flows through the forest, coursing over four beautiful waterfalls on its way to the French Broad River. There are also smaller falls on a tributary of the Little River called Grassy Creek.

DuPont State Forest has lots of waterfalls because it's an area with steep slopes and hard rock that doesn't erode easily. It's a terrific place to observe and analyze the many different ways that a stream and bedrock can interact to make a waterfall. Hooker Falls, Triple Falls, High Falls, and Bridal Veil Falls all are made of the same rock type, but they look dramatically different.

Hooker Falls is a quarter-mile walk from the Staton Road parking lot on a path carpeted with pine straw and lined with rhododendrons (Figure 7-1). The waterfall is only 11 feet high, but impressive even so. The face is nearly vertical and stretches all the way across the river, so the water falls all at once, creating the archetypal waterfall roar.

Notice the thin horizontal layering in the rock. This kind of texture, called foliation, is a result of metamorphism. Notice also the vertical cracks, called joints. Some are filled with quartz, and some are not. The quartz-filled joints tend to be slightly raised because quartz is so resistant to erosion. If you walk down to the river's edge, you can see that there are blocks of rock at the base of the falls and along the shore; these are pieces that have fallen off the face of the falls as the water has eroded the cliff. There are rocky outcrops on either side of the river here; they are in fact part of the same outcrop you see beneath the waterfall.

Why such a vertical face on these falls? It has to do with the interaction between the horizontal foliation and the vertical jointing. When horizontal and vertical planes of weakness intersect, they tend to produce blocky pieces of rock, which break off, leaving behind steep faces. In most in-

FIGURE 7-1. Hooker Falls.

stances, rock breaks off along the weaker unfilled joints rather than those that are filled with quartz. The rock here is a metamorphic rock made primarily of the minerals quartz, feldspar, and mica (the sparkly flakes are mica). The rock contains the same minerals that are found in granite, so geologists call it a granitic gneiss. A gneiss is a metamorphic rock that has distinct layers of light and dark minerals, a kind of foliation referred to as banding. This particular granitic gneiss is part of what geologists call the Table Rock Plutonic Suite, the same rock formation that is exposed at Caesars Head and Table Rock (see Chapter 14). A pluton is a large body of rock that formed underground as magma cooled and solidified. This granite pluton crystallized about 450 million years ago and was subsequently metamorphosed in a tectonic collision, although the age of metamorphism has not been determined with precision.

From the same parking lot, cross the road to hike upstream to Triple Falls and High Falls. Be careful at these falls—wet rock is more slippery than it looks. Triple Falls, true to its name, is a three-step waterfall that has

FIGURE 7-2. Triple Falls.

a total loss of elevation of about 50 feet (Figure 7-2). The foliation here is just as horizontal as it is at Hooker Falls, and you can see that Triple Falls does have a pronounced horizontal aspect—each waterfall ends on a large flat plane before the next one begins.

The horizontal foliation in these rocks and in most of the rocks in the Piedmont terrane (see Chapter 5 and Plate 4) is typical of rocks that have been metamorphosed within the lower crust, at depths of 20 miles or more. We know that these rocks were once buried that far down because of the presence of certain minerals that grow only in rocks that have been cooked at such depths. Under these conditions the rocks are hot enough that the minerals can flow plastically, like very viscous putty. It is thought that during mountain-building events the lower crust gets squeezed and extruded by the weight of the overlying rocks. This initiates a horizontal flow in the lower crust that creates a horizontal foliation. The pervasive horizontal foliation in the rocks of DuPont State Forest was very likely produced by this kind of lower crustal flow.

On the flat plane at the top of the third falls, look for a series of rounded potholes in the rock that are exposed when the river is at its average level or lower. Potholes form when sediment caught in eddies scours down into bedrock—look in the bottom of dry potholes to see if you can find the scouring sediment.

High Falls is the highest waterfall in DuPont State Forest (Figure 7-3). It has only one face, like Hooker Falls, and its face is even less steep than the faces of Triple Falls. In fact, in many places, the slope of the face is gentle enough that the water slides down the rock. Perhaps there are fewer vertical joints here than at Triple Falls. Or perhaps there is something else about the character of the bedrock here that lends itself to a gentler slope. Someone would need to take a lot of measurements and do an in-depth study of the rock and the river here to come up with a definitive answer.

Bridal Veil Falls, featured in the movie *The Last of the Mohicans*, is farther upstream. You can park at the Fawn Lake access area on Reasonover Road and hike 2 miles to Bridal Veil Falls. It is an overhang that produces a curtain of water in front of a shallow "cave." Usually an overhang like this occurs when the rock on top is more resistant to erosion than the rock beneath it.

There are other falls in DuPont State Forest—Grassy Creek Falls and Wintergreen Falls, to name two. There are also several peaks that have bare rock outcrops at the top: Big Rock, Cedar Rock, and Stone Mountain.

FIGURE 7-3. High Falls.

These are similar, on a much smaller scale, to the granite domes in Stone Mountain State Park in Wilkes and Alleghany counties (see Chapter 12).

Before it was a state forest, the land was owned by the DuPont Corporation, which operated a photographic plant here. When DuPont made plans to relocate in the mid-1990s, the corporation sold the physical plant and the land holdings separately. The state of North Carolina ended up with 7,600 acres of forest, and Sterling Imaging Corporation bought the plant and 2,200 adjoining acres, which included High Falls, Triple Falls, and Bridal Veil Falls. Sterling soon sold the buildings to Agfa and the 2,200 acres to a developer in South Carolina, who began making plans for a gated residential community of high-end homes. After public outcry and failed negotiations with the developer, the state of North Carolina obtained the land by power of eminent domain, or condemnation, which gives the government the right to force a landowner to sell land to the government for the public good. (Eminent domain is most often used to obtain land for highways.) North Carolina paid the developer $12.5 million, and the land became part of DuPont State Forest in late 2000. The photographic plant is still privately owned and operated, which explains why the protected area

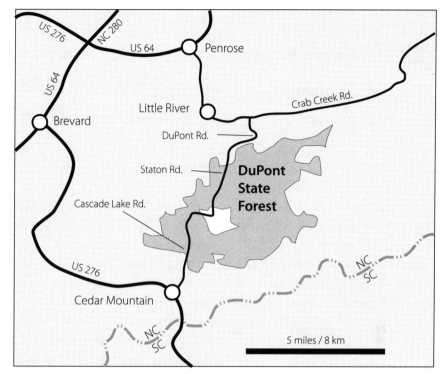

FIGURE 7-4. Location of DuPont State Forest.

is shaped like a doughnut with a rather small, off-center hole where the plant is located.

Today, DuPont State Forest contains more than 10,000 acres of land, 90 miles of hiking trails, and waterfalls aplenty.

Location and Access

DuPont State Forest is about an hour's drive south of Asheville. Camping is not permitted, although it may be in the future. Designated trails are open to horses and mountain bikes.

8

Whiteside Mountain
A Geologic Puzzle

>> JACKSON AND MACON COUNTIES, NORTH CAROLINA

Descriptive names of natural landmarks are not always precise. Forty Acre Rock comes to mind—it's only 14 acres. Then there's Grandfather Mountain—which bump is supposed to be the nose and which is the chin? And is Sugarloaf Mountain, a bit of topography that rises only 100 feet above the surrounding land, really a mountain? The name of Whiteside Mountain, on the other hand, is right on—it's a tall ridge with exposed white sides.

A terrific place to view the mountain is just southeast of it on Whiteside Cove Road (State Road 1107). Drive several miles east and northeast of the intersection of Whiteside Cove Road and Bull Pen Road (State Road 1100) for a spectacular view.

For a more up-close and personal look, go hiking on the mountain. There is only one trail, a 2-mile loop that begins in the parking lot and goes to the summit. As the trail begins, notice how sparkly the soil is in places. The sparkle is the mineral mica, which has weathered out of the bedrock here. In places on the trail on the way up, you may see outcrops of a rock rich in mica. The layers (foliation) and the abundant mica tell you this is a metamorphic rock. It has relatively coarse grains, so it's called a schist. (A similar, finer-grained rock would be a phyllite; one with even coarser grains would be a gneiss.)

As you near the top of the trail, you will see more and more exposed rock that is different from the schist. Some people mistakenly call this rock granite, but as you can see it is foliated, which means it's a metamorphic rock. The coarse mineral grains and alternating light and dark layers, called banding, tell you that this rock is gneiss. It most likely started out as granite or some other igneous rock before being metamorphosed, but in some places it's been so strongly deformed that all clues about the original rock have been erased. Because of that, it's called heterogeneous gneiss, meaning that not all of it may have started out as the same kind of rock.

FIGURE 8-1. The cliffs of Whiteside Mountain.

This rock is particularly rich in quartz and feldspar, which gives it a light color. At the top, the trail follows the ridge, and you will be treated to a series of overlooks that offer magnificent views of the valley below as well as magnificent views of the rock itself. The rock here is strongly foliated and folded, evidence that it has been exposed to intense heat and pressure. Notice also how some of the mineral grains are "smeared out," which tells you that the rock has been sheared in a fault zone (Figure 8-2).

Most of this gneiss originated as an igneous rock in a deep magma chamber about 466 million years ago. At that time, a fragment of crust, the Piedmont terrane, was colliding with Laurentia, the ancestral North America. This collision, the Taconic orogeny, was the first in a series of three collisions that occurred while Gondwana (ancestral Africa and South America) and Laurentia were moving toward each other. As the Piedmont terrane approached Laurentia, it bulldozed oceanic crust and sediments ahead of it. Included in the sediments were layers of ash and lava produced by the volcanoes on the Piedmont terrane. All of this was pushed up onto Laurentia ahead of the Piedmont terrane and then was buried and metamorphosed. The bulldozed package of oceanic crust and sediments is called an accretionary wedge; exposures of it can be seen in the western Carolinas (see Chapter 11, on Mount Mitchell, and Chapter 13, on Woodall Shoals).

Whiteside Mountain is right in the middle of the Taconic accretionary wedge. This is surprising because we don't expect molten rock to be generated in accretionary wedges; modern-day accretionary wedges very rarely have active volcanoes. In a convergent plate boundary, the accretionary wedge develops at the leading edge of the overriding plate, and the volcanoes (and magma chambers) are typically 50 to 100 miles farther back into the overriding plate. (See Chapter 3 for more information on convergent plate boundaries.) There are (at least) two hypotheses for how this igneous rock got in the middle of the Taconic accretionary wedge. One is that during the continental collision the accretionary wedge was thick enough that some of the rocks at the bottom of the wedge partially melted and formed magma. This would mean that the Whiteside gneiss originated in a similar way as the 270- to 335-million-year-old plutons that formed during the Alleghanian orogeny by crustal thickening (see Chapter 12, on Stone Mountain; Chapter 25, on Medoc Mountain; and Chapter 26, on Forty Acre Rock).

Another possibility involves a proposed flip in the direction of the subduction. Here's the hypothesis: Before the collision, the oceanic crust of the

FIGURE 8-2. Sheared gneiss at the top of Whiteside Mountain.

Laurentian plate was subducting under the Piedmont terrane. The dense oceanic crust was sinking down under the fragment, forming an accretionary wedge at the front of the Piedmont terrane. After the Piedmont terrane collided with Laurentia, that subduction stopped. Gondwana was still moving toward Laurentia, so a new subduction zone began on the trailing edge of the Piedmont terrane; but now the oceanic crust of the Gondwanan plate was diving under Laurentia and the recently accreted Piedmont terrane. This would have generated a line of volcanoes and magma bodies in the accretionary wedge that was now part of Laurentia (Figure 8-3). In any case, more data are needed before either hypothesis can begin to seem more likely than the other.

From the overlook with a white fence, there is a view to the northeast of a string of white cliffs similar to the one you're standing on. These are made of the same gneiss that's under your feet. It forms cliffs because it is more resistant to erosion than the weaker rocks in the valley.

At the next overlook (if you're walking the loop trail counterclockwise), there is a bump of rock on which is carved "ALT 4930." That's the summit of Whiteside. Soon after the summit, there is a narrow trail through a crack in the rock to another overlook. In the walls of the crack, you will see huge

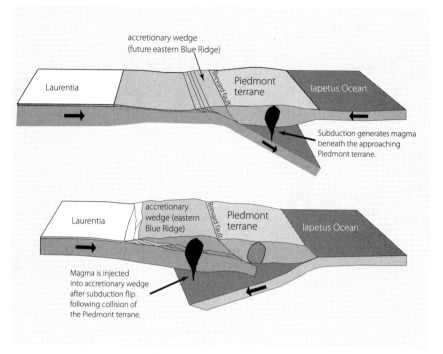

FIGURE 8-3. As Laurentia and Gondwana were converging, subduction produced volcanoes in the Piedmont terrane (upper diagram). After the Piedmont terrane collided with Laurentia, subduction may have flipped, generating new volcanoes within the old accretionary wedge (lower diagram).

feldspar and mica crystals, which are several inches across in some places. This is a pegmatite, an extremely coarse-grained igneous rock that forms from a fluid-rich magma.

If you are at Whiteside Mountain between January and July, keep your eyes open for peregrine falcons soaring above. A pair of these falcons was released here in 1985. Every spring, a pair returns. The cliff face is closed to rock climbers while the falcons are courting, nesting, and raising their brood, which is usually from mid-January or February until late June or July. The nest cannot be seen from the hiking trail, but you may hear or see the falcons, especially in the spring, when the parents spend many hours hunting other birds to feed their hungry nestlings. Wildlife biologists aren't sure where the peregrines spend the fall and winter—perhaps in the eastern Piedmont or perhaps at the coast, where there is an abundance of food in the form of overwintering shorebirds. The birds aren't banded for identification and study because attempts at banding in the past sometimes

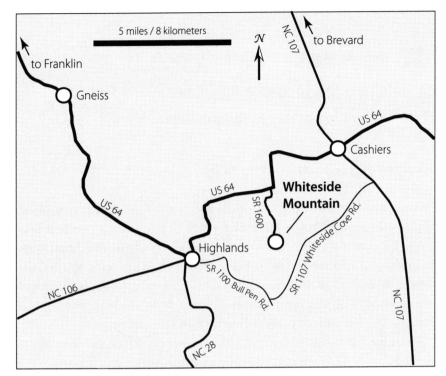

FIGURE 8-4. Location of Whiteside Mountain.

caused baby peregrine falcons to jump to their deaths out of their cliff-side nests.

We may not know exactly how the rock at this site originated or where the peregrines go in the winter, but we do know that Whiteside Mountain is a beautiful place to sit and ponder the mysteries of geology and birds.

Location and Access

Whiteside Mountain, which is in Nantahala National Forest, is off US 64 between Highlands and Cashiers. There are no facilities at the mountain.

9

Grandfather Mountain
From Valley to Peak in 750 Million Years

)) AVERY COUNTY, NORTH CAROLINA

Grandfather Mountain is where you'll find North Carolina's famous Mile-High Swinging Bridge, a suspension footbridge that spans an 80-foot deep gorge between two rocky promontories. It's also where you'll find some beautiful 750-million-year-old conglomerate rock. While most North Carolinians have heard of the bridge, probably only geologists are familiar with the conglomerate. However, once you know where to look, you too can become familiar with this fascinating rock and the story it tells.

From the Swinging Bridge, you can see in every direction waves of forested slopes dotted with rugged bare rock outcrops, often appearing to rise out of a blanket of clouds below. In the early days of our country, Grandfather Mountain was widely regarded as the tallest mountain in North Carolina, or perhaps even the East. In 1794 the famed French botanist André Michaux climbed Grandfather Mountain and believed he had reached the highest point in North America. But in 1835 Elisha Mitchell, a professor at the University of North Carolina and a geologist for the state, measured the mountain that now bears his name and found it to be higher than Grandfather (see Chapter 11).

Whereas Michaux hiked up Grandfather Mountain, today most people drive. On your way up to the spectacular views at the Visitor Center and the Swinging Bridge, be sure to stop for some geological investigations. About a mile past the entrance, you will come to a big outcrop called Split Rock. Just beyond it, there is a turnout at the switchback where you can park your car while you visit the rock. The outcrop impresses you first with its size and shape—it's about 30 feet high and has a 2-foot-wide crack running down the middle. Cracks like this one start when a little bit of water works into a joint or fissure in the rock. Each time that water seeps in, freezes, and expands, the crack gradually gets bigger. Plant roots often enlarge cracks in rock, too.

FIGURE 9-1. Grandfather Mountain.

If you look a little closer, you'll notice that the rock is made of rounded rock fragments in a fine-grained matrix—a sedimentary rock. Because the rock fragments are rounded, we can infer that they were carried some distance by a vigorous stream. As the rocks bounced along, sharp corners wore away. This kind of rock is called a conglomerate (a similar rock with angular rock fragments is called a breccia). The pebbles are made from a wide variety of rock types and are fairly large—they can be as large as baseballs. Some of the pebbles are noticeably flattened. You can also see a planar texture (foliation) in the matrix. The flattened pebbles and the foliation tell you that this conglomerate has been metamorphosed. We call this rock metamorphosed conglomerate or, more commonly, a metaconglomerate. Because the pebbles have different compositions, they responded differently to the metamorphism; that's why some are more flattened than others (Figure 9-2). Can you tell which rock compositions were stronger?

About half a mile farther down the road, you can park and take a short walk to Linville Bluffs, where there is an expansive view of mountains made of the conglomerates. The pebbles in the conglomerate under your feet are smaller than at Split Rock—about the size of grapes or cherry tomatoes. The grain size in sedimentary rocks tells us something about how fast the streams were flowing. Imagine a roaring whitewater stream high in the mountains. This fast-moving water can carry particles that range in size from clay and silt up to large cobbles. As the stream flows out of the mountains and into gentler topography, the velocity gradually decreases; and as it does, sediments settle out and are deposited on the streambed. The first sediments to settle out will be the largest ones because the stream will still be flowing fast enough to transport the smaller ones. This happens all along the stream's course. Eventually, the stream will reach its mouth and dump all its remaining sediments in the ocean (or, in some cases, a lake). The size of the grains on the streambed at any point along the course of the stream reflects how fast the stream was flowing at that point. (And velocity depends on the slope of the streambed and the water level in the stream; floodwaters move faster than low waters.) So, we know that the stream that deposited the large pebbles in Split Rock was traveling faster than the stream that deposited the small pebbles at Linville Bluffs.

When you get to the top of the mountain, you can walk across the famous Mile-High Swinging Bridge to Linville Peak, elevation 5,295 feet. Here the pebbles in the conglomerate are even smaller—about the size of peas—indicating that they were deposited by a still slower stream.

FIGURE 9-2. Split Rock, made of metamorphosed conglomerate. Look closely to see pebbles in the rock.

You've seen that the rocks of Grandfather Mountain are made of metamorphosed conglomerates and have learned that the sediments in those conglomerates were deposited by streams of varying velocity. By now you might begin wondering what kinds of streams deposited the sediments and when.

Seven hundred and fifty million years ago, when bacteria and algae were the only living things on earth, tectonic forces began to pull apart the supercontinent Rodinia. As the continent tore apart, huge faults formed in the earth's crust. Some of these continued opening up to form oceans; others created smaller features called rift basins. Similar rift basins are actively forming in East Africa today—Lake Tanganyika and Lake Malawi are in rift basins. As soon as a rift basin forms, streams and rivers begin flowing into it and depositing sediment, eventually filling the basin with sediment. When a rift basin is new, its sides are steep—the sides are, after all, faults where blocks of earth have dropped down. At first, streams flowing into the basins are moving fast and carrying big rocks. Over time, streams slow down because the topographic relief across the basin margin decreases. This happens for two reasons. The first is that erosion wears down the sides of the basins into gentler slopes and the second is that the basins fill up with sediments. So the streams slow down, depositing smaller sediments than before. Sometimes new movement along the faults makes the sides of the basin steep again. By studying the sediments in a rift basin, we can put together a history of the basin. If there were only one episode of faulting followed by basin infilling, we would expect to see progressively finer sediments traveling upward through the layers. If there are large particles on top of fine ones, that might mean that renewed tectonic activity steepened the sides of the basin again.

The rock that would eventually become Grandfather Mountain began as sediment in one of the rift basins that formed during the breakup of Rodinia. This rift basin was on the edge of the ancient continent of Laurentia, which would later become North America. The continent that was pulling away was Gondwana, which was made of parts of what would later become Africa and South America. In between lay the Iapetus Ocean. (The Carolinas experienced this same cycle of spreading and rift-basin formation over 500 million years later, during the Triassic period when Pangea broke up and the Atlantic Ocean was born.)

Millions of years after the breakup of Rodinia, Gondwana began moving back toward Laurentia. From about 460 million years ago to about 270 million years ago, the Iapetus Ocean closed up, and three landmasses collided with Laurentia—first a volcanic fragment of crust known as the Piedmont terrane, then a fragment of Gondwana, and then Gondwana itself. When Gondwana hit, Laurentia experienced an incredible amount of compression. In response, the crust thickened and rose to form the Appalachian Mountains. In many places, the crust developed almost horizontal faults along which blocks of crust were pushed up and over each other, eventually overlapping like shingles.

Such faults are called thrust faults (see Figure 2-4), and in most cases they push older rock on top of younger rock, reversing the normal order of things and alerting us to the fact that some major rearranging has gone on. A series of these thrust faults carried crustal sheets over the rift basin conglomerate, metamorphosing it into the rock you see at Grandfather Mountain today. The older rocks that were pushed over the conglomerate have since eroded away, leaving a "window" through the thrust sheet to the conglomerate below. This structure is called the Grandfather Mountain window (Figure 9-3). The lowermost fault is called the Linville Falls thrust

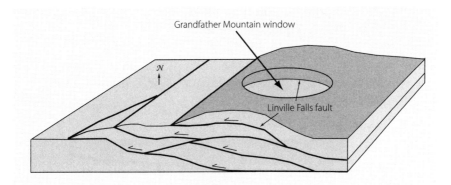

FIGURE 9-3. The Grandfather Mountain window. Movement along thrust faults during the Alleghanian orogeny put older rocks on top of younger ones. Later, erosion created a window through the Linville Falls thrust sheet, exposing the metamorphosed conglomerate of Grandfather Mountain below. Linville Falls (see Chapter 10) is located near the edge of the window, to the southwest of Grandfather Mountain, which is in the middle.

fault, and it also shows up at Linville Falls (see Chapter 10), where 745-million-year-old metamorphosed granite is on top of 540-million-year-old quartzite.

While you are at the Swinging Bridge, plan to spend time enjoying the view of the conglomerate under your feet and the panoramic view of the mountains around you. You can purchase a booklet at the Visitor Center that identifies the dozens of peaks that are visible from the Swinging Bridge on a clear day. Looking west, there are the Black Mountains, including Mount Mitchell, which is about 1,400 feet higher than where you are standing. Looking east, you can't quite see the highest point on Grandfather Mountain, Calloway Peak, because it is right behind MacRae Peak, which is almost as tall as Calloway.

Although Grandfather is not the highest peak around, it still feels pretty close to the top of the world. And that makes it seem all the more amazing that the rock of Grandfather Mountain started out 750 million years ago in the bottom of a deep rift basin.

Location and Access

Grandfather Mountain is about 70 miles northeast of Asheville and about 20 miles south of Boone. Because it is privately owned and operated, there

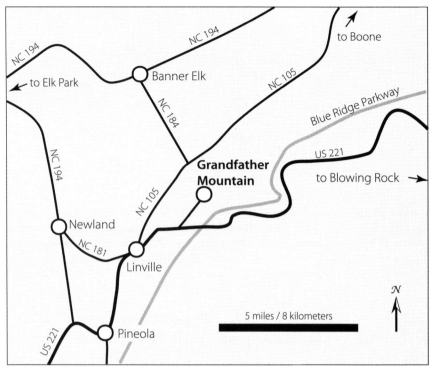

FIGURE 9-4. Location of Grandfather Mountain.

is an admission fee. Hugh Morton inherited the land in 1952 from his grand-father Hugh MacRae, who acquired it in the late 1880s. There are separate entrances available to backcountry hikers. Primitive camping is allowed.

Nearby Features

About 15 miles northeast of Grandfather Mountain, on US 321, is a large road cut that exposes some of the oldest rock in the Carolinas. It's across the street from the entrance to the Tweetsie Railroad; you can either park at Tweetsie and carefully cross the highway, or you can drive right up on the large grassy area at the base of the outcrop. The rock is called Blowing Rock gneiss, and it is 1 billion years old (1,000 million years old). The gneiss is very deformed; look for folds, boudins (which look like strings of sausages), and augen (eye-shaped crystals of feldspar).

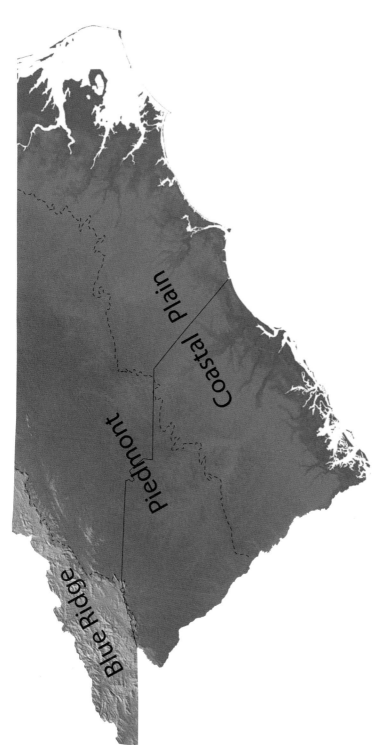

PLATE 1. The physiographic provinces of the Carolinas. The boundary between the Coastal Plain and the Piedmont is known as the Fall Zone or Fall Line.

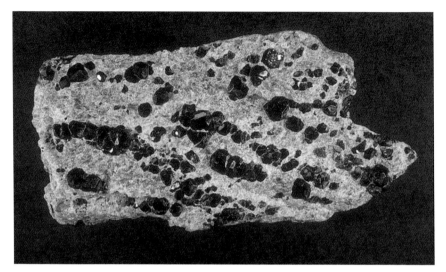

PLATE 2. A metamorphic rock with large crystals of garnet in a matrix of quartz and feldspar, from the Gudger Mine in Mitchell County, North Carolina. (In the SAS Institute Collection, North Carolina Museum of Natural Sciences.)

PLATE 3. Garnet-mica schist from Wake County, North Carolina. (In the collection of Dr. Chris Tacker, North Carolina Museum of Natural Sciences.)

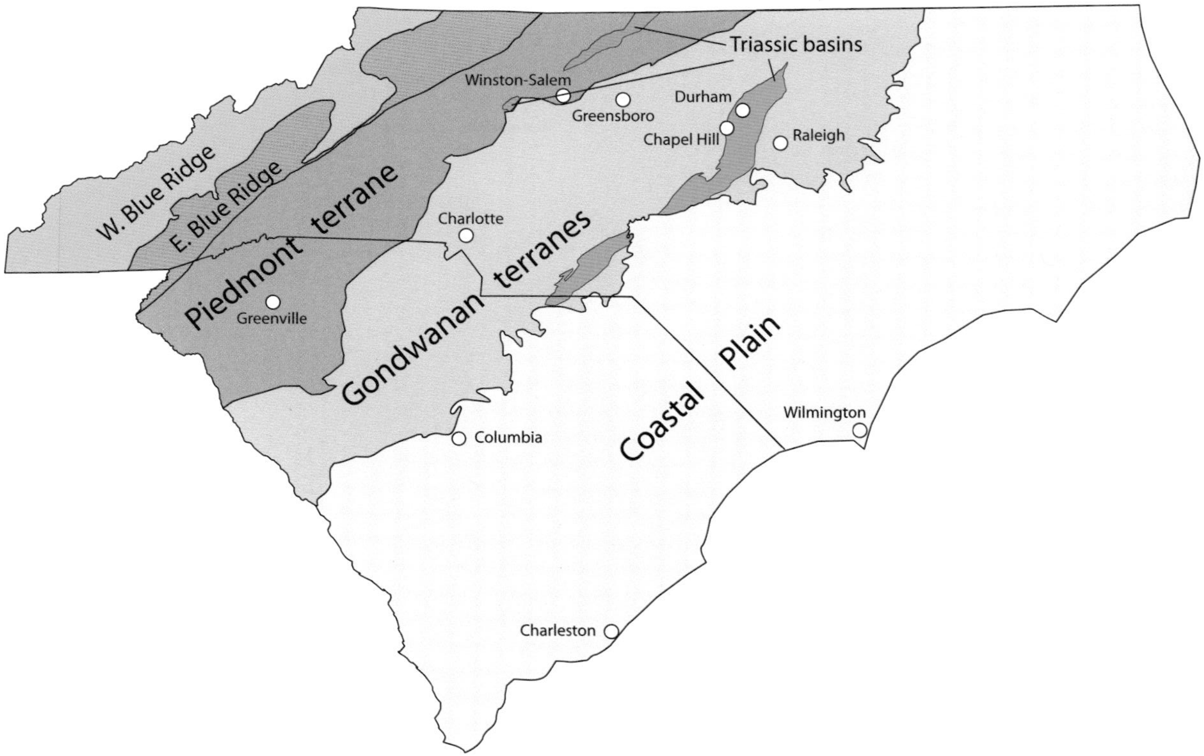

PLATE 4. Geologic map of the Carolinas. The Western Blue Ridge contains metamorphic and igneous rocks that were on the coast of Laurentia (ancestral North America). The Eastern Blue Ridge contains metamorphosed sedimentary and igneous rocks that were part of an accretionary wedge. The Piedmont and the Gondwanan terranes were added to Laurentia during collisions. Triassic basins formed when Pangea split apart. Coastal Plain sediments were deposited during past high stands in sea level.

Triassic basins

Raleigh

Durham
Chapel Hill

Greensboro

Winston-Salem

Wilmington

Coastal Plain

Gondwanan terranes

Charlotte

Columbia

Charleston

Piedmont terrane

E. Blue Ridge

W. Blue Ridge

Greenville

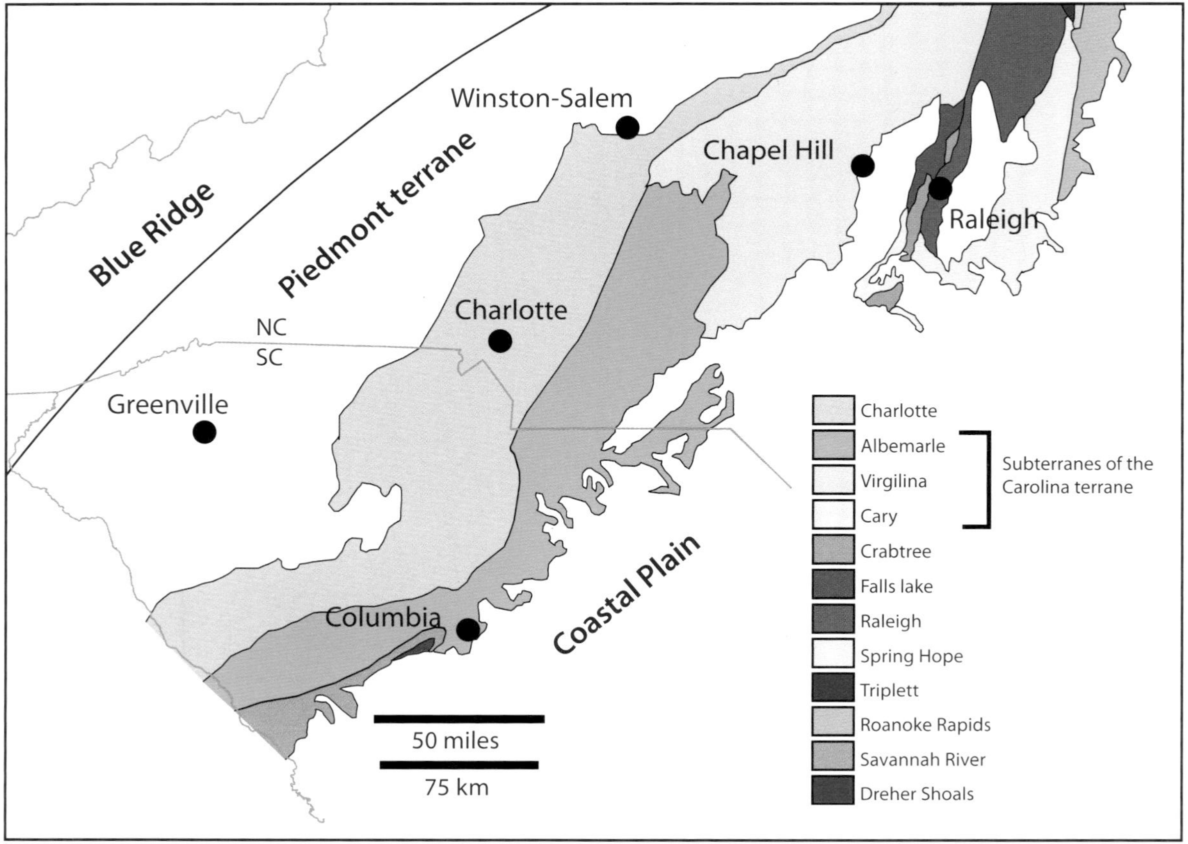

PLATE 5. Gondwanan terranes of the Carolinas. These terranes were once part of the ancient continent Gondwana before being accreted to ancestral North America. Terranes in shades of green typically experienced lower-grade metamorphism than the others.

Blue Ridge

Piedmont terrane

Winston-Salem

Chapel Hill

Raleigh

Charlotte

Columbia

Greenville

NC
SC

Coastal Plain

50 miles
75 km

Charlotte
Albemarle
Virgilina
Cary
Crabtree
Falls lake
Raleigh
Spring Hope
Triplett
Roanoke Rapids
Savannah River
Dreher Shoals

Subterranes of the Carolina terrane

PLATE 6. Whitewater Falls near Cashiers, North Carolina. At 411 feet, it is the highest waterfall east of the Rocky Mountains.

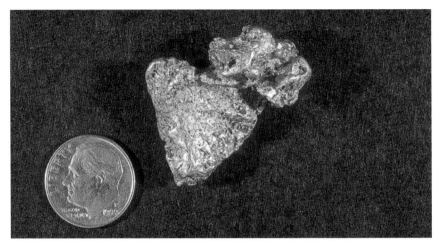

PLATE 7. A gold nugget found at Reed Gold Mine in the early 1800s. (In the SAS Institute Collection, North Carolina Museum of Natural Sciences.)

PLATE 8. Quartz veins in metamorphic rock exposed in the walls of Reed Gold Mine.

PLATE 9. Old quarry at Occoneechee Mountain; debris from the February 2001 landslide can be seen at lower left.

PLATE 10. The faceted emerald was cut from the crystal on the right, which was discovered in Hiddenite, Alexander County, North Carolina. The reddish brown, needle-shaped crystals in the emerald are rutile (titanium dioxide). (Both in the SAS Institute Collection at the North Carolina Museum of Natural Sciences.)

PLATE 11. Green emerald and black tourmaline in a matrix of feldspar, from the Crabtree Emerald Mine, Mitchell County, North Carolina. (In the SAS Institute Collection, North Carolina Museum of Natural Sciences.)

PLATE 12. Sedimentary layers at Flanner Beach. Bluish clay at the bottom was deposited 125,000 years ago, at the beginning of a 20-foot rise in sea level. Whitish layers contain abundant fossil shell fragments.

10

Linville Falls
Falls, Faults, and Geologic Windows

Travelers love Linville Falls for the spectacular scenery; geologists love Linville Falls for the spectacular geology. Just off the Blue Ridge Parkway in Burke County, the Linville River cascades first over a small cliff of metamorphosed granite (the Upper Falls) and then through a 150-foot-tall winding chute of quartzite (the Lower Falls). What separates the two rock types is a world-famous fault, the Linville Falls thrust fault, which developed during a continental collision millions of years ago. A model of the famous fault is at the North Carolina Museum of Natural Sciences in Raleigh at the waterfall on the second floor.

From the parking lot at the Linville Falls visitor center, it's an easy half-mile walk to the Upper Falls Overlook. The path to the Upper Falls Overlook splits off the main path and descends to the river. Soon after this path turns right, you will come to an outcrop on the right side of the path. At first glance, it looks like an igneous rock with visible interlocking crystals of light-colored quartz and pinkish-orange feldspar and fewer dark minerals, a rock we would call granite. But when you look closely, you will see that it is strongly layered. Many of the minerals have been stretched and flattened. The layers, which are gently inclined, tell you that the granite has been metamorphosed. This metamorphosed granite is mineralogically similar to the granite on Beech Mountain, North Carolina, as well as some other granites scattered around the area. The Beech Mountain granite has been dated at 745 million years; the granite here is likely the same age (this age refers to the granite, not the metamorphism, which happened much later).

As you continue along the trail, you will keep dropping down toward the river. At the bottom of a small set of steps, there is a low outcrop on the right. Take a look at it, then continue down to the Upper Falls Overlook, where the same rock is exposed under your feet; you can also see it in the

FIGURE 10-1. Linville Falls cascading over cliffs of quartzite. Notice the Upper Falls, top center.

walls of the Lower Falls. The most obvious feature of this rock is that it is strongly layered and folded (Figure 10-2). The rock surface also has a faint sheen, which is due to fine grains of mica. Most of the rock is made of quartz, and the strong layering and deformation, along with the mica flakes, tell us the rock has been metamorphosed into quartzite. Five hundred and forty million years ago, it was beach sand on the shores of Laurentia, the continent that would later, after the addition of several crustal fragments called terranes, become North America. A massive continental collision would change the sandstone into the quartzite you see here.

From the overlook, you can see the Upper Falls, where the Linville River tumbles over the metamorphosed granite (Figure 10-3). You can also see the top of the Lower Falls (for a better view of the Lower Falls, go to Chimney View Overlook or Erwins View Overlook). At the base of the Upper Falls, beneath the water, the metamorphosed granite gives way to the quartzite, which forms the walls of the circuitous Lower Falls.

That's right—the 540-million-year-old quartzite is beneath the 745-mil-

FIGURE 10-2. Folded quartzite at the Upper Falls Overlook.

lion-year-old metamorphosed granite. This juxtaposition of older rocks on top of younger rocks is a dead giveaway that you have crossed a fault. The granite existed before the sandstone did, and sand could not have been deposited underneath the granite. This age reversal tells us that the older rocks have been thrust over the younger rocks by movement along a fault.

It happened when Gondwana (which was made of parts of Africa and South America) collided with Laurentia, in what we call the Alleghanian orogeny. The collision was so powerful that the crust of Laurentia was compressed until huge, nearly horizontal faults developed in the crust. Blocks of crust on these fault surfaces rode up on each other like shingles, telescoping and thickening the crust and putting older rocks on top of younger ones. Each of the cracks along which movement took place is called a thrust fault (see Figure 2-4).

The Linville Falls thrust fault moved about 300 million years ago. Geologists estimate that along the fault a block of crust several miles thick was pushed as far as 50 miles to the northwest, something that probably took about 2 million years.

FIGURE 10-3. Upper Falls. Layered quartzite in the foreground has been overridden by more massive granite; Linville Falls thrust fault runs along the base of the falls.

The rocks that are right next to a fault are deformed, or "sheared," as movement is taking place. Typically, rocks in a shear zone that was active deep in the crust have very obvious fine layers that developed as a result of the shearing. When the Linville Falls fault was most active, it was buried about 10 miles below the surface, where the elevated heat and pressure allowed the minerals in the rock to deform like stiff putty. The shearing smeared out the different minerals into layers. You can see this kind of deformation in the granite and quartzite here.

Usually faults with more displacement have wider shear zones. A geologist named Chuck Trupe discovered that the shear zone of the Linville Falls thrust fault is about half a mile wide.

The folds in the quartzite show what happened to the original layers of the sandstone as the older rock was pushed over it; imagine how a rug gets folded when you push a sofa over it. (The layers of the metamorphosed granite are not strongly folded because the original rock, granite, did not have layers in it to begin with.) Notice also the dark streaks on the quartzite at the overlook. These are quartz grains that got stretched out during the faulting. We measure streaks like these to determine the direction that a fault has moved—northwest in this case.

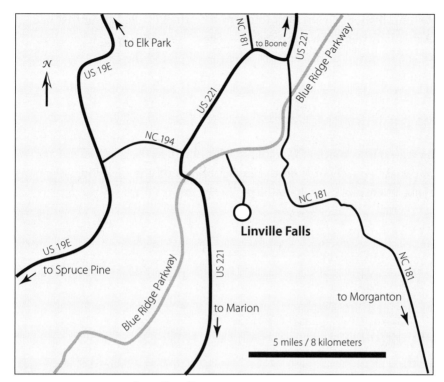

FIGURE 10-4. Location of Linville Falls.

You can see the same quartzite in North Carolina's Table Rock Mountain, just to the east. There is similar quartzite, also from the ancient Iapetus Ocean, at Pilot Mountain, but it has not been folded like this because it was not caught up in the shear zone. Its metamorphism was due to simple burial.

The rocks above the Linville Falls thrust fault are part of a large sheet of rock that covers hundreds of square miles in North Carolina. Here at Linville Falls, tectonic forces pushed up part of the Linville Falls thrust sheet, which erosion subsequently cut through, enabling us to see both the granite and the quartzite below. We call such a feature a tectonic window; this particular one, which is framed by the Linville Falls fault, is known as the Grandfather Mountain window (see Figure 9-3), named after the prominent mountain inside the window near the northwestern edge. (The quartzite at Pilot Mountain is also exposed within a tectonic window, called the Sauratown Mountain window. See Chapter 18.)

There are more than a dozen major thrust faults in the mountains of the Carolinas, and countless smaller ones. The Linville Falls thrust fault is particularly well known and well loved because of the geologic window, the huge amount of displacement along the fault, and the excellent exposure of the rocks.

Location and Access

Linville Falls is south of Grandfather Mountain in the Blue Ridge Parkway National Park. The turnoff to Linville Falls is off the Blue Ridge Parkway about 1 mile north of where the parkway crosses US 221.

11

Mount Mitchell State Park
Which Peak Is the Tallest and Why

Every schoolchild in the Carolinas knows that Mount Mitchell (6,684 feet) is the highest point east of the Mississippi. To be more precise, it's the highest point east of South Dakota. Harney Peak, in South Dakota's Black Hills, is only a few hundred feet higher.

But most schoolchildren never learn why Mount Mitchell is so tall. The answer, as we shall see, depends on the geologic history of the Carolinas and on the properties of two minerals, kyanite and quartz.

Mount Mitchell is one of about a dozen peaks on a 15-mile long ridge called the Black Mountains. Before the mid-1800s, the ridge was considered one mountain, and its peaks were not officially named. The Black Mountains run north-south, except for a hook that curves to the west at the south end. They may not be as long or wide as some other mountain ranges in the Appalachians, but they are the tallest. The highest peaks along the ridge, traveling south to north, are Clingman's Peak (6,571 feet), Mount Gibbes (6,571 feet), Mount Mitchell (6,684 feet), Mount Craig (6,648 feet), Big Tom (6,581 feet), Balsam Cone (6,596 feet), and Cattail Peak (6,584 feet). The South Toe River valley along the eastern flank of the Black Mountains is at an elevation of about 2,600 feet, giving a local topographic relief of about 4,000 feet. In fact, looking east from the top of Mount Mitchell down to the South Toe River, you will see a topographic change that is similar to that between the South Rim of the Grand Canyon and the Colorado River below.

If you visit Mount Mitchell, be sure to bring lots of warm clothes. Because of its elevation, Mount Mitchell's climate is not typical of the Carolinas. The average daily high in July is only 68°F and the highest temperature ever recorded at Mount Mitchell is 81°F. The lowest ever recorded, -34°F, occurred on January 21, 1985. Mount Mitchell receives an average of 96 inches of snow a year, and it is well known for its howling winds.

FIGURE 11-1. Looking west toward the Black Mountains. Mount Mitchell is the peak in the center.

Because of the harsh climate, the plants and animals that live in the upper elevations of the Black Mountains are typical of more northern climes. For example, northern hardwoods, red spruce (*Picea rubens*), and Fraser fir (*Abies fraseri*) grow on the high ridge tops. The dark green spruce-fir forest appears black from a distance and gave the ridge its name.

Hiking along trails in the park, you will see outcrops of dark sparkly rock that is strongly layered. This layering, called foliation, forms during metamorphism when grains of quartz, feldspar, and mica get flattened and grow in sheetlike layers. The foliation is folded and wrinkled in many places as a result of the intense heat and pressure the rock experienced deep underground (Figure 11-2). Where the rock has more quartz and feldspar than mica, it is called gneiss. Where it has more mica, it is called schist. Most of the gneiss on Mount Mitchell is not banded, but some of it has the more typical appearance of gneiss: thin alternating light and dark bands. (See Figure 2-3 for examples of banding.) In addition to the common minerals quartz, feldspar, and mica, one can find in both the gneiss and the schist here an unusual mineral called kyanite, which appears as bluish-gray bladed crystals.

In places nearly half the rock is made of kyanite. This kyanite-rich band of rock extends along the length of the Black Mountains, from Mount

FIGURE 11-2. Tightly folded kyanite- and quartz-rich schist in the Black Mountains.

Mitchell to the northernmost peak, Celo Knob. The band continues to the north, crossing US 19E east of Burnsville, North Carolina, and can be traced for a few more miles. The high peaks north of US 19E (Pig Pen Bluff and Locust Rough Mountain) are made of this same kyanite-rich rock.

The fact that the highest mountain range in the Carolinas contains kyanite is no coincidence. Both kyanite and quartz are much more resistant to weathering and erosion than lots of other minerals, such as feldspar and mica. If you've ever picked up a "book" of shiny mica flakes, you know how easy it is to pick apart and break with your fingers. Because rocks rich in kyanite and quartz stand up to erosion so well, they commonly form cliffs, hills, or mountains. Pilot Mountain and Hanging Rock, in North Carolina, are quartzite mountains, and Crowders Mountain near Charlotte, North Carolina, is a kyanite quartzite mountain.

But these two minerals are not the whole story. All of the mountains in the Carolinas are the worn-down remnants of a much higher ancient range that was pushed up by a massive continental collision that began about 330 million years ago. When continents collide, crust that is caught in the collision gets thicker, just like a sheet of clay on a table would thicken if you slowly pushed the ends toward each other. When the crust gets thicker, some of it goes down and some of it goes up, making mountains. The brand-new Appalachian mountain range was truly massive—it may have had peaks as tall as those in the Himalayas. (See Chapter 5 for more information on this collision, called the Alleghanian orogeny.) The tallest peaks in the range were probably in the Piedmont because that's where we find the most highly metamorphosed rocks.

After the collision, most of the world's landmasses were assembled in one supercontinent called Pangea. Erosion went to work on the Appalachians, tearing them down bit by bit. Then, about 220 million years ago, tectonic forces began pulling Pangea apart. As part of this rifting, a piece of crust that would become Africa began moving away from what we now call the east coast of North America. Before the two continents actually rifted apart, the crust between them stretched, getting thinner and thinner. The mountains began to sink as a result of this thinning, with those closer to the rift zone (what would become the Atlantic Ocean) losing the most elevation. As the crust in the Piedmont thinned, it no longer towered over the Blue Ridge.

Millions of years of rain, wind, snow, and ice have worn down the Appalachians even more. In this erosive environment, kyanite and quartz helped Mount Mitchell become the elevation champion.

Kyanite occurs in other places in the Carolinas, but rocks that have as much kyanite as those in the Black Mountains are unusual. To understand how the kyanite got there, we have to look far into the past, long before the collision that produced the Appalachians. The rocks that are now in the Black Mountains started out as sediments collecting on the floor of the Iapetus Ocean probably between 500 and 600 million years ago. This ocean was off the edge of ancestral North America, a continent called Laurentia. Out in the Iapetus, heading toward Laurentia, was a block of crust with active volcanoes on it (perhaps similar to Sumatra, the large island with active volcanoes at the eastern edge of the Indian Ocean). As it approached Laurentia, this piece of crust bulldozed a huge wedge of seafloor sediments and basaltic oceanic crust in front of it. When the crustal fragment collided with Laurentia in the Taconic orogeny 460 million years ago, the mass of sediments, called an accretionary wedge, was pushed up onto Laurentia and metamorphosed. They were metamorphosed again during the continental collision 330 million years ago (the Alleghanian orogeny), becoming the rocks we see in the Black Mountains today.

We know the sediments that became the Black Mountains must have been rich in silicon, oxygen, and aluminum because the first two of these elements are ingredients in quartz and all three are ingredients in kyanite.

Virtually all sediments contain quartz (silicon and oxygen), but aluminum is typically less abundant. There are two ways to explain the presence of excess aluminum in the sediments. One hypothesis is that the sediments were exposed above sea level at some point before becoming metamorphosed. Weathering tends to remove more soluble elements first, leaving behind aluminum-rich material called bauxite. (Bauxite is commonly mined today in tropical regions, where the warm, humid climate promotes rapid chemical weathering of rocks.) If the sedimentary rocks of this ancient accretionary wedge had been exposed on land and weathered into bauxite, subsequent high-pressure metamorphism would have produced a kyanite-rich rock.

Another hypothesis is that hot water percolated through the sediments, leaching the soluble minerals and leaving behind a concentration of aluminum-rich minerals. Hot water is often generated when one plate sinks under another—as the plate goes down, water in its crust is heated (because temperatures increase the deeper you go into the earth). The hot water rises, percolating through whatever rocks or sediments are above it. Hot water is a very effective agent of chemical weathering and can turn feldspar into aluminum-rich minerals. At this point, we don't know which, if either, of these explanations is correct for the Black Mountains. But we do know that it's the combination of quartz and kyanite that fends off the destructive power of erosion and gives these mountains their height.

Like many of the high peaks in the United States, Mount Mitchell was named after a prominent person. Unlike most peaks, Mount Mitchell was named after a scientist, rather than a president or an explorer. Elisha Mitchell was a professor of chemistry, geology, and mineralogy at the University of North Carolina at Chapel Hill from 1825 until his death in 1857. He also surveyed much of North Carolina while working for the state's Geological and Agricultural Survey. After an 1828 ascent of Grandfather Mountain, then believed to be the tallest mountain in North Carolina, he wrote to his wife: "It was a question with us whether the Black and Roan Mountains were not higher than the Grandfather. . . . There can be no doubt that the country around the base of the Grandfather is higher than any other tract along these elevations but I suspect the Black and Roan to be higher peaks" (quoted in S. Kent Schwarzkopf, *A History of Mt. Mitchell and the Black Mountains: Exploration, Development, and Preservation* [Raleigh: Division of Archives and History, 1985], 2).

In 1835 Mitchell calculated that the highest peak on the Black Mountain ridge was 6,476 feet tall—208 feet short of what we now know to be the actual height of Mount Mitchell. He calculated the height by taking temperature and barometric readings on the peak and later comparing them to temperature and barometric readings taken by a friend at about the same time in Morganton, North Carolina. Inaccuracies inherent in his method combined with the fact that he had miscalculated the elevation of Morganton gave him an incorrect figure.

Even though Mitchell's measurement was a couple of hundred feet short, he was still able to proclaim the Black Mountains to be not only the highest mountains in North Carolina but also the highest in the United States (which did not yet include Colorado)—higher even than the White Mountains in New Hampshire.

In the years following his 1835 measurement, Mitchell was unsure whether he had climbed and measured the highest of the Black Mountain peaks. As he wrote, "It is a matter of considerable difficulty, in the case of a long ridge like this, that swells here and there into a knob two or three hundred feet higher than its neighbors, to ascertain which it is that overtops the rest, from our inability to determine how much of the apparent elevation of one, amongst a number, is due to its nearness, & how much to height" (quoted in Schwarzkopf, *History of Mt. Mitchell*, 26).

Mitchell made more measurements in the Black Mountains in 1838 and 1844. In the 1850s a public and acrimonious debate arose between Mitchell and Thomas L. Clingman, a U.S. congressman and former student of Mitchell's, about which Black Mountain peak was the highest, whether Mitchell had measured it, and what year he had measured it. Things got confusing fast (see Table 1). In 1855 Clingman used barometric measurements to confirm that present-day Mount Mitchell (which was then called Clingman's Peak) was higher than present-day Clingman's Peak (which was then called Mount Mitchell)—in opposition to what Mitchell apparently believed. Even today, it is not completely clear which peaks Mitchell scaled in 1838 and 1844, and which of the peaks in the Black Mountain range he believed to be highest. But it is well documented and agreed upon that he measured the present-day Mount Mitchell in 1835 and, in so doing, was the first person to prove the Black Mountains to be the highest mountains in the east.

In 1857, at age 64, Mitchell traveled to the Black Mountains alone to make some new measurements to try to settle the debate. On his way down the mountain we now call Mount Mitchell, he slipped on a 40-foot water-

TABLE 1. Mitchell's measurements in the Black Mountains

	What Mitchell thought he measured	What Mitchell really measured	Mitchell's measurement
1835	at the time: the highest peak; later: not the highest peak	Mount Mitchell (actual elevation: 6,684')	6,476'
1838	at the time: the highest peak; later: not the highest peak	Clingman's Peak (actual elevation: 6,571') or Mount Gibbes (actual elevation: 6,571')	6,581'
1844	the highest peak	Mount Gibbes (actual elevation: 6,571')	6,672'

NOTE: This table uses the modern names for the peaks, which in some cases differ from the names Mitchell and his contemporaries used.

fall and fell to his death. In 1858 the peak was named Mount Mitchell in his honor, and he was buried at the top. The Department of Geological Sciences at the University of North Carolina at Chapel Hill is housed in Elisha Mitchell Hall, in tribute to its famous early faculty member.

In 1915 Mount Mitchell became North Carolina's first state park. Much of the Black Mountain range had been logged in the first decade of the twentieth century, and North Carolina's governor, Locke Craig, was concerned about the environmental degradation of the state's tallest peak. He successfully lobbied the legislature to have the area protected. The second highest peak in eastern North America, elevation 6,648 feet, now bears Craig's name.

Unfortunately, the state park has not been able to protect the trees in the Black Mountains from a recent scourge. The spruce-fir forest has largely died in the last several decades, apparently from a combination of factors. An insect called the balsam woolly adelgid, accidentally introduced in the 1950s, has killed many of the fir trees. Acid precipitation or, more precisely, acid fog has also killed trees and made others more susceptible to attacks from the adelgid. Fog frequently shrouds the peaks of the Black Mountains, and this fog is made acidic by pollutants produced when fossil fuels are burned in power plants and cars. In addition, in the past few years, the southern pine beetle has killed trees on Mount Mitchell. Before then, this beetle was not known to have survived the harsh winters above 5,000 feet.

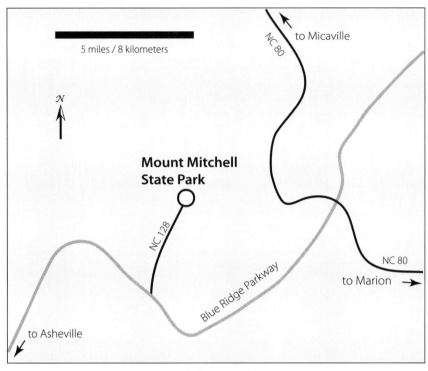

FIGURE 11-3. Location of Mount Mitchell State Park.

If you visit, you will see a forest of ghostly dead trees. You will also see Elisha Mitchell's grave and a lookout tower made of rocks from Mount Mitchell. If you climb to the top of the lookout tower, you can gaze out among the peaks of the Black Mountain range and imagine their history—from sediments on an ancient sea floor to high peaks that have inspired explorers, scientists, and politicians. Elisha Mitchell never knew the full story of the Black Mountains, but he laid the foundation for the scientists who followed him. Geologists know so much more about the Black Mountains today, and yet—as always in the field of geology—more remains to be discovered.

Location and Access

Mount Mitchell is about 30 miles northeast of Asheville on the Blue Ridge Parkway at mile marker 355. Bring warm clothes and rain gear no matter how warm and clear it is at the base of the mountain.

Nearby Features

The Museum of North Carolina Minerals, on the Blue Ridge Parkway about 10 miles north of the exit to Mount Mitchell, is worth a stop. It reopened in October 2003 after a major renovation of the facilities and exhibits. It showcases many of North Carolina's rocks and minerals and contains a wealth of information about geology and the history of mining in the state.

Emerald Village on Crabtree Creek near Little Switzerland is a commercial mining attraction where visitors can look for gems. The outcrops in and around Emerald Village feature a beautiful pegmatite (a light-colored igneous rock with unusually large crystals) that intruded a strongly foliated, dark metamorphic rock called amphibolite. Pegmatites are usually the last rocks to crystallize from molten magma and therefore have lots of elements that are magmatic "leftovers," that is, elements that don't go into making common minerals like feldspar and quartz. One of these leftovers is the element beryllium, which gets concentrated in the pegmatite magma, although still in very small amounts. Beryllium combines with the common elements aluminum, silicon, and oxygen to make the mineral beryl; and when a small bit of chromium is added to the mix, beryl turns a deep green and is known as emerald.

Recommended Reading

Schwarzkopf, S. Kent. *A History of Mt. Mitchell and the Black Mountains: Exploration, Development, and Preservation.* Raleigh: Division of Archives and History, N.C. Department of Cultural Resources, 1985.
Silver, Timothy. *Mount Mitchell and the Black Mountains: An Environmental History of the Highest Peaks in Eastern America.* Chapel Hill: University of North Carolina Press, 2003.

12

Stone Mountain State Park
A Beautiful Bare Mountain

A beautiful streaked dome of granite rises 700 feet above the valley floor. A waterfall slips down 500 feet of the mountain's steep southern slope. At the summit, bare granite is pocked with weathering pits, some of which are the tenuous toehold of little pine trees. On sunny days, hawks and vultures ride the thermals rising from its heated surface. This is Stone Mountain, in Stone Mountain State Park.

There's nothing else quite like Stone Mountain in the Carolinas (although there is something like it outside Atlanta, Georgia, also called Stone Mountain). The other mountains of the Carolinas are mostly covered with soil and vegetation. While parts of the lower slopes of Stone Mountain are wooded, it probably has a greater expanse of bare rock than any other mountain in the Carolinas.

Stone Mountain Trail is a 4.5-mile loop that takes you to the summit and to Stone Mountain Falls. The trail has some strenuous sections, including steep bare rock near the summit and hundreds of wooden steps alongside the falls. Walked clockwise from the parking area near the Hutchinson Homestead, the trail begins along a little creek through a forest. As the trail gets steeper, it gradually comes out of the woods and onto bare granite. In the transition zone between woods and bare rock, it's interesting to notice some of the stages of soil formation. In places you will see (and perhaps slip on) patches of brownish-orange sand and pebbles. These are some of the products of weathered granite. The most abundant mineral in granite is feldspar, which chemically weathers to clay. When the clay washes away, it leaves behind loose bits of rock. These angular fragments that collect on granite as it weathers are called grus. If grus accumulates on a flat area, it retains moisture and attracts plants. Next thing you know, the organic particles from the plants have mixed in with the grus, and you've got soil.

FIGURE 12-1. Stone Mountain. The black streaks running down the mountain are mineral stains from flowing water. Photograph by Edward Farr.

A positive feedback cycle is set up because the acidity of the soil greatly
enhances the rate of grus formation. Grus forms at a much slower rate on
steep, soil-free slopes.

At the top of the mountain, you can observe other kinds of weathering in
action. The dark streaks visible from the valley floor are where rivulets of
water have stained the rock. Up close, you can see that the streaks are also
slightly indented; the force of the water and the waterborne sediments have
eaten away the rock. Sometimes you will see chains of deep circular depressions in the dark streaks, where swirling sediments have scoured holes.
It's easy to imagine water running through the rivulets during a storm, cascading from pothole to pothole, gradually deepening the holes.

You will also see weathering pits of various sizes all over the granite, not
just in the streaks (see Figure 26-1). These form where puddles of water
have chemically degraded the rock, making it more easily erodable (rainwater is naturally somewhat acidic). Some of the larger weathering pits
have accumulated enough sediment to support plants. The smaller weathering pits look like hoof prints.

FIGURE 12-2. Slabs of rock break off in pieces parallel to the mountain's surface in a process known as exfoliation.

You can also see places where the top layer of the granite seems to be peeling off (Figure 12-2). In fact, that is exactly what is happening, on account of a process called exfoliation. As erosion removes overlying rock, pressure on the rock is released, which causes cracks to form in the granite very near and parallel to the surface. Eventually, parts of the rock break off and slide away, releasing more pressure and creating more cracks. Exfoliation is the primary way in which the rock is weathering here, and it is a common process in smooth bare rocks, like those exposed in Yosemite National Park in California. The rate of this kind of mechanical weathering is slower than the rate of chemical weathering that occurs underneath the vegetated parts of the rocks.

On the far side of the loop, you will come to Stone Mountain Falls (Figure 12-3). Here, the water slips down 500 feet of granite. The granite is steep, but not quite steep enough for the water to ever lose contact with the rock. The falls are slippery and dangerous; wooden steps provide a way to walk safely along the falls to the bottom, where you can relax on a boulder and enjoy the sights and sounds of moving water. As your mind begins to wan-

FIGURE 12-3. Stone Mountain Falls.

der over what you've seen today, you might begin to ask yourself how this great big bare mountain came to be.

It's a story of erosion. All things being equal, areas of high relief erode faster than areas of low relief. In other words, erosion works to smooth out the surface of the earth. In the real world, all things are never equal. For one thing, the forces of tectonic plates moving around sometimes push up mountains faster than erosion can smooth them down. Also, the bedrock on the surface of the earth varies tremendously. Many mountains in the Carolinas exist as a result of being more resistant to erosion than the surrounding landscape. For example, Pilot Mountain (see Chapter 18) is made of highly resistant quartzite. Crowders Mountain (see Chapter 16) and Mount Mitchell (see Chapter 11) are chock-full of quartz and kyanite, which is just as resistant as quartz. However, this is not the case with Stone Mountain—the valleys are underlain by the same granite that makes up Stone Mountain and the smaller granite domes in the park.

In general, in an area underlain by one kind of bedrock, with no active tectonic forces, the topography gets smoother over time. But if the bedrock is a uniform igneous rock like granite, sometimes the opposite happens. In areas where the bedrock is hard and uniform, like granite, low areas can erode faster than high areas. In other words, the relief between hilltops and valley floors can stay the same or even increase over time. This kind of counterintuitive weathering process takes place only in certain areas. If it occurred everywhere on earth, the surface would be composed of towering mountains and cavernous valleys, with no smooth spots anywhere.

First of all, this particular weathering process only occurs in areas of massive igneous bedrock that is not highly fractured. "Massive" means the rock is of uniform strength throughout, with no natural planes of weakness. Rocks that are strongly metamorphosed are not massive because they tend to have layers of different minerals, some of which are stronger than others.

Another requirement for this counterintuitive weathering process is that some areas are bare and other areas are covered with soil. Soil cover increases the rate of weathering because soil retains moisture and chemical compounds that hasten rock decomposition. Soil also attracts plants, whose roots work to break up rock. So the lower areas that are covered by soil and vegetation erode at a faster rate than the bare areas. Over time, the relief between soil-covered areas and bare areas increases. This process continues as long as the bare areas have steep slopes, because there is little chance for soil to develop and accumulate on the steep slopes. And it only works if the bedrock is massive and unfractured: if the bedrock were jointed or had layers of weak minerals, a high, bare exposure of the rock would tend to fall apart along the joints or weak layers and would lose elevation faster than its soil-covered valley counterpart.

Stone Mountain is made of relatively young granite. It was formed 335 million years ago, during the Alleghanian orogeny, the massive continental collision between Laurentia (ancestral North America) and Gondwana (ancestral South America and Africa). (The granite of Medoc Mountain in North Carolina and Forty Acre Rock in South Carolina formed during the same collision. See Chapters 25 and 26.) Because there have been no collisions in the Carolinas since then, the rock has not been metamorphosed (which would make layers of weak minerals) or fractured. The vast majority of the bedrock in the western Carolinas is metamorphosed and fractured because it is older and has been through multiple tectonic events. That's why we don't have lots of big bare rock mountains in the Carolinas.

If you're not quite ready to head home after hiking to the top of Stone Mountain and enjoying Stone Mountain Falls, there are many other trails and several other waterfalls to discover. Fairly short, strenuous trails lead to the smaller granite domes called Cedar Rock and Wolf Rock. There are some beautiful little waterfalls at the very beginning of Widow's Creek Trail, less than a couple of hundred yards off the road that winds through the park. There is also in the park a restored homestead that includes a log cabin, a barn, a corncrib, a meat house, and a blacksmith shop. The log cabin, built in 1855, was home to the Hutchinson family here at the base of Stone Mountain for four generations.

Location and Access

Stone Mountain State Park is north of North Wilkesboro. Take either US 21 or NC 18 to State Road 1002 and follow it to the John P. Frank Parkway, which will take you into the park.

Nearby Features

One of the largest open-face quarries in the world is operated by the North Carolina Granite Corporation in Mount Airy. The company mines a huge body of granite that underlies about 35 square miles of the area, including

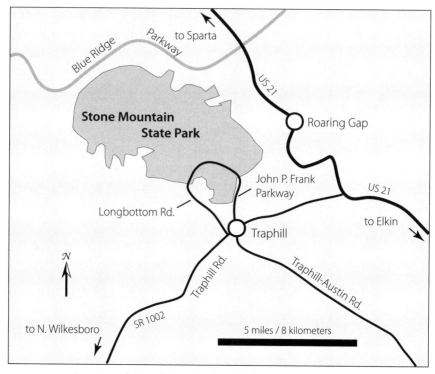

FIGURE 12-4. Location of Stone Mountain State Park.

the city. The granite intrusion was formed at the same time as the Stone Mountain granite, during the collision of Laurentia and Gondwana about 335 million years ago; like Stone Mountain, it is massive and undeformed. Mount Airy granite is light gray with shiny black specks of mica and is widely used as building stone in North Carolina and the rest of the United States. Some examples: the Arlington Memorial Bridge in Washington, D.C.; the Wright Brothers Memorial in Kill Devil Hills; and the Mount Airy Post Office. There are several large outcrops of the granite along US 52 and US 601 near Mount Airy.

13

Woodall Shoals
Beautiful Rocks That Have Been Through a Lot

The Chattooga River begins in Jackson County in western North Carolina and then snakes south, marking the border between Georgia and South Carolina. Outcrops of metamorphic rock create rapids and waterfalls, making the Chattooga a picturesque river and a popular destination for photographers, canoeists, and kayakers. The Chattooga is a designated Wild and Scenic River, with the Sumter National Forest on the South Carolina side and the Chattahoochee National Forest on the Georgia side.

Woodall Shoals is on the Chattooga almost due west of Walhalla, South Carolina. It is a set of rapids running over and along a fascinating outcrop of rock that may contain a record—albeit a cryptic one—of three important geologic events that have affected the Carolinas during the past 460 million years. The outcrop is an 8,000-square-foot broad, flat area of rock in the streambed, about a quarter-mile walk from the Woodall Shoals recreation site parking lot. Once you get to the river, walk a few yards upstream, and you will see Woodall Shoals. If the river is high, some of the outcrop may be underwater. Apparently, years ago this outcrop was underwater virtually all the time, but then a Mr. Woodall dynamited the west side of the river to create a deeper channel for floating his logs downstream.

Woodall Shoals is a feast for the eyes of anyone interested in geology. You will see light and dark layered rocks that are folded and squished together like colored play dough. There are simple U-shaped folds and more complicated zigzag folds. Some folds are smaller than your hand; others are bigger than a car. The tiniest wrinkles are called crenulations. In some places folds of different ages interfere with each other, similar to the way that waves in water coming from different directions produce interference patterns. Some of the interference patterns appear as domes or basins in the folded layers. Also look for layers that have been stretched apart so that

FIGURE 13-1. Woodall Shoals on the Chattooga River.

they look like strings of sausages. These are called boudins, a French word for sausages.

All of this deformed rock is metamorphic rock; it was the metamorphism that produced the layers, folds, and boudins. Metamorphism is the result of increased temperature and pressure, and the high pressure squeezed the rock into the contorted shapes that we see today. At Woodall Shoals, there is schist, gneiss, and amphibolite. The rock that is mostly mica, with the flakes aligned into closely spaced layers, is schist. Where you see light and dark bands, the rock is gneiss. And where the rock is almost completely black, it's amphibolite.

The highly deformed metamorphic rocks have been intruded in places by some very coarse-grained igneous rocks called pegmatite. Pegmatite forms by the underground crystallization of magma that contains water as well as other elements and compounds that inhibit the nucleation of mineral crystals. In fact, it appears that most pegmatite magma gets significantly cooler than its freezing point before the mineral crystals nucleate (a phenomenon known as supercooling). This kind of cooling history tends to create fewer—but larger—crystals than the normal cooling of magma.

As on many other river outcrops, you will find potholes, those smooth, circular, deep holes scoured out by waterborne sand and pebbles. Some of the potholes may have water in them; others will be dry. Most will have sand and pebbles in them. When the river is high and flowing over these potholes, eddies cause the sediment to whirl around, scouring the holes still deeper.

Finding an exposed outcrop of 8,000 square feet is like hitting a geological jackpot in the Carolinas, where so much of the rock is covered by vegetation. What makes this outcrop even more exciting is that it contains a wealth of information—the folds and other structures can tell us about events that happened millions of years ago.

Small folds are essentially scale models of the larger structures in a region. This relationship is called Pumpelly's Rule after Raphael Pumpelly, a geologist from New York who first discovered and articulated this association in 1894. The rule says that the orientations of the small folds are parallel to the orientations of the large-scale regional folds. That's important because we can infer the direction of tectonic forces by studying the orientation of folds. Structural geologists even study the arrangement of the mineral grains of metamorphic rocks under the microscope to learn more about the large-scale tectonic forces that have affected a region. In simplest terms, the hinge or "spine" of a fold is commonly perpendicular to the tectonic forces that produced it (although with stronger deformation fold hinges can become reoriented).

Geologists have spent a lot of time measuring the orientation of folds, layers, and fractures at Woodall Shoals in order to find out more about the geologic history of the area. Between about 500 and 600 million years ago, these rocks started out as horizontal layers of sediments interspersed with an occasional layer of basalt from a lava flow. These layers were deposited on the floor of the Iapetus Ocean between Laurentia (the ancient North America) and Gondwana (the continent that would become South America and Africa).

About 500 million years ago, Laurentia and Gondwana began moving toward each other, as if on a slow-motion conveyor belt. They came together in a series of three collisions. First, a strip of crust with volcanoes on it—the Piedmont terrane—collided with Laurentia (see Figure 5-2). Next, a piece of Gondwana broke off and collided with Laurentia (see Figure 5-3). Finally, Gondwana itself collided with Laurentia, creating the supercontinent Pangea.

The first collision, the Taconic orogeny, took place about 460 million

FIGURE 13-2. Amphibolite boudin. Notice that the foliation within the boudin is not parallel to the foliation in the shist surrounding it, indicating at least two episodes of metamorphism.

years ago. As the Piedmont terrane approached Laurentia, it scraped off the sediments and basalts that were on the floor of the Iapetus Ocean and shoved them up onto the edge of Laurentia, like dirt before a bulldozer. These bulldozed rocks formed what we call an accretionary wedge, and the rocks of Woodall Shoals are part of the Taconic accretionary wedge.

The sediments and lava flows were folded, compressed, and stretched as they were bulldozed ashore. The sandy layers became quartz-rich gneiss, the muddy layers became schist, and the basalt layers became amphibolite. The rocks may have been deformed again during a second collision, the enigmatic Acadian orogeny (see Chapter 5). They were deformed yet again when Gondwana collided with Laurentia in the Alleghanian orogeny. Geologists who have studied Woodall Shoals have noticed that there are at least five different generations of folds, which they have interpreted to be related to all three orogenies. This outcrop is a good illustration of just how much deformation rocks can go through as a result of the movement of tectonic plates. In some boudins, you will be able to see metamorphic layers or folds that are oriented differently than the metamorphic layers or folds of the surrounding rock (Figure 13-2). That means the rock in the boudins has gone through at least two episodes of metamorphism. The first

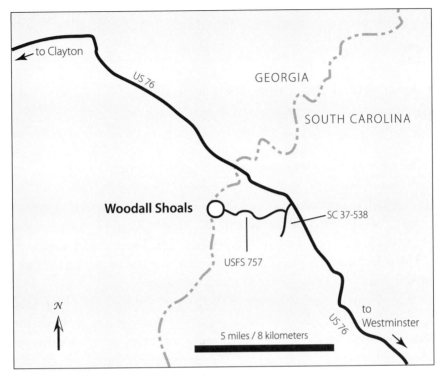

FIGURE 13-3. Location of Woodall Shoals.

episode created the layers or folds you see in the boudins. The second episode turned the rock into boudins, but it was not strong enough to "erase" the layers or folds of the first episode.

Woodall Shoals may be a perfect spot to do geological research, but you certainly don't have to be a geologist to appreciate the place. Folds and crenulations, boudins and pegmatites, potholes and pebbles all have stories to share, but they are also just plain beautiful.

Location and Access

Woodall Shoals is at the Woodall Shoals Boat Launch on the Chattooga River in the Sumter National Forest. The boat launch is at the end of U.S. Forest Service Road 757, a gravel road that branches off US 76. US 76 enters the national forest from Westminster, South Carolina. Note that there are three different parcels of Sumter National Forest in South Carolina. This is the one that borders Georgia. There are no facilities at Woodall Shoals.

14

Caesars Head and Table Rock State Parks
The View from the Blue Ridge Escarpment

The top of Caesars Head in Greenville County, South Carolina, is a glorious place to be on a warm fall afternoon. You are standing on a cliff 3,266 feet above sea level. Below you, miles and miles of Piedmont stretch eastward, ablaze with autumn foliage. Above you, migrating hawks soar on the thermals rising from the sun-warmed bare rock mountain.

It's such a good view because you're standing on the edge of the Blue Ridge escarpment, which is the topographic dividing line between the Piedmont and Blue Ridge. The escarpment is an abrupt change in elevation of up to 2,000 feet that runs from Virginia through North Carolina into South Carolina. In some places, such as Caesars Head, the escarpment is essentially vertical. In other places, it is not a cliff, but rather a steep slope. One way to experience the escarpment in your car is to drive from Old Fort to Black Mountain on I-40 in North Carolina—you will gain 1,500 feet in elevation over the course of 5 miles, making this one of the steepest sections of interstate in the country.

What is the origin of the Blue Ridge escarpment? Usually, abrupt changes in topography correspond to changes in rock type—the weaker rock wears away faster, leaving a cliff of hard rock. This does not explain the Blue Ridge escarpment here because the rock type at the top of Caesars Head is the same as that in the valley below Caesars Head. Is the Blue Ridge escarpment a fault scarp? A fault scarp is a cliff caused by a fault, where rocks on one side have dropped down relative to rocks on the other side. There is an obvious and extensive fault, called the Brevard fault, that corresponds to the Blue Ridge escarpment in places—but not here (Figure 14-2). At Caesars Head, the Brevard fault is more than 5 miles to the northwest. There might be an undiscovered fault through here, but so far no evidence of it has been found.

The most recent—and most convincing—hypothesis for the Blue Ridge

FIGURE 14-1. Caesars Head.

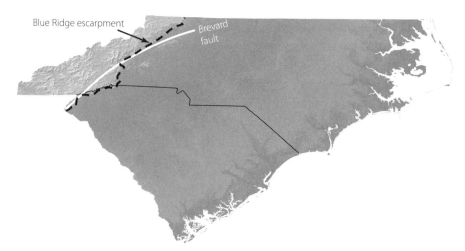

FIGURE 14-2. Caesars Head and Table Rock are located between the Blue Ridge escarpment and the Brevard fault.

escarpment is that it began as a feature known as a rift-flank uplift in the Triassic, about 220 million years ago, when Africa began to pull away from North America. Rift-flank uplifts are long ridges of slightly higher elevation that run along the edges of continents that have rifted apart. When continents begin to rift, the crust gets stretched out and thinned, much as Silly Putty does before it snaps. After the rift occurs, the edges of the two new continents rise as a result of two processes. Continental crust is buoyant, and when part of the crust is broken off and faulted away, the thinned crust can rebound, regaining some of the elevation it lost when it was being stretched out. In addition, rifting causes hot mantle rocks to well up into and fill the widening gap. Because hot rocks are less dense than cold rocks, the crust here will tend to be buoyed up. When Pangea split up in the Triassic, a rift-flank uplift would have developed along the eastern edge of North America. This uplift would have been far to the east from where the Blue Ridge escarpment is now, but over the past couple of hundred million years it could have retreated to the west as a result of erosion.

One might ask, if the rift-flank uplift has been eroding for hundreds of millions of years, why is it still so steep in places? One hypothesis has to do with climate and sea level. During the Cretaceous, about 90 million years ago, sea level was the highest it has been in the past 600 million years (see Chapter 29, on the Cliffs of the Neuse). The climate was warm, and all the glaciers and the ice caps had melted. Warm temperatures also caused the ocean waters to expand, so sea level rose even more. Geologists have estimated that sea level during the Cretaceous was about 800 feet higher than it is today. These estimates come primarily from deposits of ocean sediments that cover a huge part of the low-lying areas of the world's continents; North America even had a vast inland sea from Texas to central Canada. With sea level so high, the eastern part of the Carolinas would have been flooded, and ocean waves would have been battering rocks at the foot of the rift-flank uplift, eroding it back and keeping it steep, much like the sea cliffs we see today along the mountainous shorelines of the western United States (although the coastal mountains of the western United States are not part of a rift-flank uplift).

Caesars Head, located between the Blue Ridge escarpment and the Brevard fault, is in an area that would be classified as Piedmont according to its bedrock and as Blue Ridge according to its topography. Table Rock (3,197 feet) in Pickens County, South Carolina, is also in this exceptionally elevated part of the Piedmont. Situated likewise on the edge of the Blue Ridge escarpment, it, too, has a glorious view from the top. However, you've got to earn that view—while you can drive to the top of Caesars Head, you must hike about 7 miles round-trip to enjoy the top of Table Rock.

Both Caesars Head and Table Rock are made of granitic gneiss. Gneiss is a metamorphic rock that typically has bands of dark minerals alternating with bands of light minerals. Sedimentary, igneous, or metamorphic rock can metamorphose into gneiss; in this case, the gneiss started out as granite that crystallized from magma 450 million years ago.

About 460 million years ago, a fragment of crust with volcanoes on it was colliding with Laurentia (proto–North America) in an event called the Taconic orogeny (see Figure 5-2). The granite that turned into the gneiss of Table Rock and Caesars Head may have started out in a magma chamber feeding the volcanoes on this crustal fragment, which we call the Piedmont terrane. However, the age of these rocks may be a little too young to fit that model. One hypothesis that would explain the younger rocks is that after the Piedmont terrane had already been added to Laurentia, new volcanoes arose in the terrane. This might have happened if oceanic crust began subducting under the Piedmont terrane after it had been added to Laurentia. This flip in the subduction would have produced volcanoes on the land. (See Figure 8-3, keeping in mind that Caesars Head and Table Rock are in the Piedmont terrane, not the accretionary wedge as Whiteside is.)

FIGURE 14-3. A cross-sectional view of folds in gneiss at Carrick Creek in Table Rock State Park.

Later, the granite was metamorphosed. The metamorphism happened when another fragment of crust, probably the Gondwanan terranes, hit Laurentia, although the timing of this collision is not well established (see Chapter 5).

In some places, the gneiss is weakly metamorphosed and looks very much like granite—speckled, with minerals of different colors distributed evenly throughout. In other places, the gneiss is thinly banded and some of the bands are folded. When you see bands and folds, that means the gneiss was strongly metamorphosed.

A good place to see strongly metamorphosed gneiss is along Carrick Creek in Table Rock State Park. The 2-mile Carrick Creek Trail begins and ends at the Nature Center. Soon after you start on the trail, you will come to a small waterfall over some rocks that are very impressively folded, like big wrinkles in a rug (Figure 14-3). The folds are evidence that the rock experienced pressures and temperatures high enough to cause it to flow like putty. During metamorphism, minerals in the granite recrystallized into

FIGURE 14-4. Looking down the troughs and ridges of the folds at Carrick Creek.

light and dark layers. The lighter layers are rich in quartz and feldspar. The darker layers are rich in black mica called biotite. Actually, all the layers look fairly dark on the weathered surfaces that you are likely to see in the park. What distinguishes the layers here by the creek is not coloring but differential weathering. The biotite-rich layers have weathered away faster than the layers rich in quartz and feldspar. That creates the ledges in the folds, which makes them easy to see.

When you come to a wooden bridge that crosses Carrick Creek, stop and look at the rock in the streambed. You are now seeing the same series of folds as you saw at the waterfall, but from a different perspective. The creek has taken a right-angle turn: before this point, the creek was cutting across the folds; now it is running along in the troughs of the folds. Seeing both of the views on the same short walk can help you visualize the rock in three dimensions (Figure 14-4).

The gneiss at Caesars Head is similar to that at Table Rock, but less layered and folded and not as weathered. Caesars Head has some pretty impressive cracks, called joints. (A joint is a crack in rock along which no significant movement has taken place, whereas a fault is a crack along which movement has taken place.) One of the joints near the top of Caesars Head has been eroded into a narrow passageway called the Devil's Kitchen. It is just large enough for one person to walk through. In and around Devil's Kitchen, you will see some historic graffiti—names and dates carved in the rock many years ago.

At Caesars Head State Park, you can hike 2 miles to Raven Cliff Falls along a marked trail. Raven Cliff Falls is where Matthews Creek plunges 400 feet down the face of the Blue Ridge escarpment. From there, if you're wearing your fully loaded backpack, you can set off on 50 miles of trails in the Mountain Bridge Wilderness and Recreation Area, which connects Caesars Head and Jones Gap to the east. The same escarpment that gives you such a good view atop Caesars Head and Table Rock also makes for some rugged and inspiring hiking.

Location and Access

Caesars Head and Table Rock State Parks are both about 20 miles northwest of Greenville, South Carolina. Caesars Head is just off US 276 and Table Rock is just off SC 11. South Carolina state parks charge a nominal admission fee.

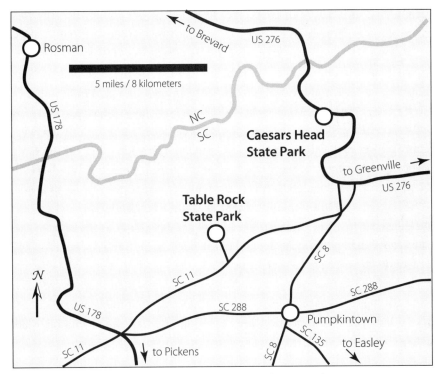

FIGURE 14-5. Location of Caesars Head and Table Rock State Parks.

Nearby Features

Two other great places to see the Blue Ridge escarpment are Gorges State Park and Whitewater Falls, both in North Carolina.

Gorges State Park is west of Caesars Head. Between the two state parks, the escarpment runs east-west. At Gorges, the drop-off is not as abrupt as at Caesars Head, although the total elevation change is greater. This is one of those places where the escarpment is a long slope rather than a vertical cliff. At the entrance to the park near the town of Sapphire, North Carolina, you are at the top of the escarpment; the base of the escarpment is about 4 miles away and 2,000 feet below you. The bedrock at the top of the escarpment is called the Toxaway gneiss. It's a billion-year-old gneiss that was metamorphosed during the continental collisions that led to the assembly of the ancient supercontinent of Rodinia. To the southeast, the slope of the escarpment is developed in more easily erodable rocks from the Tallulah Falls Formation, which are metamorphosed sediments. So, unlike at Caesars Head and Table Rock, the escarpment here could be attributed to differences in rock type. Furthermore, the Tallulah Falls Formation has been rendered even less resistant by the Brevard fault, which runs along the base of the escarpment here. The Brevard fault is almost 370 miles long, stretching from Alabama almost to Virginia. The fault is not a line, but rather a zone, varying in width from about a half a mile to a mile and a half. Motion along the Brevard fault may have taken place during each of three collisions that occurred as Laurentia and Gondwana were approaching each other. As the rocks moved past each other on the fault, they were deformed, broken, crushed, and sheared. Here, the Tallulah Falls Formation was subjected to this treatment, making it even easier to erode.

South from Sapphire along NC 281 is Whitewater Falls, the highest waterfall east of the Rockies with a height of 411 feet (Plate 6). It is also on the Blue Ridge escarpment. At the end of the parking lot toward the falls, there are some large boulders that show the kind of rock that the falls cascade over. Notice the intensely deformed layering, a sure sign that we are dealing with highly metamorphosed rock. This is more of the Toxaway gneiss, the billion-year-old metamorphic rock that you can see at Gorges State Park.

Recommended Reading

Wooten, Richard M., Mark W. Carter, and Carl E. Merschat. *Geology of Gorges State Park, Transylvania County, North Carolina.* Information Circular 31. Raleigh: North Carolina Geological Survey, 2003.

The Piedmont

15

South Mountains State Park
Stuck between a Continent and a Hard Place

>> BURKE COUNTY, NORTH CAROLINA

The High Shoals Falls Loop Trail is one of the most popular trails in South Mountains State Park, and for good reason. High Shoals Falls is a spectacular waterfall that plunges 80 feet over a cliff into a huge jumble of boulders, some larger than cars.

The trail to High Shoals Falls begins from the Jacob Fork parking area. A few dozen yards beyond the restroom, there are some small rock outcrops on the bank on the right side of the trail. Notice the sparkly mica and the layering, known as foliation. Both the mica and the foliation tell you it's a metamorphic rock, in this case schist, which began as a fine-grained muddy sediment before being metamorphosed into what you see here. After the trail crosses Shinny Creek (pronounced "Shiny"), you will come upon an outcrop on the right, some of which is overhanging, marked by a post labeled "2." (The numbered posts along the trail are keyed to a booklet describing the geology along the High Shoals Falls trail; the booklet is available at the park office.) Notice the white veins that run through the outcrop; they contain very large crystals of feldspar and quartz—some of the crystals are a half inch or more in diameter. These veins are a large-grained igneous rock called pegmatite; the veins have undergone metamorphism, as evidenced by the faint foliation within the pegmatite. The size of the crystals in an igneous rock depends on how easily individual atoms can move through the molten rock and the abundance of "nucleation points" for the individual crystals. If conditions in the molten rock are such that atoms can move faster than usual or if there are fewer nucleation points, there will be larger crystals. Atoms can move faster through magma that contains volatile compounds such as water, and water also inhibits the nucleation of crystals.

The rock that surrounds the pegmatite began as a sedimentary rock, a

FIGURE 15-1. High Shoals Falls.

"dirty" sandstone with a lot of mud mixed in with the sand. These kinds of sediments are common on the seafloor just off the coasts of landmasses, where rivers dump a mixture of sediments onto the continental shelf. The dirty sandstone has since undergone metamorphism.

As you are walking along the west bank of the Jacob Fork River, through rhododendrons and ferns, you will come upon a post marked "3" at a large, steep, exposed area of slightly metamorphosed granite. You can see big rock slabs that have moved down the slope and piled up at the base of the outcrop (Figure 15-2). The slabs break off in a process called exfoliation, a type of weathering that occurs in rocks having a uniform texture—that is, few or no cracks or layers of weak minerals. As erosion removes rock, the underlying rock responds to the decreased pressure by expanding upward, and cracks form in the outcrop parallel to the surface. Eventually, rocks break off along these fractures. You can think of exfoliation as rock layers "peeling" off one by one like layers of an onion. Exfoliation is common in exposed bodies of igneous rock; it is also taking place at North Carolina's Stone Mountain (see Figure 12-2), Georgia's Stone Mountain, and Yosemite National Park. In 1989, when Hurricane Hugo came through South Mountains State Park, the tremendous amount of rainfall made it possible for many loose rocks to slide off this outcrop at once, which is why some people call it the Hugo rockslide. Water facilitates landsliding in several ways. It can act as a lubricant; it can increase the weight of the rock or sediment; and it can also percolate into fractures and partially lift the rock, thereby reducing the force required to get it to slide.

Soon after the Hugo rockslide, the trail crosses the Jacob Fork River on a wooden bridge. From the bridge you can see water tumbling over and around huge boulders. Some of them have ferns and even small trees growing on them, which tells you that the boulders have been here a long time. How did these boulders get here? Were they carried down the stream in a flood? Not likely. Even in a flood, the amount of water in the creek would not be enough to move boulders this large. You'll see a clue to their origin farther along the trail.

After hiking up many wooden steps, you will come to the base of High Shoals Falls; there is a wooden overlook for viewing the water as it cascades over a near-vertical surface. This is a waterfall that makes you want to stand quietly for a while, enjoying the majesty of the rocky cliffs and the power of the water. When you come out of your reverie, look closely and notice the

FIGURE 15-2. Bare rock exhumed by the Hugo rockslide.

fractures in the rock. Planar fractures like these are called joints; they form when relatively cool and brittle rock is stressed, by movement of tectonic plates, for example. Once a joint is formed, it can get wider when water seeps in and freezes, and when plant roots push their way in and expand. Follow the wooden steps up along the steep river banks to the near-vertical cliffs. Now you can look at the joints up close (Figure 15-3). Every once in a while, a block of rock separates from the cliff along one of these joints. The catalyst for a piece of rock falling may be an earthquake (rare here), heavy rain, or simply the passage of years. For example, in 2003 large pieces of rock fell off of the Old Man in the Mountain in New Hampshire, ruining the famous profile that graces the New Hampshire commemorative quarter. Even though the state had put in bolts to try to forestall the inevitable, a round of rain, wind, and freezing temperatures finally did the Old Man in. North Carolina has its share of major rock falls, too. A large rock slide along I-40 during the summer of 1997 closed the highway in western North Carolina for months, and smaller slides are a frequent problem along this stretch of I-40.

The boulders in the stream fall from these cliffs, the face of the waterfall, and the cliffs on the other side of the stream. Decades or even hundreds of years may pass between episodes of rocks tumbling off a cliff and crashing down into the stream. If one had fallen recently, you would see severed tree trunks (which the authors did not see in 2003). However, the stream is full of rocks. This gives you an idea of how long the stream has been flowing here. In geologic time, a boulder every hundred years is practically an on-going landslide of rocks. The cliffs form a bowl shape because the cliffs under the waterfall are eroding back faster than the cliffs on the banks—the force of flowing water in the Jacob Fork encourages joints to widen and rocks to break off.

As you continue on the trail you will come to the top of the falls. Notice that there are no boulders in the Jacob Fork here. You are above the cliffs, so there is no longer a source for big boulders. In the flat bedrock next to the stream channel, you will see large, smooth holes, called potholes. They form when sediment gets caught in a depression in the rock and the stream swirls sediment around in the depression, eventually scouring out a smooth, circular hole.

Also in the streambed you can see numerous mineral-filled fractures trending straight across the stream. These are part of the system of joints that produced the steep cliff face of the falls.

FIGURE 15-3. Nearly vertical joints in the cliffs near High Shoals Falls.

The rock that makes up the cliff and the streambed also makes up the bulk of the South Mountains. It's a weakly metamorphosed granite called the Toluca granite. Because it has been metamorphosed, it's technically a gneiss, but the name signifies its origin as an igneous rock. We commonly add a geographic name, like "Toluca," to a rock name because it indicates that the rock is of a distinct age and mineralogy and that it belongs to a large and traceable body that can be shown on a geologic map.

All the rocks that you see in South Mountains State Park are metamorphic. When you encounter that much metamorphic rock at once, it is evidence of a large regional event, such as a collision between plates.

In fact, the granite and sediments were metamorphosed when they got caught in the collision between a continent and a continental fragment. The timing of this collision is the subject of controversy: there is some evidence that it may have happened as early as 440 million years ago, while other data indicate it may have happened much later, about 350 million years ago. (See Chapter 5 for more information about the mysterious Acadian orogeny.) Two continents—Laurentia and Gondwana—were creeping inexorably toward each other. (Laurentia would later become North America. Gondwana consisted of parts of present-day South America and Africa.) But before the two continents collided, portions of Gondwana rifted off and headed on their own toward Laurentia. The rifted-off fragments are called the Gondwanan terranes (see Figure 5-3). Sediments on the seafloor were caught between the Gondwanan terranes and Laurentia and were accreted onto Laurentia during the collision. The intense heat and pressure of the collision metamorphosed the sediments. Magma generated deep underground during the collision intruded the metamorphosed sediments and cooled to form large bodies of igneous rocks such as granite. Continued heat and pressure metamorphosed the granite, too. The metamorphosed sediments and granite that were squashed between Laurentia and the Gondwanan terranes are now exposed in the gorges and peaks of the South Mountains.

Including the High Shoals Fall Loop, which is a couple of miles long, South Mountains State Park has more than 40 miles of trails. So you can take your pick of many places to explore the park and examine the rocks that were created and deformed millions of years ago.

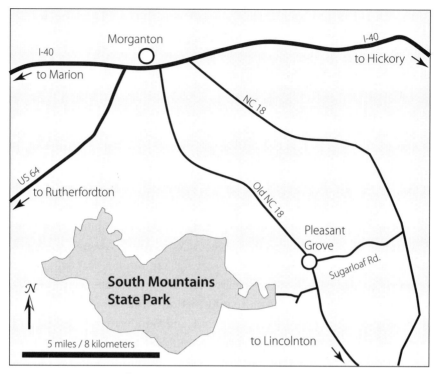

FIGURE 15-4. Location of South Mountains State Park.

Location and Access

South Mountains State Park is about 20 miles south of Morganton. Take NC 18 south from I-40; after about 10 miles, you'll start seeing signs to the park.

16

Crowders Mountain State Park
A Mountain of Quartz and Blue Daggers

>> GASTON COUNTY, NORTH CAROLINA

The mountaineer climbs a mountain because it is there. But why is the mountain there? Some mountains are there because of plate tectonics: the collision of continents pushes up a mountain range. Other mountains are there because of differential erosion: water and wind wear away soft rocks leaving hard rocks behind to form mountains. Then there are volcanoes: lava flowing up from fissures in the earth's surface creates a cone over time. And some mountains are there because of a combination of these three factors.

So why is Crowders Mountain there? A hike to the top will begin to answer that question. There are actually two peaks in Crowders Mountain State Park: Crowders Mountain, elevation 1,625 feet, and The Pinnacle, (which some maps call Kings Pinnacle), elevation 1,705 feet. To get to the top of Crowders Mountain, walk about a mile along Backside Trail from the visitor center parking lot. The first part of the hike is on an old roadbed through a forest of pines and hardwoods. Occasionally along the trail, you encounter large boulders. As you continue on, there are fewer trees and more rock, and the trail becomes quite steep. Finally the forest gives way to stunted trees here and there, and the roadbed turns into a narrow trail that climbs hundreds of railroad-tie steps through the rocks.

When you reach the top of Crowders Mountain, you will be atop jagged hundred-foot-tall cliffs—a perfect vantage point from which to enjoy the view of the Piedmont, including the Charlotte skyline. From this height, the Piedmont looks surprisingly flat, and you can really appreciate how much higher Crowders Mountain is than the surrounding terrain.

Turn your view to the rocks themselves; they are full of light gray elongated crystals about half an inch long (Figure 16-2). In places, the crystals are reddish, stained by groundwater high in iron. Notice how these crystals often project above the surrounding surface of the rock. Where they

FIGURE 16-1. The view from Crowders Mountain. Notice the vertical foliation and gently dipping (almost horizontal) fractures in the rock cliffs.

FIGURE 16-2. Elongated crystals of kyanite in the quartzite at Crowders Mountain.

have weathered out of the rock, the long crystals are loose on top of the soil. You can guess that this mineral must be pretty resistant to weathering to maintain its shape even when it has been eroded out of the rock; less durable minerals would have long since broken to bits or been altered to clay. The mineral is kyanite, and it's well known for its toughness. Kyanite tells you that this rock is metamorphic because the mineral only occurs in rocks that have experienced intense pressures. These metamorphic rocks are rich in quartz, and they also contain some mica.

Notice also the white quartz veins. Millions of years ago, hot, silica-saturated fluids were circulating through cracks in this rock. As the fluids cooled, quartz precipitated out of solution. We know this because when we look at thin sections of quartz veins under the microscope, we find tiny fluid inclusions—microscopic bubbles of water that were trapped in the crystals of quartz as it solidified. Even though they are called quartz veins, keep in mind that in three dimensions they are more like quartz sheets. Quartz, like kyanite, is very resistant to weathering and erosion.

The rock that forms these cliffs is quartzite, and we call it kyanite quartzite to indicate that it is rich in kyanite. It is one of the most erosion-resistant rocks around. What happens when there is a lot of erosion-resistant rock in one place? You get a mountain. The rocks in the surrounding countryside are mostly mica-rich schist, which is more easily eroded. Schist is a foliated metamorphic rock with relatively large grains; here it is composed mostly of mica, which makes the rock split easily into thin slabs. So we have our answer: Crowders Mountain is here because the schist has eroded faster than the kyanite quartzite. This kind of mountain, formed by differential erosion, is called a monadnock.

If you shift your focus to looking at the overall texture of the rock, you will notice thin, almost vertical layers in the rock. The layers, called foliation, originated during metamorphism. The rock tends to break off along the layers, which is why the cliffs are nearly vertical, rather than rounded. If you look more closely, you can find little folds in the foliation in some places. These were caused by high pressures associated with the metamorphism.

The metamorphism was caused by a continental collision. The rock here started out as part of another continent called Gondwana, which was made of up of parts of what would later become Africa and South America. Beginning about 570 million years ago, Gondwana and Laurentia (which would eventually become North America) were on a collision course. Oceanic crust was sliding underneath the leading edge of Gondwana, causing volcanoes to erupt. In the shallow waters at Gondwana's edge, layers of sandstone and volcanic ash accumulated. Deep underground, magma-heated water began circulating through the layers. The hydrothermal activity carried soluble calcium, sodium, and potassium away from the rocks and left behind the silica (silicon plus oxygen) and aluminum in certain places. This set the stage for the eventual formation of quartz (which is made of silicon and oxygen) and kyanite (which is made of silicon, oxygen, and aluminum).

Millions of years later, the leading edge of Gondwana broke away from the rest of the continent and collided with Laurentia. During the collision, the rocks were deeply buried and metamorphosed, producing quartz and kyanite. These rocks make up a belt of rocks known as the Kings Mountain belt, which is part of the Charlotte terrane (see Chapter 5 and Plate 5 for more information about the Charlotte and other Gondwanan terranes). Today you can see rocks of the Kings Mountain belt in Crowders Mountain and The Pinnacle. The vertical foliation in the rocks is a result of the strong horizontal pressure associated with the collision and accretion of these rocks. Rocks that share a similar history to those on Crowders Mountain, but did not undergo such intense metamorphism, are exposed at Occoneechee Mountain in Hillsborough, North Carolina (see Chapter 20).

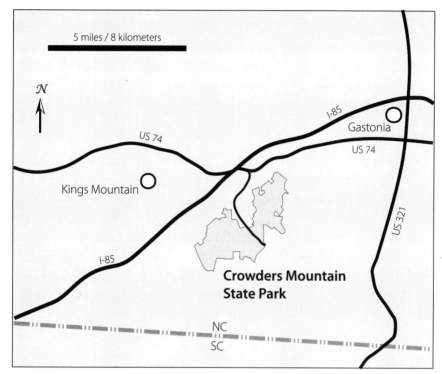

FIGURE 16-3. Location of Crowders Mountain State Park.

Hydrothermal processes akin to those that led to the formation of pockets of quartz and kyanite also concentrated gold, which is why this region of the Piedmont had so many gold mines in the 1800s (see Chapter 17, on Reed Gold Mine).

Just across the border, in York County, South Carolina, is another kyanite quartzite mountain called Henry's Knob. Kyanite was mined from that mountain from 1947 to 1970. Kyanite is an ingredient in ceramics that can withstand high temperatures, for use in products such as sparkplugs and bricks that line blast furnaces. Miners called kyanite "blue daggers" because of its shape and color (on Crowders Mountain it's more gray than blue). Strip mining left Henry's Knob a bare mess, pockmarked with pits and piles, and almost 400 feet shorter. Crowders Mountain and The Pinnacle might well have suffered the same fate had it not been for the efforts of a local group of concerned citizens, the Gaston County Conservation Society. In 1973 Crowders Mountain State Park was established to preserve Crowders Mountain and The Pinnacle for the enjoyment of all.

Location and Access

Crowders Mountain State Park is not far off I-85 near Kings Mountain, west of Charlotte. Take US 74 east from I-85; turn right on Sparrow Springs Road. Camping is allowed at backcountry camping sites.

Nearby Features

Work is under way on a 6-mile hiking trail that will connect the southern edge of Crowders Mountain State Park with the northern edge of Kings Mountain State Park and Kings Mountain National Military Park in South Carolina. Contrary to their names, these two parks in South Carolina are mountainless. They are the site of a famous Revolutionary War battle where a scrappy band of American soldiers defeated a British army. It is thought that the battle was named after Kings Mountain, a ridge just south of Crowders Mountain State Park, which is visible from the battle site but is not within the boundaries of either of the South Carolina parks.

17

Reed Gold Mine
The Glory Days of Gold

>> CABARRUS COUNTY, NORTH CAROLINA

Imagine going out for a walk on your farm and finding a 17-pound gold nugget flashing in a shallow stream. That's what happened to twelve-year-old Conrad Reed in 1799. He lived in Cabarrus County, North Carolina, with his parents, John and Sarah Reed, and his seven brothers and sisters. No one in the family realized the rock was gold, but because it was both pretty and heavy, they saved it and used it as a doorstop. Three years later, John Reed took it to a jeweler on his annual trip to Fayetteville. The jeweler identified it as gold and told Reed to name his price. Reed asked for $3.50, and the jeweler paid him on the spot. The gold was probably worth about $3,600 in the currency of the day, and would be worth about $160,000 in 2006. (Some say Reed later sued the jeweler and received more money.)

Conrad Reed's pretty yellow rock was the first recorded and authenticated gold nugget discovered in the United States, although in 1781 Thomas Jefferson described a rock containing specks of gold that he said had been found in Virginia. Native Americans and early explorers may have found gold as well.

John Reed and a few of his neighbors entered into a partnership. They and their slaves panned and dug for gold in and around the creek during the slow seasons of the farming year. In 1803 a slave named Peter found a 28-pound nugget.

Other nearby farmers who'd heard of Reed's good fortune were beginning to turn up gold in their own creeks. In the next few years, the Harris and the Dunn mines opened in Mecklenburg County, and the Parker mine opened in what is now Stanly County. Gold was discovered in Greenville County, South Carolina, in 1802.

At first, miners simply looked for flakes and nuggets that had been eroded out of bedrock and deposited in streambeds (Plate 7). This is called placer (pronounced "plasser") mining. Miners panned for gold, dug shallow pits

FIGURE 17-1. The tunnel leading into Reed Gold Mine.

in and around creek beds, and used sluices and half-barrel rockers to wash large amounts of sediment (Figure 17-2). Rockers were sometimes connected by a long handle that was used to rock all the troughs at once. Panning and rocking exploit the fact that gold is so dense that it quickly settles to the bottom of a container when swirled around with rocks and sand. Gold is almost 20 times as dense as water, and about three times as dense

FIGURE 17-2. This photograph, taken in Cabarrus County in the 1880s, shows some of the equipment miners used to find gold, including a pan and a half-barrel rocker. Courtesy of the North Carolina Office of Archives and History, Raleigh, North Carolina.

as iron. (A bowling ball made of gold would weigh about 270 pounds. Conrad Reed's 17-pound nugget was probably no larger than a baseball.)

Because there was not much currency in the brand-new nation, many Carolinians used raw gold to purchase goods. Denison Olmsted, an early North Carolina geologist, noted that "almost every man carries about with him a goose quill or two of it [gold], and a small pair of scales in a box like a spectacle case. The value, as in patriarchal times, is ascertained by weight, which, from the dexterity acquired by practice, is a less troublesome mode of counting money than one would imagine. I saw a pint of whiskey paid for by weighing off three and a half grains of gold" (Denison Olmsted, "On the Gold Mines of North Carolina," *American Journal of Science* 9 [1825]: 12–13).

During the first two decades of the 1800s, Reed Gold Mine was the biggest producer of gold in North Carolina, which was the only state where gold was being mined. The Reed mine was famous for the quantity of its large nuggets. From 1803 to 1835, 14 sizable nuggets were found there; they ranged in weight from 1 pound to 28 pounds, for a total of 115 pounds.

Underground or hard-rock mining began in North Carolina in 1825. In that year, Matthias Barringer was panning in a stream on his property in Stanly County when he noticed that there was no gold upstream from a certain point, and plenty of gold downstream. The bedrock at that point, he reasoned, must be the source of gold: as the stream eroded the bedrock, some gold would wash downstream, but none of it would move upstream. So he began digging into the creek banks, and was rewarded by striking a quartz vein full of gold.

Barringer's discovery reinvigorated mining activity in the Carolinas. Many miners left behind their pans and rockers for hard-rock mining. They tunneled underground looking for quartz veins, which they broke up using hammers, mallets, picks, and shovels. They brought the chunks of quartz to the surface, to be crushed even finer. After the quartz was crushed, miners added mercury, which dissolved any gold that might be in the mix. The mercury-gold solution would be distilled later, boiling off the mercury and leaving behind gold. (Present-day gold panners working the streams of the Carolinas sometimes find mercury in the bottoms of their pans.) There were several well-known hard-rock mines in or near Charlotte, including the Capps, Rudisill, and St. Catherine's mines. Reed Gold Mine did not put in a shaft until 1831. A few years later, a family legal squabble over the ownership of a 10-pound gold nugget effectively shut down the mine for a decade.

Until 1828, North Carolina was the only state in the union supplying the U.S. mint in Philadelphia with gold. In 1827 Benjamin Haile found gold in his stream in Lancaster County, South Carolina, and he began sending gold to the Philadelphia mint in 1829. The Haile mine would eventually produce more than $6 million worth of gold, making it one of the richest gold mines in the eastern United States.

In 1842 gold was discovered near what is now called Gold Hill in southeastern Rowan County, North Carolina. In the next five years, at least 15 underground mines operated in and around Gold Hill. Twelve thousand people lived there during the 1850s when it was the most productive and best known of the Carolinas' mines. Today it is a quiet little village of about a hundred people.

Because the trip to Philadelphia was slow and dangerous, Carolinians needed a mint of their own, so Christopher and Augustus Bechtler opened a private mint in Rutherfordton in 1831. Six years later, the U.S. government opened a mint in Charlotte. Bechtlers' mint closed in 1857 after having coined at least $4 million (and probably much more) in gold. The Charlotte mint closed in 1861, at the outbreak of the Civil War, after having coined about $5 million in gold. Today, the Mint Museum of Art occupies the former U.S. mint building; among the art collections is a numismatic collection, including gold coins minted by Bechtler and by the Charlotte Mint.

The 1849 Gold Rush in California was the beginning of the end of the glory days of gold in the Carolinas. Reed Gold Mine was worked off and on by different owners over the next several decades, with mostly poor or mediocre returns. In 1896 Jacob Shinn found the last large nugget on the property. It weighed 22 pounds. From the 1890s until 1971, the mine was owned by the Kelly family from Ohio. After 1910 very little organized mining took place there. The Kelly family hung onto the land, but for the most part let it lie fallow. From a historical perspective, this was fortunate because the old tunnels and mining equipment were spared the bulldozers of progress. In 1971 North Carolina purchased the tract and designated it a state historic site.

Today you can visit the museum at Reed Gold Mine, tour a mine shaft, and even pan for gold—although the gravel for panning comes from the Cotton Patch Gold Mine in Stanly County. All the easy-to-find gold at the Reed mine has already been removed.

If you take the underground tour at Reed Gold Mine, you will walk through tunnels in the hard rock, see leftover mining equipment, and peer into old shafts. If you look at the rock walls, you'll also see plenty of veins of milky white quartz, which is what the miners were after (Plate 8). They knew that the gold was in those quartz veins, but they didn't know why. It's a story that begins on an ancient continent called Gondwana, which consisted of parts of what we now call South America and Africa.

About 570 million years ago, Gondwana had an active convergent plate boundary along at least one of its edges. As oceanic crust dove under Gondwana, volcanoes developed on the edge of the continent. Layers of volcanic ash, as well as sand and silt, accumulated in the shallow waters off Gondwana and were cemented into rock. The underground magma chambers feeding the volcanoes heated the groundwater that was trapped in this rock, causing the water to cycle through the rock in huge convection currents—heated water rose, then cooled, then sank, then got hot and rose again.

This kind of hot-water circulation tends to concentrate gold over time. Gold is actually present in minute quantities in many kinds of rocks, but it's spread out in microscopic particles here and there. Hot water dissolves gold out of bedrock and carries it upward as it rises through porous and fractured rock. Eventually, the water becomes too cool to keep the gold in solution anymore, and solid gold is deposited in the bedrock. Slight changes in the acidity of the water can also cause gold to precipitate out of solution. Hot water dissolves and concentrates other substances as well—for example, silica, which makes quartz, and iron and sulfur. That's why you'll often find gold and pyrite (which is iron sulfide) near or in quartz veins.

Geologists studying the gold deposits in the Carolinas have found that most of the gold was deposited in the rocks at nearly the same time as those rocks were formed, which is consistent with the idea that the gold was deposited by hot water flowing through rocks within an active volcanic system. Yellowstone National Park is a good example of an area where hot-water currents are operating today. The water that bubbles out of the hot springs and geysers at the surface percolates down into the bedrock. When it goes deep enough, it gets hot and rises back to the surface. There could already be a significant gold deposit beneath Yellowstone. Another modern-day example is the active Galeras volcano in Colombia; each day it is venting hydrothermal gases that have been measured to contain about a pound of gold mixed with the gas, and geologists estimate that about 50 pounds of gold are being deposited inside the plumbing system of the volcano every year. At this rate it will take only about 10,000 years to create an ore deposit containing 250 tons of gold, an amount that would make this a particularly rich lode.

Sometimes gold deposits can be clustered around a fault zone. For example, many of the gold mines in the Gold Hill region lie along the trace of a fault zone known as the Gold Hill fault. It is likely that hot water circulating through the fault zone remobilized the existing gold and concentrated it in quartz-filled fractures.

But how did the gold get from Gondwana to the Carolina Piedmont? Millions of years after the gold and quartz were deposited in the rock made of sediments and ash, the leading edge of Gondwana broke off and collided with Laurentia (proto–North America). The heat and pressure of the collision metamorphosed the rock into slate, but they did not destroy the gold-filled quartz veins.

Erosion eventually brought the slate to the surface. Streams eroded out some of the quartz and gold, including Conrad Reed's 17-pound nugget that started the Carolina gold rush. Commercial gold mining essentially stopped in North Carolina in 1963. South Carolina, however, has had active mines more recently. In 1992 South Carolina ranked seventh in the nation in gold production and was the only gold-producing state east of the Mississippi. The Haile mine was worked as recently as 1991. The Ridgeway mine in Fairfield County operated from 1988 to 1999 and was the most productive gold mine on the East Coast. Modern mines crush all the rock, not just the quartz veins, because extremely fine particles of gold are disseminated throughout the rock. The Ridgeway mine crushed 31 tons of rock for every troy ounce of gold recovered. (Gold is weighed in troy ounces instead of "regular" ounces, which are technically known as avoirdupois ounces. A troy ounce weighs 31.103 grams. An avoirdupois ounce weighs 28.41 grams.)

The Ridgeway produced 1.5 million ounces of gold—more than all the gold produced by North Carolina from 1799 to 1963. No one knows what North Carolina's total is, but it is probably between 720,000 and 1.2 million ounces. While that is minuscule compared to the output of California (115 million ounces between 1848 and 1995), gold played a major role in the history of the Carolinas. The mechanical engineering that Carolinians learned while mining gold may have set the stage for the Piedmont's later success in manufacturing businesses, such as textiles and furniture. And gold mining and minting put Charlotte on the road to becoming the financial center it is today. One of the early banks formed by gold investors was Commerce National Bank. Many years and mergers later, it has become Bank of America.

In 1969—170 years after Conrad Reed made his historic find—construction workers digging the foundation of the First Union National Bank building in Charlotte unearthed a gold nugget. It was a fitting reminder of the golden history of the Carolinas. Though the Carolinas' gold rush is little remembered, Charlotte's banking prowess and the Piedmont's manufacturing success are, in part, built on gold.

Location and Access

Reed Gold Mine is a North Carolina Historic Site. Admission is free. It is northeast of Charlotte, a few miles southeast of the intersection of US 601 and NC 200.

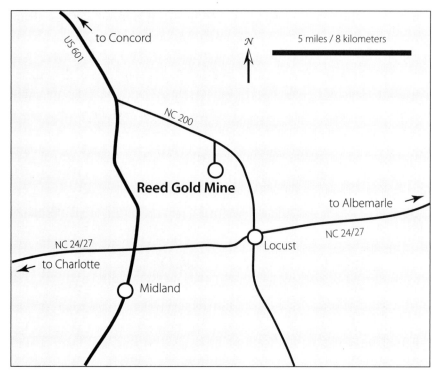

FIGURE 17-3. Location of Reed Gold Mine.

Recommended Reading

Carpenter, P. Albert, III. *Gold in North Carolina*. Information Circular 29. Raleigh: North Carolina Geological Survey, 1993.

Knapp, Richard F., and Brent D. Glass. *Gold Mining in North Carolina: A Bicentennial History*. Raleigh: Division of Archives and History, 1999.

18

Pilot Mountain State Park
Beach Sands in a Mountain

According to legend, there are two footprints somewhere in the rock on the very top of Pilot Mountain—Noah's footprints, made as he stepped out of the ark. Pilot Mountain was actually called Mount Ararat for a time, after the mountain in Turkey where tradition says Noah's ark landed. Travel a bit northwest of Pilot Mountain, and you will find a town named Ararat on the banks of a river of the same name. The name Mount Airy is also a derivative of Mount Ararat.

Pilot Mountain is a place of many legends—just as you'd expect. Anyone who has seen the distinctive mountain remembers it. It rises abruptly almost 1,500 feet from the surrounding Piedmont and is capped by a large 200-foot-tall knob. The knob, called Big Pinnacle, has light-colored, nearly vertical sides and is vegetated only on its flat top. Just west of the Big Pinnacle is a small saddle, beyond which is a smaller peak called Little Pinnacle.

One persistent myth is that Pilot Mountain is an extinct volcano, which, as we shall see, is not the case. Another legend has it that Indians, early settlers, and mountain men, including Daniel Boone, used the mountain as a landmark. There's no reason not to believe this one—such a visible and unusual feature no doubt guided many a traveler.

If you want to know why this unusual mountain is here, a good place to start is the Jomeokee Trail, which begins at the eastern end of the park's parking lot and leads to the base of the Big Pinnacle. The trail starts off following some stepping stones downward. Stop on the "landing" where the railing ends and look at the outcrop on your right (Figure 18-2). You'll notice that there seems to be more than one kind of rock in this outcrop. Some of the rock is foliated and folded, and it sparkles with flakes of mica. This is a metamorphic rock called mica schist, and it is composed mainly of mica, with some quartz grains and minor amounts of iron oxides. The little

FIGURE 18-1. A view of the Big Pinnacle from the Little Pinnacle overlook. Photograph by Mark P. Johnson.

folds in the schist are a result of metamorphism. Other parts of the rock look almost like sand, but they are not as crumbly as sandstone would be. This is metamorphosed sandstone, called quartzite; it's almost all quartz, a mineral that is very resistant to erosion.

As you continue on the trail, you will be walking in the saddle between the Little Pinnacle (which is back near the parking lot) and the Big Pinnacle, which is in front of you. When you get to the Big Pinnacle, you will see that it is made of thick layers of really pure, hard quartzite. That's why Pilot Mountain is here. While the quartzite in it has held firm, weaker rocks surrounding the mountain have eroded away. But even quartzite must eventually erode. On Pilot Mountain, for whatever reason, the quartzite in the saddle is weathering away faster than the quartzite in Big Pinnacle, giving us the shapes that make the mountain's silhouette so distinctive.

Pilot Mountain is part of the Sauratown Mountains, which rise above the Piedmont north of Winston-Salem, and the quartzite you see here can be found on the higher peaks throughout the range, including Hanging Rock.

FIGURE 18-2. An outcrop of light-colored quartzite and darker, folded schist on the Jomeokee Trail. Photograph by Mark P. Johnson.

The mountains are named for a tribe of Native Americans called the Saura, Saraw, or Cheraw Indians. The tribe maintained a settlement on the Dan River not far east of Pilot Mountain from about 1700 to 1720, when they were driven farther south by attacks of the Iroquois. The mountain range includes Moores Knob and Cooks Wall, which are in Hanging Rock State Park in Stokes County, and Sauratown Mountain, also located in Stokes County.

Although Pilot Mountain is 2,421 feet above sea level today, its cliffs originated as white beach sands on the shores of an ancient ocean. About 540 million years ago, the Iapetus Ocean was lapping on the shores of Laurentia, the continent that would later become North America. Laurentia's sandy beaches were probably similar to the beaches of the Carolinas today, except that they were made up of almost pure quartz grains. Among geologists, the Sauratown quartzite is known for its purity: it's more than 98 percent quartz. Our beaches today are mostly quartz, but they also contain minor amounts of feldspar, mica, heavy minerals, and shell fragments.

Over time, the sands on the Laurentian coast became deeply buried under other rocks and sediments. Across the Iapetus Ocean from Laurentia was Gondwana, which was made of parts of modern-day Africa and South America. Between 460 and 270 million years ago, Gondwana and Laurentia came together in a series of collisions. The final collision, known as the Alleghanian orogeny, began about 330 million years ago and created the Appalachians. This event metamorphosed the beach sand into hard quartzite rock. When the Alleghanian orogeny was over, all the world's continents were assembled into the supercontinent Pangea.

As you're hiking along the Jomeokee Trail, look for dark streaks in the quartzite; the streaks are where dense minerals were concentrated in layers in the beach sand. You may have seen similar swirls of dark minerals on Carolina beaches or at Jockey's Ridge (see Chapter 33). In both the Sauratown quartzite and today's beaches, the dark minerals are usually ilmenite (iron-titanium oxide) and magnetite (iron oxide).

At the base of the Big Pinnacle, you may notice thin layers in the quartzite that are inclined at different angles. This is called cross-bedding, and it reflects the way the sand was originally deposited (Figure 18-3). The kind of cross-bedding preserved in the quartzite is commonly found in modern-day beach sands, especially those deposited in the surf zone and in shallow water. These features provide some of the strongest evidence for the quartzite having originated as beach sand. Also look for more of the folded schist you saw at the beginning of the Jomeokee Trail. In some places, weathering has exposed three-dimensional views of the little folds, which resemble folds in a rug that has been scooted across the floor.

Back when the quartzite was beach sand, the schist was sandy mud. Heat and pressure changed it into the banded, folded rock you see here. The small folds in the schist mimic the shape and orientation of a very large arch or fold, called an anticlinorium, that affects the entire Sauratown Mountains. On the south flank of the Sauratown Mountains, the layers of rock tilt south, and on the north flank, the layers tilt north, forming the very large arch. The Big Pinnacle of Pilot Mountain is at the crest of the fold, so the strata are nearly horizontal. Both the large fold and the small ones were caused by the continental collisions that created the Appalachians.

The vegetation on Pilot Mountain includes many plants that are more typical of the Blue Ridge highlands to the northwest, such as rhododendron (*Rhododendron catawbiense*), mountain laurel (*Kalmia latifolia*), pitch pine (*Pinus rigida*), and table mountain pine (*Pinus pungens*). During the

FIGURE 18-3. Cross-beds in quartzite on the Big Pinnacle. Photograph by Mark P. Johnson.

Great Ice Ages, these and other plants inhabited much of the Piedmont. As the climate became warmer, they were replaced in the lower elevations by plants more suited to the warmth. They stayed on Pilot Mountain, where the exposed slopes provide harsher conditions.

Pilot Mountain is also home to some birds that usually roost farther west: ravens. Big Pinnacle is one of only two places in North Carolina's Piedmont where ravens nest. You may hear their distinctive barking calls or see them soaring around the Big Pinnacle.

After exploring the Big Pinnacle close up, step back for a broader view. Take the Little Pinnacle Trail from the parking area about 100 yards to an overlook. Here you'll have a good view of the Big Pinnacle and the rest of the Sauratown Mountains, most of which lie in Hanging Rock State Park to the east. The highest point is Moores Knob, elevation 2,579 feet.

From the overlook, the Piedmont land surface appears almost flat. Relief in the Piedmont rarely exceeds 200 feet. On a clear day, you can see the Winston-Salem skyline to the south-southeast. To the northwest, you can see the highlands of the Blue Ridge physiographic province, which looks almost like a plateau from here. The boundary between the Piedmont and the Blue Ridge is an abrupt change in elevation, called the Blue Ridge escarpment or Blue Ridge front. About 20 miles west of Pilot Mountain, US 21 climbs the Blue Ridge escarpment, going from about 1,300 feet to 2,856 feet at the top. The Eastern Continental Divide follows the crest of the escarpment here, as does the Blue Ridge Parkway. West of the divide, the New River flows northeast; its waters ultimately travel 2,500 miles to the Gulf of Mexico, by way of the Ohio and Mississippi Rivers. East of the divide, tributaries cascade down the escarpment to the Yadkin River flowing northeast across the Piedmont. The Yadkin then turns southeast and heads toward the Atlantic Ocean, a trip of only 300 miles.

Interestingly, the rock under your feet on Pilot Mountain is much more similar to rock found in the western Blue Ridge than it is to rock that surrounds the Sauratown Mountains. Most of the metamorphic rock in the Sauratown Mountains is either the 540-million-year-old quartzite and schist exposed along the Jomeokee Trail (which were later metamorphosed during the Alleghanian orogeny) or rock that was metamorphosed about 1,200 million years ago. (The older rock was so thoroughly metamorphosed that it's not as easy to tell what it originated as.) These two groups of rocks are similar to rocks in the western Blue Ridge that were metamorphosed 1,000 to 1,200 million years ago and to 540-million-year-old quartzite we find even farther to the west in Tennessee. But between here and there, in the eastern Blue Ridge, we don't see these rocks at the surface. That's because they are buried underneath thrust sheets, which are thick slabs of crust that have been pushed over the top of the billion-year-old rocks and the quartzite along low-angle faults called thrust faults (see Figure 2-4). These thrust sheets formed during the continental collision between Laurentia and Gondwana, and the direction of their movement is from southeast to northwest. The rocks of the Sauratown Mountains were originally covered by one of these thrust sheets, but because the rocks have been uplifted here, erosion has worn a hole through the thrust sheet, giving us a view to the rocks below. The leading edge of this thrust sheet is in the western Blue Ridge; past that, we again see rocks similar to those exposed in the Sauratown Mountains.

The view through the thrust sheet to the rocks below is called a tectonic window (see Figure 9-3 for an example); this particular one is called the Sauratown Mountain window. Tectonic windows give us valuable informa-

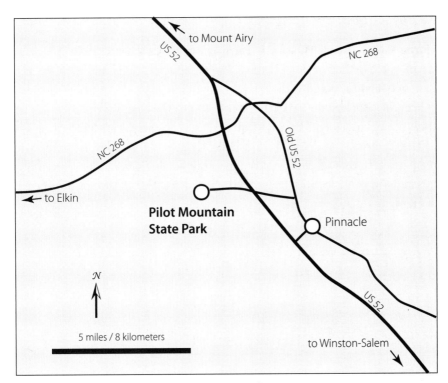

FIGURE 18-4. Location of Pilot Mountain State Park.

tion about the nature of thrust faults and how much movement has taken place along them. (See Chapter 9, on Grandfather Mountain, and Chapter 10, on Linville Falls, for more information about tectonic windows.)

Some people might be disappointed to learn that Pilot Mountain is not really an extinct volcano. But to a geologist trying to untangle Carolina geologic history, not much could be more exciting than the chance to peer through a thrust sheet and find rocks that are related to western Blue Ridge rocks scores of miles away.

Location and Access

Pilot Mountain State Park is just west of US 52, 24 miles north of Winston-Salem and 14 miles south of Mount Airy. The Pilot Mountain State Park exit from US 52 leads directly to the park entrance. The old tollhouse near the turnoff for the campground is made of Sauratown quartzite.

Nearby Features

Horne Creek Living Historical Farm is off US 52, near Pinnacle. Horne Creek is a North Carolina Historic Site demonstrating rural life in the region between 1900 and 1910.

Hanging Rock State Park, about 14 miles to the east, has many miles of trails along ridges and knobs of quartzite, and somewhat different views of the Piedmont and the distant Blue Ridge. The geology is similar in many ways to that of Pilot Mountain. Larger-scale folds can be seen in the quartzite in some locations, especially at Cooks Wall in the southern part of Hanging Rock State Park.

19

Morrow Mountain State Park
A Beautiful Quarry

Morrow Mountain is covered with millions of tons of quarrying debris. You'd never guess it while driving up the road that winds through an idyllic hardwood forest or hiking along wooded trails there. But stop and pick up a rock—an angular gray rock, that may have a whitish rind on one side. The inside is a uniform dark gray to black, with crystals so small you can't see them. You're holding one piece of the millions of tons of quarrying debris (Figure 19-2).

Human hands quarried this stone long before Europeans arrived in the New World. In fact, humans began using the rock at Morrow Mountain about 11,000 years ago, for making arrowheads, spear points, and stone tools. As late as A.D. 1200 to 1500, people of the Pee Dee culture were still using it. Morrow Mountain is one of the most extensive prehistoric quarries in the United States. Virtually the entire mountain is covered by a mixture of soil and rock chips, in some places 10 feet thick.

Morrow Mountain rock was popular among many generations of native peoples because it is uniform, hard, and extremely fine grained. Uniformity makes it easy to work with; hardness makes it durable; and the tiny grains allow for sharp blades and points. The hardness is due to an abundance of the mineral quartz. The tiny grains indicate that this igneous rock cooled quickly (above ground). In most cases, a quartz-rich, fine-grained rock is called rhyolite, which is the extrusive equivalent of granite. Geologists and archaeologists alike have called this rock Morrow Mountain rhyolite for decades, and many continue to do so. However, chemical analyses have shown it to be midway in composition between rhyolite and dacite, which contains more plagioclase feldspar than rhyolite. So the precise technical name is metarhyodacite, the "meta" indicating a minor amount of metamorphism. If you choose to follow tradition and call the rock rhyolite, as we do, know that you are sacrificing some precision in doing so.

FIGURE 19-1. Morrow Mountain. Photograph by J. Robert Butler.

Most rhyolite in the world has at least a few grains that are large enough to be seen with the naked eye, but Morrow Mountain rhyolite has virtually none, making it unusual in its uniformity. The same quartz-rich rock that makes good stone tools also makes good mountains. Rocks high in quartz, such as rhyolite, granite, and quartzite, are not easily eroded and often form peaks and cliffs (see Chapter 16, on Crowders Mountain, and Chapter 18, on Pilot Mountain).

A good spot to see the full depth of the quarrying debris that prehistoric people left behind is on the south flank of Morrow Mountain. Walk to the lower (southern) end of the parking lot at the top and take the trail that begins at the steps over the low wall. This trail is the Mountain Loop Trail. Follow the trail for about 200 yards to a wooden bridge over a gully, which was carved by water running off the parking lot. Continue on the trail until it doubles back to a second bridge where you can get a good view of the eroded walls of the gully (Figure 19-3). The walls are 10 feet tall, and they are made of broken rhyolite pieces embedded in brown clay. The pieces you see are dark gray and unweathered, at least on some sides; many of the pieces do have a whitish weathered "rind" on one or more sides. The fresh surfaces tell you that these chips are the product of human activity; undisturbed rhyolite would be covered with the light-colored rind. Prehistoric people chipped off the rind to get at the harder fresh rhyolite underneath.

FIGURE 19-2. A sample of Morrow Mountain rhyolite. Photograph by J. Robert Butler.

Although rock chips and flakes are everywhere, it's highly unlikely that you will find any arrowheads because the prehistoric quarriers generally didn't make tools on the mountain—they simply broke out large chunks of the rhyolite and took them down to their camps to work them further. (Please remember that collecting rocks or artifacts is prohibited in state parks.) One of their camps was at the famous Hardaway archaeological site just east of Badin, about 5 miles north of Morrow Mountain, which began to be occupied perhaps 10,000 years ago. At the Hardaway site, prehistoric people shaped and trimmed pieces of Morrow Mountain rhyolite into points and tools, leaving behind tons and tons of very fine rock chips.

Archaeologists have found tools made of Morrow Mountain rock not just near the mountain, but as far as 120 miles away—from southern Virginia to the coast of South Carolina.

Morrow Mountain is in the Uwharrie mountain range. From the overlook just beyond the upper end of the parking lot, you can see some of the other peaks in the Uwharries, most of which are also made of rhyolite. The only other one with rhyolite as uniform as Morrow Mountain's is Tater Top, the small peak in the foreground to the east. There is also a nice view here of the Pee Dee River (dammed to form Lake Tillery), about 650 feet below the overlook.

FIGURE 19-3. The walls of this gully expose 10 vertical feet of clay embedded with chips of rhyolite. Photograph by J. Robert Butler.

The rhyolite in this area originated 570 million years ago as lava flowing out of volcanoes and as magma that cooled quickly just below the surface on a continental fragment that had broken off of Gondwana, an ancient continent that contained parts of present-day Africa and South America. In addition to rhyolite, the volcanoes erupted quartz-poor lava, which formed basalt. In the shallow seas around the volcanoes, layers of volcanic ash, mud, and silt settled on the seafloor, forming sedimentary rock. Millions of years passed, and the rhyolite, basalt, and sedimentary rocks were buried under more lava and sediments. The continental fragment was moving toward Laurentia, the ancient precursor to North America, and the two landmasses eventually collided. The remains of part of the continental fragment—a belt of weakly metamorphosed rhyolite, basalt, and sedimentary rocks—stretches across central North and South Carolina and is called the Carolina terrane. (See Plate 5 for a map showing the Carolina terrane.)

You won't see many rhyolite outcrops on Morrow Mountain because almost all of them have been quarried away. In fact, in later years people probably had to dig pits in the debris to reach rock. Any such pits would have long since been filled with soil that crept down the mountainside.

However, there are several places to see outcrops of the metamorphosed sediments and basalt. As you approach the park, there is an outcrop of weakly metamorphosed sedimentary rock called argillite on the right side of Morrow Mountain Road soon after you leave Valley Road. The rock is layered, and fractures have cut the layers into small blocks.

A bit farther along the road, near the sharp bend at Shiloh Church, is a good outcrop of basalt (the quartz-poor lava). The rock was slightly metamorphosed from the collision; geologists call it metabasalt or greenstone. If you look closely, you will see that it is composed of angular blocks of varying sizes. This type of rock is called a volcanic breccia, and its presence tells us that these rocks were not extruded as a quiet lava flow; instead, an explosive eruption threw blocks of hardened lava into the air.

At the park entrance, take a look at the information building. It's made of argillite, as are most of the buildings and walls in the park. The Civilian Conservation Corps (CCC) built these structures in the 1930s from argillite quarried in the northern part of the park. (You can visit the quarry by following Quarry Trail.) Also notice the cedar trees near the entrance. Some are shaped like cones, while others are more like columns. Columnar cedars grow in soil that is high in calcium, typically soils on limestone bedrock. Columnar cedars are common on the limestone soils in Tennessee. Although there is no limestone here, the metabasalts contain small amounts of calcite, which is the mineral form of calcium carbonate, and large amounts of calcium-rich feldspar.

Another interesting spot in the park is the parking lot near the boat launch—to get there, go all the way to the end of the road that passes the campgrounds to the river. You'll see many smaller rhyolite chips scattered on the sandy floodplain near the parking lot (although many of the rocks are pieces of crushed stone brought in to construct the parking lot). This was an encampment where Indians made tools from the rhyolite hunks.

In the late 1700s this was the site of Lowder's Ferry, which carried travelers on the Fayetteville-Salisbury road across the Pee Dee River; it operated until the 1920s, when a bridge was built downstream. A town, Tindallsville, sprang up here around 1760. Although it served as county seat for a short while, Tindallsville fell into ruin around 1830. Shortly thereafter, in 1834, Dr. Francis Kron moved to this area to practice medicine. His house has been restored for visitors.

Walk out on the small dock over the river. To the north, the river is called the Yadkin; to the south, the Pee Dee. This river, like many others, was given different names by explorers in different areas. The name change takes place here, where the Uwharrie River enters straight across from you. Another nearby river with two names is the Catawba in North Carolina, which becomes the Wateree in South Carolina's Coastal Plain.

To the northwest you can see Falls Mountain. Upstream from Falls Mountain lies a section of river once called the Narrows. Before dams were built early in the twentieth century, the Yadkin went from 1,000 feet wide to 60 feet wide here as it coursed over rhyolite boulders. The hard rhyolite bedrock prevented the river from eroding a wider channel. In the early 1900s a French company decided to harness the power of the river to generate electricity. The Narrows was the obvious place to do it because the narrow channel combined with the hard rock walls made it easier to build a dam. Construction of the dam was interrupted by World War I; eventually Alcoa bought out the French company and completed the dam in 1917. This dam and others built by Alcoa still power an aluminum plant in nearby Badin. The town, by the way, was named after the president of the French company, Adrien Badin.

Human beings find some rocks more useful than others. For as long as

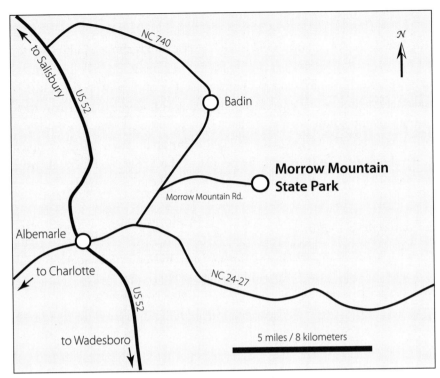

FIGURE 19-4. Location of Morrow Mountain State Park.

people have been around Morrow Mountain's rhyolite, they have been using it. For 11,000 years, people used it to make arrowheads and spear points. For the last century, people have been generating electricity from dams constructed in a rhyolite-walled river bed. Although we no longer fashion tools from its rhyolite, the mountain still provides something it no doubt provided prehistoric people as well—beautiful scenery and a glimpse into the past.

Location and Access

Morrow Mountain State Park is in the Uwharrie Mountains northeast of Charlotte. From Albemarle, take NC 24-27 east to NC 740. Go north on NC 740, and then east on Morrow Mountain Road, following it into the park. From the north, take NC 740 to Badin, and then follow signs to the park. As is true in all state parks, collecting rocks and artifacts is prohibited here.

Nearby Features

The Town Creek Indian Mound State Historic Site is about 23 miles south-east of Morrow Mountain, off NC 731, east of Mount Gilead. This famous archaeological site has a museum and a number of reconstructed features, including palisades that enclose a temple mound and mortuary. Excavation at the site and studies of the artifacts have provided a wealth of information on the Native Americans who lived in the area. The site was occupied from about A.D. 1200 to 1500 by people of the Pee Dee culture. (Closed Mondays.)

Recommended Reading

Daniel, I. Randolph, Jr. *Hardaway Revisited: Early Archaic Settlement in the Southeast.* Tuscaloosa: University of Alabama Press, 1998.

Ward, Trawick H., and R. P. Stephen Davis, Jr. *Time before History: The Archaeology of North Carolina.* Chapel Hill: University of North Carolina Press, 1999.

20

Occoneechee Mountain State Natural Area
A Mine with a View

)) ORANGE COUNTY, NORTH CAROLINA

The highest point in Orange County, North Carolina, is Occoneechee Mountain, at 867 feet. The actual peak is just outside the borders of the Occoneechee Mountain State Natural Area, and it really doesn't have much of a view because it's covered with trees and transmission towers. The real view is in the park, from the overlook at the top of the mountain's cliffs (elevation, approximately 700 feet). To get there, hike the gravel road up the mountain, and then take the Overlook Trail spur. From the overlook, you can see for miles and miles out over the Eno River valley and into West Hillsborough and the trees beyond. It's an unusually long view for this part of the Piedmont. One thing you can't see from here is the face of the cliffs below you, which are worth a look for several reasons. A landslide at the cliffs in February 2001 damaged an earlier overlook structure, and the scars of the landslide are still visible from below.

The trails that will take you to good views of the cliffs and landslide are unnamed, but they are marked on the park's map and are well maintained. These trails fork off from the Occoneechee Mountain Loop Trail at the power-line cut. One fork offers a view of the cliff faces about halfway down, and another fork goes to the very bottom of the cliffs. There are several signs prohibiting rock climbing, which would obviously be unwise on these highly unstable surfaces.

Probably the most arresting aspect of the cliffs is their unusual color— white with areas of orange, pinkish red, and gray. These are actually the walls of an old quarry. In the 1800s people mined the rock here to use in railroad beds, leaving behind these cliffs. From this vantage point, it's easy to see that there is steep-to-vertical layering, or foliation, in the rocks. The steep foliation is what led to the landslide—after a day of hard rain, followed by a freeze, the rocks gave way along planes of weakness (the foliation) to slide down the face of the cliffs. From the foot of the

FIGURE 20-1. Boulders of quartzite at the top of Occoneechee Mountain.

cliffs, the landslide rubble is impressive—there are boulders the size of cars (Plate 9).

The foliation and lack of distinct sedimentary grains tells you this rock is metamorphic. In places, it's schist; in other places, it's phyllite; and, in still others, it's quartz-rich enough to be called quartzite. As its name suggests, quartzite is a metamorphic rock with abundant quartz. Schist and phyllite are metamorphic rocks that are foliated and rich in platy minerals (mica or chlorite). Schist is medium- or coarse-grained, and phyllite is fine-grained. Because the names do not necessarily indicate a particular mineral composition of the rocks, we often add mineral names to the front of the rock names to be more descriptive. So the rocks here are called quartz-sericite phyllite and quartz-sericite schist. Sericite is a fine-grained kind of silvery mica. The quartz and sericite give the rocks their unusually light color. Their high quartz content explains why Occoneechee Mountain is here—quartz is very resistant to erosion. This area became a mountain when softer metamorphosed volcanic rocks eroded away, leaving a peak of quartz-rich rocks behind. Mountains formed this way are called monadnocks. While quartz and sericite are the most prominent minerals here,

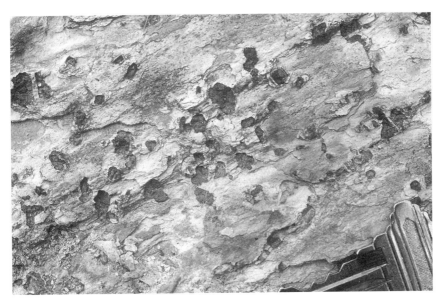

FIGURE 20-2. Pyrophyllite-sericite schist with large, dark crystals of andalusite.

there are some other important minerals in these rocks, including pyrophyllite and andalusite (Figure 20-2). Pick up a piece of the rock, which is scattered everywhere along the trails; you will notice that although the rock itself is quite hard, if you rub a foliation surface, it feels a little powdery—like talc. The powdery feeling is due to the mineral pyrophyllite.

These cliffs are no longer mined, but a very similar rock is currently being extracted on Eno Mountain Road just east of here by Piedmont Minerals. You can see the buff-colored cliffs of the modern mine in the distance from where the Occoneechee Mountain Loop Trail intersects the powerline cut. The rock is being mined for pyrophyllite and andalusite, both of which are used to manufacture high-temperature ceramics for products like sparkplugs and blast furnaces. This mine is the only place where andalusite is being extracted in the United States today.

The geologic history of the rock at Occoneechee Mountain and the Piedmont Minerals mine is almost identical to that of Crowders Mountain (see Chapter 16) with one important difference: the degree of metamorphism that the rock experienced. The rock of Crowders Mountain is rich in quartz and kyanite, an erosion-resistant mineral that has the same chemical formula as andalusite (they are each made of the same proportions of aluminum, silicon, and oxygen). Minerals like andalusite and kyanite, which have the same chemical formula but different crystal geometry, are known as polymorphs. Kyanite is the mineral that forms from this compound at high pressure and moderate-to-high temperature. Andalusite forms at low-to-moderate temperature and low pressure. The presence of kyanite at Crowders Mountain tells us that those rocks were buried deeper and subjected to higher temperatures than the rocks at Occoneechee Mountain. There is a third mineral polymorph of this compound that is called sillimanite. Sillimanite typically forms at a wide range of pressures and at temperatures that are even higher than those at which kyanite forms. Sillimanite is abundant in the Piedmont terrane (Plate 4) and in parts of the Blue Ridge; rocks containing sillimanite have experienced some of the most intense metamorphism in the Carolinas.

The rocks of Crowders Mountain are part of the Charlotte terrane and the rocks of Occoneechee Mountain are part of the Carolina terrane (Plate 5). Both of these terranes are "exotic" terranes with the same genesis—they originated as part of another continent (Gondwana) before being plastered onto ours (Laurentia) during a tectonic collision. These rocks started out as layers of sediment and volcanic ash on the continental shelf of Gondwana about 600 million years ago. Gondwana and Laurentia were being pulled toward each other by the conveyor belt of subduction, which caused volcanoes to erupt on Gondwana, spewing ash on top of the shallow-water sediments. Hydrothermal activity, also generated by subduction, removed elements like potassium, sodium, and calcium and concentrated silica and aluminum in the layers of sediment and volcanic ash. Millions of years later, this part of Gondwana rifted off and collided with Laurentia (see Figures 5-2 and 5-3), metamorphosing the sediments and ash into kyanite-rich rocks in the case of Crowders Mountain and into andalusite-rich rocks in the case of Occoneechee Mountain.

So the rocks of Crowders Mountain and Occoneechee Mountain share the same origins—as ash and sediments on an ancient continental shelf—and the same outcome—as monadnocks in the North Carolina Piedmont.

Location and Access

Occoneechee Mountain State Natural Area is administered by Eno River State Park. To get there, take exit 164 off I-85 near Hillsborough. Turn north onto Churton Street, and then take a quick left onto Mayo Street. Turn left

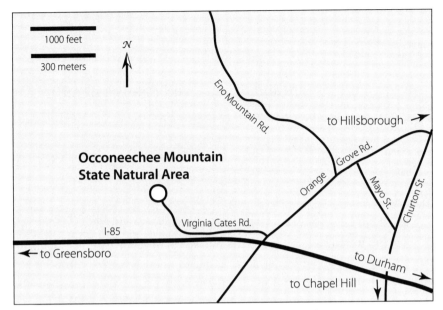

FIGURE 20-3. Location of Occoneechee Mountain State Natural Area.

onto Orange Grove Road, and then right onto Virginia Cates Road; follow the signs to the parking area. No camping or rock climbing is allowed; there are two fishing ponds.

Nearby Features

There is a reconstructed seventeenth-century Occaneechi Indian village in Hillsborough that shows how Native Americans were living in the area at the time when the English explorer John Lawson made his famous journey through North Carolina. The reconstructed village is maintained by the Occaneechi Band of the Saponi Nation of Alamance and Orange counties.

21

The Museum of Life and Science and Penny's Bend
Diabase Sills in the Durham Triassic Basin

>> DURHAM COUNTY, NORTH CAROLINA

There are not too many places in Durham County where you see a lot of exposed bedrock; one place where you can is at the Museum of Life and Science in Durham. If you go to the museum's outdoor exhibit called Explore the Wild, you will walk down a big wooden boardwalk into an old abandoned quarry. The floor of the quarry is covered with water; the walls are cliffs of rock left behind when the city of Durham stopped quarrying here in the 1930s. (The rock was used as gravel on Durham's dirt streets.)

At the overlook to the bear enclosure, which is partially bounded by the quarry walls, you can examine the rock up close. Make sure that you can tell the difference between the fake concrete rock, on the right as you're looking at the bears, and the real rock, which is on the left. Most of the real rock surface has weathered to a brownish color, but if you can find a fresh surface to look at, you'll see the rock itself is very dark gray, almost black. The grains are small, but definitely not microscopic; you can see individual light and dark minerals; and there is no obvious layering or foliation. The grains and texture tell you this is an igneous rock; the very dark color tells you it's basaltic in composition. If the rock had microscopic grains, you would know that the molten rock cooled quickly on the surface of the earth, and you'd call it basalt. If it had large grains, you would know that it cooled slowly deep underground, and you'd call it gabbro. The grains of this rock, however, are intermediate in size, which tells you it cooled underground, but quite near the surface. We call this kind of rock diabase.

The story of this igneous rock begins 220 million years ago, during the Triassic, when the supercontinent Pangea first began to break up (see Figure 5-4). Two of the pieces of Pangea were destined to become the continents of Africa and North America, and as they started to pull away from each other, hundreds of cracks appeared in the crust, most of which ran roughly perpendicular to the directions the continents were moving. These "rift ba-

FIGURE 21-1. Old diabase quarry wall at the Museum of Life and Science (bear for scale). Photograph by Cynthia Gurganus.

sins" were bounded on one or both sides by normal faults (see Figure 2-4). Some of the basins continued to widen until ocean waters came flooding between the continents: this is how the Atlantic Ocean was born. (A good modern example of this stage of the birth of an ocean is the Red Sea, which is a flooded rift basin that opened between Africa and the Arabian Peninsula. See Figure 3-1.) The other rift basins stopped growing and eventually filled in with sediment brought in by rivers. These rift valleys, called Triassic basins, can be found all along the east coast of North America and the west coast of Africa.

North Carolina's two main Triassic basins are the Deep River basin and the Dan River basin. There is also a small Triassic basin that straddles the line between Davie County and Yadkin County. The Deep River basin has three named subbasins: the Durham, Sanford, and Wadesboro basins. South Carolina's Triassic basins are buried beneath the more recent sediments of the Coastal Plain, although there are a few small exposures of Triassic sediments where the southernmost end of the Deep River basin extends into South Carolina (Plate 4 and Figure 21-2).

In North Carolina, Triassic basins commonly show up as valleys because the sedimentary rocks in them are more easily erodable than the surrounding igneous and metamorphic rocks. If you have ever driven downhill out of Chapel Hill toward Durham, you have descended into the Durham Triassic basin. You climb out of the Durham basin and cross the Triassic Jonesboro normal fault as you drive up the hill going east on I-40 near the Harrison Avenue exit in Cary.

Now we're finally getting to the part of the story where igneous rocks make their appearance. As plates begin to diverge, the crust stretches out and thins, and as it does so, the reduced weight of the crust promotes partial melting of the uppermost mantle, which produces basaltic magma. The same process produces basaltic magma whether the plates are continental crust (as in this case) or oceanic crust (as in the case of seafloor spreading). So while North America and Africa were pulling away from each other, and the rift basins were filling with sediments, basaltic magma was shooting through the sediments and cooling into diabase rock.

Where diabase intrudes across sedimentary layers, we call the structure a dike, and where it intrudes between layers, we call it a sill. The abandoned quarry at the Museum of Life and Science is a diabase sill. This rock extends far beyond the walls of the quarry and is periodically exposed at the surface over an area of several square miles. If you walk on the path out of the quarry to the other parts of the Explore the Wild and Catch the Wind exhibits, you will see some boulders of diabase scattered along the edges and in the woods. Rounded, reddish-brown boulders are weathered diabase; angular, dark boulders are fresh, unweathered diabase. The fresh

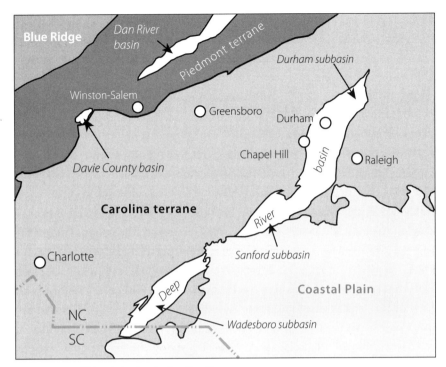

FIGURE 21-2. Triassic basins in the Carolinas.

pieces have been more recently removed from the bedrock, either by the actions of humans or by the natural process of erosion.

Another diabase sill in Durham County is at Penny's Bend on the Eno River (Figure 21-3). Although it can't be traced continuously to the sill at the museum, the two exposures were likely of the same body of rock before erosion destroyed parts of it. At Penny's Bend, most of the diabase is actually under a thick layer of soil; there are only a few outcrops along the shore of the river. Nevertheless, the diabase sill has two quite visible effects at Penny's Bend. The first is that the Eno River follows a horseshoe bend here as it takes the path of least resistance around the hard diabase rock and through the easily erodable Triassic sediments. The second visible effect is the unusual group of plants that grow at Penny's Bend. As the sill weathers into the soil, its high calcium content (from the mineral plagioclase feldspar) gives the soil a higher pH (more alkaline, less acidic) than is normal in this area, where most soil is acidic. Many of the plants that grow at Penny's Bend are more likely to be found in the alkaline soils of the midwestern prairies, including smooth coneflower (*Echinacea laevigata*), tall larkspur (*Delphinium exaltatum*), prairie dock (*Silphium terebinthinaceum*), hoary puccoon (*Lithospermum canescens*), and eastern prairie blue wild indigo (*Baptisia minor var. aberrans*). The smooth coneflower is a federally endangered species, and the others are either threatened or endangered in the Carolinas or under consideration for being added to the those lists.

If you go to Penny's Bend, the trail starts from the western corner of the parking lot (the corner farthest away from Snow Hill Road). There is a short trail with interpretive signs through the prairie wildflowers, and then a 2-mile loop along the river and back. You'll see lots of rounded diabase boulders on the path; their surfaces have weathered from the original dark gray to brownish orange. Soon after the short interpretive trail, you will cross a small wooden footbridge, and then soon after that, the trail meets the river. Here you will see an outcrop of the diabase on the shore. A casual observer might think it was just a bunch of boulders rather than what it is—an exposure of bedrock. One way to tell is that you can notice a continuity of fractures throughout the rock. Weathering along the fractures is what is beginning to make this outcrop look like a pile of distinct rocks.

We'd like to point out a good place to see some interesting Triassic sediments in Durham, but that's hard to do. Whenever the sediments are exposed—along a new road cut, for example—they quickly crumble and become covered with plants. However, if you keep your eyes open, you can occasionally see layers of sediments or cross-beds during highway construction or behind new buildings. One clue is to look for red rocks. The Triassic sandstones and shales are usually colored deep brick red or maroon.

The sediments in North Carolina's Triassic basins have been mined for coal, sand, and clay. The sand and clay is often used to make bricks: North Carolina is the nation's leading producer of bricks. Coal was mined from the Deep River's Sanford subbasin, mostly in Chatham County, from the mid-1800s until the early 1950s.

Before 1994 the sediments of the Triassic basin were not known for being particularly rich in fossils, but that may be changing. In 1994 a University of North Carolina geology student named Brian Coffey discovered a 220-million-year-old fossil in the Deep River basin south of Durham. Subsequent work by the paleontologist Joe Carter and his students at UNC–

FIGURE 21-3. An outcrop of a diabase sill at Penny's Bend on the Eno River.

Chapel Hill revealed a mass of bones that turned out to be from six different animals. The two most exciting were a rauisuchian and a sphenosuchian, both of which resemble dinosaurs, but are much older. The rauisuchian is one of only about 30 such skeletons known in the world, and it was the first found in eastern North America. It bears a passing resemblance to a *Tyrannosaurus rex* and was probably about 7 feet tall and 11 feet long. The sphenosuchian was an ancestor of crocodiles, but it had longer legs. The four other fossils included two forebears of mammals.

A couple of years after Coffey's discovery, a bulldozer operator in a Triassic basin turned up another fossil. This prompted Vince Schneider, curator of paleontology at the North Carolina Museum of Natural Sciences, to begin systematically searching for more fossils at several mines in the Deep River basin. Since then he has found and collected hundreds of fossil bones from a variety of early reptiles. He has also found dozens of fossils from a group of mammal ancestors called traversodonts, which looked like a cross between a rat and a lizard. Scientists from around the country are studying the assemblage of fossils, owned by the Museum of Natural Sciences, to

FIGURE 21-4. A skeleton of a reptile that lived in the Triassic period. This is a rauisichid, a type of rauisuchian. (In the collection of the North Carolina Museum of Natural Sciences.)

learn more about animals that roamed the Carolinas in the Triassic (Figure 21-4).

Two hundred and twenty million years later, rauisuchians and traversodonts are extinct; dinosaurs have come and gone; and mammals have evolved into creatures that write and read books. But the diabase sill that was injected into Durham County's Triassic sediments all those years ago remains. It's been used for street gravel and as a bear enclosure, and it encourages the growth of unusual flowers that people enjoy. For anyone who's interested, this diabase sill tells an important segment of the Carolinas' geologic story, about a time when a supercontinent rifted apart and the Atlantic Ocean was born.

Location and Access

The Museum of Life and Science has indoor and outdoor science exhibits, a live insectarium, and a three-story butterfly house. There is an admission fee. To get to the museum, take the North Duke Street exit off I-85 in Durham, and then turn right onto Murray Avenue.

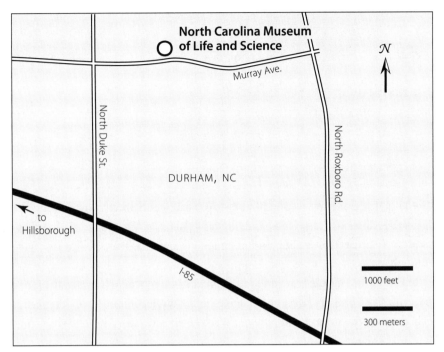

FIGURE 21-5. Location of the North Carolina Museum of Life and Science.

Penny's Bend is on the Eno River. To get there, take Roxboro Road north from I-85 in Durham. Turn right onto Old Oxford Road and go to the intersection with Snow Hill Road. It is administered by the North Carolina Botanical Garden. There are no facilities at Penny's Bend.

22

Landsford Canal State Park
Transportation and Geology

>> CHESTER COUNTY, SOUTH CAROLINA

Geology, transportation, and history are inextricably intertwined along the Catawba River at Landsford Canal State Park. At times the geology has made transportation easier, and at times it has made transportation more difficult.

In the 1700s people traveling on horseback or in wagons naturally chose to cross the Catawba here, at a place where a large rock outcrop in the riverbed made the crossing shallow and relatively smooth. The crossing soon became known as Land's Ford, because Thomas Land owned the land and operated a store here in the mid-1700s. The ford was used by local settlers, explorers, Native Americans, and immigrants traveling both north and south (it was part of the Great Wagon Road connecting Philadelphia and the Carolina Piedmont); Revolutionary War troops crossed here, as did, much later, Civil War troops.

The rocks at Landsford Canal are a kind of igneous rock called diorite. It has been slightly metamorphosed, but there is no visible foliation. Most of the diorite you will see here is in the river and has a brown, weathered surface; along the trail, however, there are a few boulders whose fresh surfaces display diorite's salt-and-pepper color and texture (Figure 22-2). Diorite was also used to line the walls of some of the locks. Diorite, like granite, forms in magma chambers and has large (visible) mineral grains. It has less silica than granite and more calcium, iron, and magnesium, which is typical of magma that feeds volcanoes that form above subduction zones (see Chapter 3 for more on subduction). The age of these particular rocks has not been measured, but they are similar to other rocks in the area that are between 535 and 570 million years old. These rocks formed on the volcanic edge of the ancient continent Gondwana. Later, the volcanic edge rifted off of Gondwana and collided with the continent that would later become North America. The fragment became part of the Carolinas and is called

FIGURE 22-1. Spider lilies blooming among diorite boulders in the Catawba River.
Photograph by Brian Gomsak.

the Charlotte terrane, one of the major terranes within the exotic Gondwanan terranes (see Figures 5-2 and 5-3 and Plate 5).

The same rock that made it easier to cross the river made it more difficult to travel on the river. The rock at Land's Ford wasn't the only problem; there are rapids just upstream as well. In the early 1800s cotton growers in the Piedmont needed a safe and reliable way to get their cotton to the markets on the coast. If there were a way to get past the rapids, the Catawba River would carry them to the Wateree River and then on to Charleston. In 1820 South Carolina began funding an ambitious project to build a canal at Landsford to bypass the rapids. This was one of four canals built on the Catawba and the Wateree in the early 1800s.

Robert Mills was the architect for these canals. Born in Charleston in 1781, he has been called America's first architect. He designed almost twenty county courthouses in South Carolina and several public buildings in Columbia. He later designed buildings in Philadelphia, Baltimore, and Washington, D.C.—including the Department of the Treasury, the U.S. Post Office, and the Washington Monument. Describing the Catawba River at Landsford, he wrote, "Ten thousand rocks and grassy islets meet the traveller's eye, ten thousand murmuring streams meander through them. During

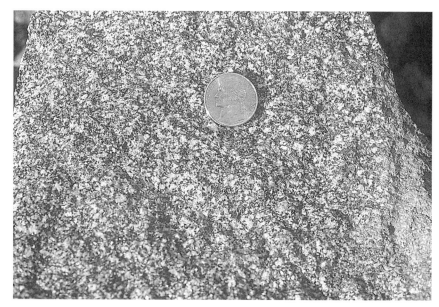

FIGURE 22-2. Diorite at Landsford Canal State Park.

low water the cattle delight to graze upon the islets . . . at such times they furnish a curious spectacle in the midst of a mighty river" (Robert Mills, *Statistics of South Carolina* [Charleston: Hurlbut and Lloyd, 1826], 53).

A river's bed constantly loses elevation between its source and the sea. If it didn't, the water wouldn't flow. A canal, on the other hand, must be perfectly level. If it weren't, the water would run out one end.

Traveling downstream, boats first left the Catawba River and entered Landsford Canal at 444 feet above sea level. The canal rejoined the Catawba about a mile and a half later, at 412 feet. The canal lost those 32 feet of elevation in two pairs of locks. Locks are like elevators for boats, powered by gravity. A boat traveling downstream enters a lock through an open gate. That gate is closed and water slowly let out until the water level matches that of the next portion of the canal. Then the second gate is opened, and the boat travels on.

Beginning in 1820, workers dug the canal by hand and lined it with clay to make it waterproof. To keep it level, the first part of the canal had to be dug into the ground. Farther downstream (but before the locks), the canal had to be built up above the level of the river.

Once in the canal, boats were towed by mules or horses. In the river, boats were often propelled by poles, but poles weren't allowed in the canal

FIGURE 22-3. A lock whose walls are lined with diorite rock.

because they could puncture the waterproof clay lining. The boats were about 60 feet long and 7 feet wide and could carry 50 bales of cotton.

It took three years of manual labor to complete the canal. It opened in 1823. Public funding was cut off in 1838, and the canal was no longer in use after 1846. By then, railroads and improved roads were beginning to solve the problem of transporting crops to market.

At Landsford Canal State Park, you can walk the same trail the horses trod as they pulled boats through the canal; it's a 1.5-mile trail (one way). Of course, the canal is dry now—no water is being diverted into it from the river. The state park provides a trail guide containing information about the canal and its locks. In some places the canal remains in good shape, and in other places (particularly where it had been built up) it is mostly eroded away. The locks, whose walls are made of field stones and lined with clean-cut rocks from a nearby quarry, are well preserved (Figure 22-3). It's interesting to notice the ways in which the canal is being incorporated back into nature. For example, there are very large trees growing between the canal and the path. These trees could not have been growing here when a horse on this path was towing boats with a rope. Even though the canal is dry, you can tell that water does flow in it at times, probably during heavy storms, because you can see places where water has deposited sediment in

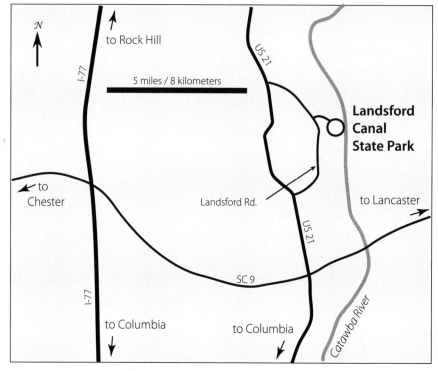

FIGURE 22-4. Location of Landsford Canal State Park.

miniature sand bars, just like a natural meandering river (see Chapter 27, on the Roanoke River). At the end of the trail, you come to Land's Ford. You can see the remains of a wagon path coming right down into the river and continuing on into the woods on the other side.

Along the river's edge, there is also a short nature trail that offers views of the rapids that the canal was designed to circumvent. One of the sets of rapids contains the largest population of the rocky shoals spider lily (*Hymenocallis coronaria*), which blooms in late May and early June. These white-blooming flowers spring from bulbs wedged among the rocks. They are found in South Carolina, Georgia, and Alabama. For many people, the spider lilies in bloom are reason enough to visit Landsford Canal State Park.

These days, we travel quickly and easily by car and train and plane. A few rock outcrops here or there don't slow us down. Landsford Canal is a good place to imagine the way things were 100 or 200 years ago. A fortuitously placed outcrop in a streambed became a pivotal point in local travel and

was a part of the Great Wagon Road connecting North and South in colonial times. Later, rapids that thwarted river travel inspired a mammoth
engineering project whose remains still stand today.

Location and Access

Landsford Canal State Park is 15 miles west of Lancaster, South Carolina,
off US 21. It is not open on Tuesdays and Wednesdays. South Carolina state
parks charge a nominal admission fee. There is no camping.

23

The North Carolina Museum of Natural Sciences
Gems and Meteorites

An unusual number of gems and meteorites have been unearthed in the Carolinas. Sometimes the discoveries were pure happenstance; other times the discoveries were the result of many years of hard work. If, for whatever reason, you have not chanced to find a meteorite or an emerald in the wilds of the Carolinas, we suggest you pay a visit to the North Carolina Museum of Natural Sciences in Raleigh and enjoy a free look at some interesting things other people have dug up.

The museum has an extensive geology exhibit with many beautiful North Carolina minerals on display, including emeralds and rubies. It also has in its holdings more than a dozen North Carolina meteorites, two of which are on display. (The Museum also has some fantastic dinosaur skeletons, including a *Tyrannosaurus rex* skull and a large *T. rex*–like *Acrocanthosaurus* that was found in southeastern Oklahoma.)

Though millions of meteors streak through our atmosphere every day, most burn up before hitting the ground. The few that survive are called meteorites. So far, 30 meteorites have been found in North Carolina, and six in South Carolina. The largest meteorite on record was found in Namibia and weighs between 60 and 70 tons. The largest meteorite ever found in North Carolina is the 160-pound Uwharrie meteorite (Figure 23-2), which you can see at the Museum. In 1922 T. L. Russell came across this meteorite while plowing in Randolph County. Not knowing its extraterrestrial origin, he used it as an anvil for eight years. In 1930 it made its way to the museum, where it was identified as a meteorite. No one knows when it hit the earth. The museum also displays another meteorite found in North Carolina called the Farmville meteorite.

Sometimes there are witnesses when a meteorite falls. The Moore County meteorite, which weighed 4 pounds, 2 ounces, fell in a farm field where three men were working on the evening of April 21, 1913. One of the men

FIGURE 23-1. The North Carolina Museum of Natural Sciences.

described it as "a red hot ball followed by a trail of blue-black smoke, estimated to be about 15 feet long" (E. P. Henderson and Harry T. Davis, "Moore County, North Carolina, Meteorite—a New Eucrite," *American Mineralogist* 21 [1936]: 215).

A portion of the Moore County meteorite is at the museum, although it is not usually on display. Meteorites are often cut into pieces and sent to different museums. The British Museum of Natural History in London, the Smithsonian Institution in Washington, D.C., and the American Museum of Natural History in New York all have massive collections, including portions of many Carolina meteorites.

By studying meteorites, scientists learn about the origin of the earth and the formation of our universe. Most meteorites are pieces of asteroids, which are large rocky bodies in our solar system, or of comets, which are similar to asteroids but contain more volatile compounds, such as frozen water. Asteroids and comets are thought to represent remnants of our early solar system—pieces that were shed off passing comets or were never accreted into planets. A few meteorites appear to be pieces of Mars and of the moon that were blasted off by large impacts.

Meteorites may also have been important in the origin of life on earth.

FIGURE 23-2. The 160-pound Uwharrie meteorite.

Certain kinds of meteorites contain amino acids that are essential building blocks for life. Others contain the element phosphorus in a form that is readily soluble in water. Phosphorus is an essential ingredient in DNA, but most of the phosphorus on earth is bound up in minerals that are highly insoluble. Early bombardment of the earth by meteorites may have been a source for these life-sustaining ingredients.

Meteorites can be divided into three basic categories: stony (silicates with iron particles), metal (iron and nickel), and stony-iron (iron filled with rock materials). Most meteorites are stony; about 5 percent are metal; and less than 2 percent are stony-iron. The Moore County meteorite is stony, and the Uwharrie meteorite is metal. The Farmville meteorite is a chondrite: it has blobs of stony minerals in a metal matrix.

At least two of the six meteorites that have been found in South Carolina were seen as they fell. The Bishopville meteorite, which weighed about 13 pounds, fell on March 25, 1843, in Lee County. Many people saw and heard the explosion. The object fell in a field of slaves, who fled from the overwhelming smell of sulfur. When the meteorite was dug up the next day, it still smelled strongly of sulfur. The Bishopville meteorite is an aubrite, a kind of stony meteorite that often contains an abnormally high amount of sulfur.

The other observed fall in South Carolina was that of the Cherokee Springs meteorite, which landed in Spartanburg County on July 1, 1933. As it fell, it broke into two pieces that hit the earth about 6.5 miles apart—one weighing about 12.5 pounds and the other 6 pounds. Mr. G. E. Mayfield, who owned a store near where the larger piece fell, described the incident as follows:

> The morning of July 1 I was sitting on the porch of the store talking with Arthur Swafford. We heard a noise like an airplane and for two or three minutes the approach sounded nearer. Finally we went to the edge of the porch to look for the plane, and as I caught around the post at the corner of the porch it sounded as if the plane was just over the building.
>
> On looking for it to come into view I caught sight of the meteorite just as it struck the limb of a hickory tree, to the rear and to one side of the Methodist church, and strike the ground. As soon as it struck the sound died away. It went into the ground, which was sandy, about 15 to 18 inches, then bounced out and was lying 15 inches from the hole it made.
>
> I hurried to the spot and picked it up, but found it was so hot that I had to change it from one hand to the other to keep it from hurting my hands. It fell in a grove of trees. It struck a hickory limb about three-quarters of an inch in diameter and cut it off as if cut by shears. The leaves from the tree fluttering down showed us to the spot.
>
> When we first heard it, the noise was like a plane with the motor racing, but the nearer it came the slower it turned and just before it struck the ground it sounded like a plane with the motor idling. (Stuart H. Perry, "The Cherokee Springs Meteorite," *Popular Astronomy* 42 [1934]: 349)

Meanwhile, Mrs. E. P. Cash heard and saw the fall of the smaller part of the meteorite:

> On the morning of July 1 my husband called me from the field down below the house to bring him some peas. When I reached the

barn to get the peas I heard something like a blast, but it sounded like it was way up in the elements. It was to the north. It made me feel queer. I started to go back to the house for my little girl, but I didn't; I picked up the peas and started, and my husband's brother (E. H. Cash) was coming to meet me.

I heard something in the air like an airplane. I looked. He had his hat off and was looking. I saw something, still thinking it was an airplane real high in the air. By the time I saw it, it came over my head and fell at the corner of our lot fence, made a hole in the ground four or five inches deep, and bounced out on top of the ground. (Perry, "Cherokee Springs Meteorite," 352)

The way people describe the sound of a meteorite falling has changed over the years as our modes of transportation have evolved. Whereas Mr. G. E. Mayfield and Mrs. E. P. Cash both said the meteorite made the noise of an airplane, North Carolina residents in 1849 likened the sound of a meteorite that fell in Cabarrus County to "loaded wagons jolting down a rocky hill." This description was reported the following year in an article in which it was noted that the same description was used by observers of another fall in a different part of the country in 1807 ("Miscellaneous Intelligence: 1. Meteorite in North Carolina," *American Journal of Science* 9, no. 25 [1850]: 145). More recently, a married couple who witnessed a meteorite fall in Kentucky in 1990 said it sounded like a helicopter.

South Carolina's largest meteorite is the Ruff's Mountain, weighing about 117 pounds, which was found in Newberry County in 1844. It is on display at the McKissick Museum on the campus of the University of South Carolina in Columbia.

Somewhere in South Carolina there are horseshoes, nails, and a gate hinge made of a meteorite. In the 1840s a farmer found a 36-pound meteorite in a field in Chester County. Not knowing what it was, he kept it behind a barn for a few years. He later took it to a blacksmith, who discovered that it was malleable because it was mostly iron. The blacksmith used most of the meteorite to make horseshoes, nails, and hinges. Later, what remained came into the hands of a scientist, who identified it as a meteorite. Today small portions of the Chesterville meteorite are at the British Museum of Natural History and at Harvard University.

In all likelihood, all over the world there are old horseshoes and nails made of metal meteorites. Meteorites are not beautiful, nor are they easily recognized as objects of scientific interest. In preindustrial times, if someone found a big hunk of metal, it would be natural to put it to use—as an anvil, like the Uwharrie meteorite, or as raw material for metal goods, like the Chesterville meteorite. (For that matter, the 17-pound gold nugget found in North Carolina in 1799 was initially used as a doorstop; see Chapter 17.)

Gems, on the other hand, are beautiful and easily recognized as something of value. If you found an emerald, you might not know what it was, but you'd know it was something to keep. North Carolina is well known for its gems—minerals that are valued because of their beauty and rareness. All of the four so-called precious gemstones—ruby, sapphire, emerald, and diamond—have been found in North Carolina. Ruby and sapphire are actually the same mineral—corundum. Red corundum is called ruby, and corundum of every other color (blue, purple, pink, orange, brown) is called sapphire. North Carolina's geologic history includes events that tend to produce gemstones. South Carolina has shared basically the same history, but its borders don't encompass as much of the gem-bearing rocks.

Gems are often found in pegmatites, which are veins of igneous rock with extra-large crystals. Imagine a body of molten rock—magma—underground. As a rule, magma mostly contains common elements, like silicon, oxygen, aluminum, iron, magnesium, calcium, sodium, and potassium. As the magma starts to cool, these common elements first crystallize into common minerals, such as quartz, feldspar, mica, pyroxene, and amphibole. Unusual elements like beryllium or lithium don't readily fit into the structure of these common minerals, so they tend to become concentrated in the remaining melt, along with small amounts of leftover common elements. This slowly cooling fluid produces big crystals of unusual minerals, such as beryl (which is made of beryllium, aluminum, oxygen, and silicon). Green beryl is the precious gem emerald; it owes its color to the presence of chromium.

Corundum (ruby or sapphire) is made of aluminum and oxygen, with no silicon. Rocks from the crust usually have abundant silicon, which combines with any aluminum and oxygen that are around to make minerals like kyanite and andalusite. (For more on kyanite, see Chapter 11, on Mount Mitchell, and Chapter 16, on Crowders Mountain; for more on andalusite, see Chapter 20, on Occoneechee Mountain.) It's unusual to have aluminum with no free silicon around because silicon is one of the most common elements on earth. However, rocks from the mantle have less silicon and can produce corundum when metamorphosed. Rubies and sapphires can also form when sedimentary rocks that are exceptionally rich in aluminum are metamorphosed.

In the Carolinas, the tectonic collisions that occurred from about 460 to 300 million years ago (see Chapter 5) produced many magma chambers and metamorphosed many sedimentary rocks, setting up conditions for the formation of rare minerals that humans would later value as gems.

The emerald is North Carolina's state gemstone (Plates 10 and 11). The area around Hiddenite, in Alexander County, has long been a source of large and beautiful emeralds, as well as the less valuable gem known as hiddenite. In 1969 a 1,438-carat emerald was found in Hiddenite—at the time the largest on record in North America. In the early 1980s a 1,686-carat emerald from Hiddenite took over the title. In 2003 an emerald weighing more than 1,800 carats was unearthed in Hiddenite (unfortunately, in four pieces). Hiddenite has also been the source of some of the most beautiful emeralds found in North America: the 18-carat Carolina Queen, the 7-carat Carolina Prince, and the 13.15-carat Carolina Emerald, the last of which is on display at the Smithsonian.

Diamonds, which are made of the element carbon, have also been found in the Carolinas. Between the mid- and late-1800s, gold miners found 13 diamonds in the gravel of mountain streams in North Carolina. One of these is in the collections at the Museum of Natural Sciences (although not always on display). The largest North Carolina diamond was found near Dysartsville in 1886; it weighed 4.33 carats. Diamonds are the hardest of all minerals, which means they can scratch any other mineral; however, they are brittle, which means they can be shattered with a hammer. One of the diamonds found in North Carolina was reportedly broken to bits by a miner who attempted to test the stone's hardness with a hammer blow; a geologist examined a fragment of it later and confirmed it to be a diamond. No one has ever discovered the source rock for these diamonds.

Semiprecious gems found in the Carolinas include garnet, aquamarine (a form of beryl), and varieties of quartz, such as amethyst, rose quartz, rutilated quartz, and smoky quartz.

If you go gem hunting, always ask permission before doing so on private land. If you visit commercial gem mining establishments, be aware that some "salt" their buckets with gemstones from elsewhere.

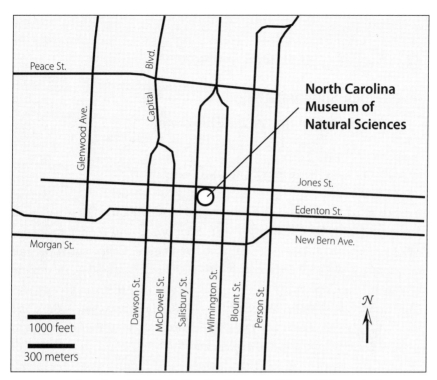

FIGURE 23-3. Location of the North Carolina Museum of Natural Sciences in downtown Raleigh.

Location and Access

The North Carolina Museum of Natural Sciences is located in downtown Raleigh. Admission is free. Only a portion of what is in the museum's collections is on display at any given time; so if you are interested in seeing a particular meteorite or gemstone, call before you go to find out if you will be able to see it. There are also outstanding geologic displays scattered throughout the museum. Spending a few hours there is a great way to get a taste of the rich geologic history of North Carolina.

Recommended Reading

Streeter, Michael. *A Rockhounding Guide to North Carolina's Blue Ridge Mountains.* Almond, N.C.: Milestone Press, 2003.

24

Raven Rock State Park
Everything's Happening at the Fall Zone

>> HARNETT COUNTY, NORTH CAROLINA

In 1739 a ship full of Highland Scots arrived in Wilmington. They had been enticed to North Carolina by glowing descriptions and monetary incentives from Gabriel Johnson, a Scot who lived on the Cape Fear River and was governor of the Province of North Carolina. These Scottish settlers traveled up the Cape Fear River until they found hills that reminded them of the Scottish Highlands. Many settled in Harnett County, where the Cape Fear tumbles over rapids and falls. To harvest fish, they stacked rocks to enhance natural chutes in the rapids, and then they constructed traps of woven sticks to catch the fish that were funneled through the chutes. (Native Americans may have built similar fish traps here earlier; the English explorer John Lawson journeyed through the Piedmont in 1701 and wrote in *A New Voyage to Carolina* that the native peoples caught fish with "great Wares, with Hedges that hinder their Passage only in the Middle, where an artificial Pound is made to take them in; so that they cannot return" [John Lawson, *A New Voyage to Carolina*, ed. Hugh Talmage Lefler (Chapel Hill: University of North Carolina Press, 1967), 218]). The Scottish settlers also used energy from waterfalls and rapids on the Cape Fear to power mills for grinding grain or sawing logs.

If you visit Raven Rock State Park today, you can see rapids on the Cape Fear River and visit Lanier Falls and Northington Falls (also called Fish Traps), where Scottish settlers operated fish traps.

The waterfalls and rapids on the Cape Fear in Harnett County are there because the river is leaving the Piedmont and entering the Coastal Plain. The river wears away the sediments in the Coastal Plain faster than the hard rocks of the Piedmont, giving rise to waterfalls at the boundary between the two. Falls and rapids are a characteristic of all rivers leaving the Piedmont for the Coastal Plain. That's why the boundary between the two physiographic provinces is called the Fall Line or the Fall Zone (Plate 1).

FIGURE 24-1. Raven Rock.

Because settlers built mills on waterfalls, and because waterfalls often marked the end of upstream navigation from the sea, many towns arose in the Fall Zone near the Atlantic coast—cities like Baltimore, Washington, D.C., and Richmond. Fall Zone towns in the Carolinas include Roanoke Rapids, Rocky Mount, and Columbia.

A little farther downstream from Raven Rock State Park, at Smylie's Falls, the Cape Fear loses more than 20 feet of elevation in 2 miles. These falls powered the original Erwin Mills for which the town of Erwin was named.

To allow upstream navigation past the Fall Zone, the Cape Fear Navigation Company built locks and dams on the river during the early to mid-1800s, including one at Fish Traps. The locks and dams were damaged during the hurricanes of 1858 and 1859, scavenged during the Civil War, damaged again during a flood in 1865, and then dealt a final blow when the government allowed timber-raft operators to breach the dams to get down the river safely. By then, the rapids were no longer obstacles to transportation because railroads had overtaken the rivers as thoroughfares.

The same hard rock that forms rapids in the river also forms Raven Rock, a series of steep and sculpted cliffs more than 100 feet high that follow the banks of the river for about a mile. To get to the cliffs, take Raven Rock Loop Trail. At the bottom of a flight of wooden stairs you will have a chance to examine the cliffs up close. Notice the layers of different rock type. In places, the rock is massive (that is, not layered), and it is mostly made of light-colored quartz and feldspar grains. This is quartzite, which is metamorphosed sandstone. Other parts of the rock contain more mica and are banded—that is, there are bands of light-colored minerals and bands of dark-colored minerals. This is a metamorphic rock called gneiss (Figure 24-2).

Look for veins of white quartz shooting across portions of the rock. In other places, you can see where layers of quartz have been pulled apart into blobs shaped like sausage links by the huge pressures the rocks experienced while being metamorphosed. These blobs are called boudins. Upstream of the wooden stairs, you can find rows of tiny, uneven holes in the rock. These were left behind when layers rich in calcium carbonate minerals were leached away by rainwater. If you look among the rocks that have fallen off the cliffs, you will find larger, more regular holes that were drilled in the rock when it was being quarried.

Because these cliffs are full of quartz, they are very hard and resistant

FIGURE 24-2. Gneiss cliffs at Raven Rock.

to erosion. The rocks around them have eroded away, leaving the cliffs behind.

These rock layers are part of what is known as the Carolina terrane (Plate 5). The Carolina terrane is an exotic terrane—a fragment of crust that originated in one place on earth and ended up somewhere else through the movement of tectonic plates. In fact, the edges of most continents are made of a series of exotic terranes that are remnants of past collisions. The Carolina terrane was once part of an ancient continent known as Gondwana, which consisted of parts of what we now call Africa and South America. Oceanic crust was subducting under Gondwana, producing volcanoes that spewed out lava, gas, and ash. This edge of Gondwana rifted off and collided with Laurentia (ancestral North America). As that happened, layers of volcanic ash and sediments were metamorphosed into the quartzite, gneiss, and schist that are exposed at Raven Rock today. These rocks, which are about 570 million years old, are part of a body of rock that extends from Umstead State Park west of Raleigh to this area. The unit is called the Big Lake–Raven Rock schist, but it includes a range of metamorphic rocks, including the coarse-grained gneiss and the quartz-rich quartzite here at Raven Rock.

On the northern leg of the Raven Rock Loop Trail, look for some huge white boulders on the south side of the trail. These are made of quartz and have weathered out of quartz veins in the bedrock. Quartz veins are common in metamorphic rocks; they form when hot subterranean water containing dissolved quartz fills deep cracks in the rocks. As the water cools, quartz precipitates from the water. Lots of quartz veins are as thin as bed sheets, but from the size of these boulders, you can tell that some veins are quite thick.

Raven Rock Loop Trail, besides taking you to the cliffs, also has an overlook where you can see back down the river to Fish Traps. If you want to see Fish Traps (Northington Falls) at close range, take the Fish Traps Trail. It's hard to tell whether the jumble of rocks in the river still represents any human handiwork—or whether nature has completely dismantled the fish traps. Look at the rock outcrops above the river here and see if you can find any drill holes dating from when these rocks were quarried in the mid-1800s.

The Campbell Creek Trail takes you to a deposit of ancient river gravels. Near the beginning of the trail, before it drops down to the creek, you may notice some cobbles on the trail and also in the woods to the north (right)

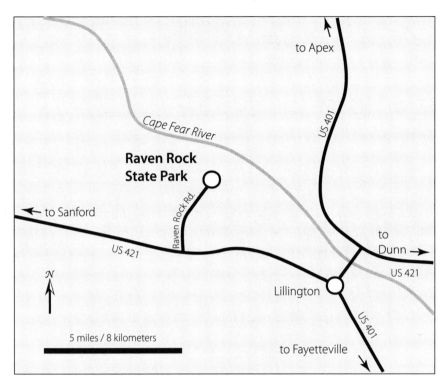

FIGURE 24-3. Location of Raven Rock State Park.

of the trail. Some have an orange-colored stain, a result of the oxidation of iron in the rocks. They are smooth and rounded, which is a clue they were tumbled along in a river—not the modern Cape Fear River, which is far below, but an ancient river. As the ancient river continued to erode the rocks and cut the cliffs, the cobbles were left high and dry.

Notice the number of downed trees at the beginning of the Campbell Trail. Most of these trees were knocked over by the high winds of Hurricane Fran in September 1996. Geologists like to look in the upended roots of trees because the bits of rock trapped in the roots usually represent the bedrock of the area. You might try this yourself and see what you find. Even if you don't discover anything too interesting among the tree roots, a trip to Raven Rock State Park will always be geologically satisfying because of its impressive cliffs.

The cliffs were called Patterson's Rock until about 1850. According to legend, in the mid-1700s a man named Gilbert Patterson wrecked his canoe on some rapids. He managed to get to shore and camped under the cliffs for several days, with a broken leg, before he was rescued. Some say the name was changed to Raven Rock in the 1850s because of the ravens that were nesting on top of the cliffs. Others say it had been called Raven Rock much earlier, the name having come from a Native American legend involving a brave named Raven. In any case, the name stuck, and Raven Rock State Park was established in 1969 to preserve the river, forest, rapids, and cliffs for outdoor recreation—and for the enjoyment of those who like to look at beautiful rocks.

Location and Access

Raven Rock State Park is on the Cape Fear River about midway between Fayetteville and Raleigh; it is reached from US 421, a few miles west of Lillington. Pack-in primitive camping is allowed.

25

Medoc Mountain State Park
Granite and Grapes

>> HALIFAX COUNTY, NORTH CAROLINA

Okay, so maybe Medoc is not exactly a "mountain." The summit is only 325 feet above sea level, and only 150 feet higher than the surrounding land. It's so unimposing that the first question many visitors to the park ask is "Where is the mountain?" Still, in eastern North Carolina, right at the border between the Piedmont and the Coastal Plain, Medoc Mountain is a significant topographic high. And hiking a steep trail through shady stands of mountain laurel (*Kalmia latifolia*) does give you the feeling of being much farther west in the state. The park is the easternmost occurrence of chestnut oak (*Quercus prinus*), which thrives in the western half of the state, petering out in Wake and Vance counties before showing up again on the slopes of Medoc Mountain.

The mountain is called Medoc after a famous vineyard that flourished near here for almost a century. The vineyard took its name from the wine-producing Medoc region of France. Sidney Weller started the vineyard in the early 1800s, along present-day State Road 1002, between NC 48 and Medoc Mountain. At the time, most wine was imported from Europe. Weller was not content to use traditional European cultivation methods in his vineyard; instead, he experimented with new methods and adopted the most successful ones. He also developed a hybrid of the native scuppernong grape, which he called the Halifax Grape. Weller frequently wrote articles for progressive farming magazines and was one of the movers and shakers behind the first North Carolina state fair in 1853. Thanks in large part to the success of Weller's vineyard, North Carolina led the nation in wine production in 1840. The vineyard itself was a tourist attraction: for 50 cents apiece, visitors could picnic on the grounds and eat as many grapes as they wanted, all while being serenaded by choirs.

After Weller's death in 1854, the vineyard was sold to the Garrett family, which named it Medoc. Paul Garrett developed and produced a scupper-

FIGURE 25-1. Medoc Mountain. Photograph courtesy of North Carolina Division of Parks and Recreation.

nong wine called Virginia Dare, using grapes not just from Medoc Vineyards but from other regional vineyards as well. Virginia Dare was the most popular wine in America in the early 1900s. Prohibition closed the wine cellars, but the vineyard existed at least until the 1940s. Today, virtually no trace of it remains.

If you visit Medoc Mountain State Park, you might soon ask yourself, why is this "mountain" here? Virtually the entire area is vegetated, so it's not immediately obvious what kind of rock underlies the mountain. But if you go hiking on the Summit Loop Trail, along the eastern bank of Little Fishing Creek you will come across a fairly large flat outcrop of granite above the trail (Figure 25-2). The surface is weathered, making it difficult to distinguish individual mineral grains. Look for slightly raised veins on the rock—these are probably quartz veins. This granite underlies the entire mountain. It formed deep underground when melted rock (magma) slowly cooled and crystallized. Millions of years of erosion eventually exposed it at the surface. The rocks surrounding Medoc Mountain are metamorphosed sedimentary and volcanic rocks that are less resistant to erosion than the granite, which explains why Medoc Mountain is here.

The granite of Medoc Mountain is 300 million years old; it solidified during a continental collision that resulted in the formation of the super-

FIGURE 25-2. The granite outcrop along the shores of Little Fishing Creek. Photograph courtesy of North Carolina Division of Parks and Recreation.

continent Pangea. The collision was between Gondwana (parts of present-day South America and Africa) and Laurentia (the ancient core of North America). We call this collision the Alleghanian orogeny, and it was the most recent of the mountain-building events that have affected the Carolinas.

When two continents hit each other, a tremendous amount of continental crust is squeezed together in a tight space. The crust has got to go somewhere. It responds by folding and faulting, both of which cause the crust to thicken. This thickened crust starts to warm up because of natural heat production in the rocks from the decay of radioactive elements like uranium and thorium. Since rock is a poor conductor of heat, the rock gets hotter and eventually can melt. When the magma cools later, it forms a large body of igneous rock, called a pluton. So in an area where there has been at least one continental collision, you expect to find plutons. Indeed there are many granite plutons besides Medoc Mountain in the Carolinas that are 270 to 335 million years old: for example, Stone Mountain (see Chapter 12), Mount Airy granite, Rolesville granite (northeast of Raleigh),

Sims granite (just west of Wilson), and Castalia granite (west of Rocky Mount) in North Carolina, and Forty Acre Rock (see Chapter 26) and Liberty Hill granite (north of Columbia) in South Carolina. Granite plutons that formed during the Alleghanian orogeny can be found in Virginia and Georgia as well.

Some granite plutons, such as Stone Mountain and Forty Acre Rock, have huge expanses of bare rock. Medoc, on the other hand, is completely forested. The Medoc granite must have properties that promote the growth of vegetation, such as more intense chemical weathering or abundant fractures.

Even though the bedrock is for the most part hidden by soil and plants, you will see some interesting "float" in the park. Float is the name for loose rocks on the surface that have weathered out of the bedrock. Keep your eyes open for red- or yellow-stained quartz cobbles. These have weathered out of veins of milky quartz in Medoc's granite. Some of the quartz contains deposits of pyrite and molybdenite. Pyrite, or fool's gold, is shiny and yellow, and it often occurs in cubic shapes. When pyrite weathers, it stains the quartz red. Molybdenite is bluish gray and metallic; when it weathers, it stains the quartz yellow. Molybdenite is made of sulfur and molybdenum, a strong, lightweight metal that is an important constituent in some kinds of stainless steel. Medoc Mountain State Park has one of the largest molybdenum deposits in the eastern United States. However, there are larger deposits in the western United States that make it unprofitable to try to extract it here.

The summit of Medoc has no vista because of the thick cover of trees. But you can see some cement support posts that are the ruins of an old dance pavilion that was used in the early part of the twentieth century. According to local residents, flappers danced the nights away on top of Medoc Mountain in the 1920s.

Standing in the quiet forest in a quiet part of the state, it may be hard to imagine the bustle and commotion of flappers dancing all night or nineteenth-century merchants and tourists flocking to the vineyard. It may be even harder to imagine the slow-motion violence of continents colliding hundreds of millions of years ago, pushing up mountains and melting rock that would later solidify into granite. Today's Medoc Mountain offers gentler diversions: a peaceful retreat, a beautiful setting in which to ponder human and geological history, and a rare chance to hike a steep trail at the edge of the Coastal Plain.

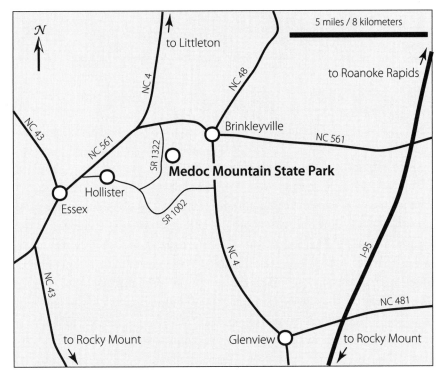

FIGURE 25-3. Location of Medoc Mountain State Park.

Location and Access

Medoc Mountain State Park is about 20 miles southwest of Roanoke Rapids
and a little over 20 miles north of Rocky Mount. Take NC 561 west off I-95,
and then turn onto State Road 1322.

Recommended Reading

Gohdes, Clarence. *Scuppernong: North Carolina's Grape and Its Wines*. Durham:
Duke University Press, 1982.
Jones, H. G., ed. *Sketches in North Carolina, USA, 1872 to 1878: Vineyard Scenes
by Mortimer O. Heath*. Raleigh: Division of Archives and History, 2001. (Note:
This book contains sketches and watercolors of Medoc Vineyards made by
Mortimer O. Heath, an Englishman who worked there for a short while.)

26

Forty Acre Rock
The Battle between Rock and the Forces of Erosion

Bare bedrock is not something you often find in the Carolinas. The entire Coastal Plain is covered with sand and other sediments, and even in the Piedmont and the Blue Ridge, you don't see nearly as much rock as you do out in the western United States. Our wet and warm climate encourages the growth of vegetation, which thoroughly covers most of the Carolinas. That's why geologists in the Carolinas spend so much time at road cuts and quarries—places where vegetation and soil have been removed, revealing a view of the rock below. Even when a road cut exposes a nice fresh rock surface, it's usually not too many years before kudzu or poison ivy reclaims it.

Forty Acre Rock provides a spectacular opportunity to see a wide expanse of bare rock with virtually no vegetation or soil cover. To reach the rock, you walk down a sandy path lined with pine trees that looks like it could be in the Coastal Plain. In fact, this area is right on the border between the Coastal Plain and the Piedmont. After about a quarter mile, the sand and pines give way to bare rock—14 acres of it (not 40). Unfortunately, you may also see a lot of spray-paint graffiti and broken glass. The Heritage Trust Fund, a division of the South Carolina Department of Natural Resources, manages this area and has made great strides in cleaning it up in the last few years; however, vandalism is an ongoing problem.

Probably one of the most noticeable things about this outcrop is its very homogeneous texture. The mineral grains are evenly distributed and, for the most part, similar in size, and there is no layering of any kind. The interlocking mineral grains and nonlayered texture tells you this is an igneous rock. The fact that the grains are big enough to be visible tells you it's intrusive (it cooled underground), and the light color, caused by a preponderance of quartz and feldspar, tells you it's granite. We call this kind of outcrop "massive," which means that it is homogeneous, with minerals distributed evenly and no planes of weakness, such as layers or folds; it also

FIGURE 26-1. Weathering pit on Forty Acre Rock. Photograph by J. Robert Butler.

is relatively free of fractures. Massive, unfractured granite tends to stay un-vegetated, even in the Carolinas, because it has so few irregularities where plants can gain a foothold. The same qualities make it hard for rain, wind, and gravity to erode granite. For this reason, in many places granite forms mountains, as at Stone Mountain (see Chapter 12). But here the granite forms a "flatrock" exposure. That's because this area, right on the edge of the Coastal Plain, was beveled off by the ocean when sea level was higher. The ocean is extremely efficient at eroding bedrock; not even granite can withstand the ocean's onslaught.

Even today, with the ocean miles away, Forty Acre Rock is being eroded—just more slowly than most rocks. Look for loose or semiloose slabs of gran-ite on the rock face. In a process called exfoliation, the slabs are "peeling" off the main rock body. As the weight of overlying rock is removed, granite expands upward. This expansion causes cracks to form parallel to the rock surface. Pieces of the rock eventually break off along these cracks, like lay-ers of an onion (see Figure 12-2).

Weathering is also taking place in the numerous shallow pools on the surface of the rock (Figure 26-1). These pits get started when small irregu-larities in the rock collect rainwater. Rain is naturally somewhat acidic and eats away at the rock. Even a tiny bit of pooled water can sustain hardy plants, whose roots crumble the rock bit by bit, enlarging the pit. Lichens and mosses are the first colonizers. (Lichens are actually two organisms that live together—fungi and algae.) Other plants that live in the weathering pits at Forty Acre Rock include red-moss or elf orpine (*Diamorpha smallii*), pool sprite (*Amphianthus pusillus*), oneflower stitchwort (*Minuartia uniflora*), Small's purslane (*Portulaca smallii*), and wingpod purslane (*Portulaca coronata*). Because it is such an unusual and specialized habitat, Forty Acre Rock is home to nearly a dozen rare, threatened, or endangered plant species.

In many of the pits, you can see little broken bits of granite in the bottom. Over time, these broken bits combine with decaying plant matter to produce soil, which will attract more plants until the weathering pit becomes an island of vegetation in a sea of rock. You may also notice small aquatic insects in the pools.

The granite exposed at Forty Acre Rock is called the Pageland granite; it's named after a nearby town that is located within the granite body. Pageland granite extends about 30 square miles, much of it underneath soil and vegetation. Granite forms when a body of magma rich in silica cools slowly deep underground; here at Forty Acre Rock you are looking at the inside of an ancient magma chamber. The Pageland granite formed about 300 million years ago, at the tail end of the continental collision that generated the Appalachian Mountains. Gondwana, the ancient continent made of parts of present-day Africa and South America, collided with Laurentia, which later became North America. This collision is called the Alleghanian orogeny, and after it was over, all the world's continents were grouped together in the supercontinent Pangea.

The force of plates coming together during a collision squeezes crust from the sides, forcing the crust to thicken by expanding both upward and downward. Imagine a thin sheet of clay on a table. If you put your hands on either side of the clay and slowly bring them together, the clay will change shape to become shorter horizontally and thicker. The thickened crust heats up and can melt to form magma. This is how the Pageland granite originated.

In the Piedmont and Blue Ridge, there are many granite bodies that formed during the Alleghanian orogeny, between 270 and 335 million years ago. North Carolina's examples include Stone Mountain in Wilkes and Alleghany counties (see Chapter 12), Mount Airy granite in Surry County,

FIGURE 26-2. A dark, fine-grained xenolith in the granite of Forty Acre Rock. Photograph by J. Robert Butler.

Rolesville granite in Wake County, Medoc Mountain in Halifax County (see Chapter 25), Sims granite in Wilson County, and Castalia granite in Nash County. In South Carolina, in addition to the Pageland granite exposed at Forty Acre Rock, there is the Liberty Hill granite in Kershaw County.

Although the texture of the Pageland granite is regular for the most part, in some places you may notice dark spots that are 10 or 20 inches across. These are called xenoliths, a name that comes from the Greek words for "foreign" and "stone." The xenoliths here may have broken off from the walls of the magma chamber, or they may be blobs of a different kind of magma that got incorporated into the mix (Figure 26-2). The magma was obviously not hot enough to melt these xenoliths, but you can see that some changes have taken place around their edges, where they have been partially "digested" by the surrounding magma.

Down below the main outcrop of Forty Acre Rock is a trail to a waterfall. When you first reach the expanse of granite (from the path from the parking lot), go left down to where the granite meets the woods and you will find the trail. The 20-foot waterfall slides down a rounded granite face most of the way. Only at the bottom does the water actually fall. Behind the waterfall is a shallow cave, completely covered with graffiti. The area around the waterfall is full of slick wet rocks, so it's probably not a good place to take small children.

Near Forty Acre Rock is an exposure of a rock that is not particularly attractive, although it's famous among geologists. It's visible in a road cut along US 601, about a third of a mile south from the intersection of 601 and Reserve Road. The road cut was made in 1966, and, unfortunately, vegetation has made a lot of progress since then. While there are no longer any fresh rock surfaces here, you can still see large blocky dark rocks protruding from the bank among the weeds and saplings.

Like the granite at Forty Acre Rock, this rock is igneous, but it has a different composition and is much younger—it's about 200 million years old. At the time it formed, the supercontinent Pangea was breaking up. As Gondwana and North America pulled away from each other, the Atlantic Ocean opened up between them. During the breakup, enormous fractures called rift valleys developed in the continents on both sides of the brand-new ocean. These valleys, known collectively as the Triassic basins (see Chapter 21), are found all along North America's east coast, from Nova Scotia down into Alabama, and also on the other side of the ocean in West Africa. At about the same time that the rift valleys were taking shape, deep vertical cracks broke through the rifting rocks and filled with magma. This magma was basaltic in composition rather than granitic, giving the rock a much darker color than Forty Acre Rock. Because it cooled underground but fairly near the surface, its grain size is intermediate between that of an intrusive igneous rock and that of an extrusive igneous rock. A basaltic igneous rock like this, with crystals that are visible but small, is called diabase. The structure it forms—a tabular igneous body that cuts across the enclosing rock formations—is called a dike. (An igneous body that is injected parallel to existing rock layers is called a sill.) The diabase dike near Forty Acre Rock is famous because this particular dike is one of the widest discovered—it is more than 1,000 feet across. Typical dikes may be as much as two or three miles long, but they are rarely more than 100 feet wide.

In not too many years, this diabase dike will be completely covered with vegetation. Even Forty Acre Rock will not be able to win the battle against the plants. But it should be able to hold them off for another thousand years or so.

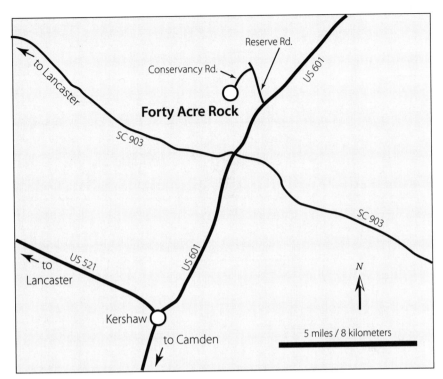

FIGURE 26-3. Location of Forty Acre Rock.

Location and Access

To get to Forty Acre Rock, take US 601 going northwest out of Kershaw, in Lancaster County. About 1.5 miles after you pass the intersection with SC 903, turn left onto Reserve Road. Go 1.7 miles and then turn left onto unpaved Conservancy Road. Follow this road for about a mile; there is a parking lot at the end of it. Hike about a quarter mile to get to Forty Acre Rock. There are no facilities, and camping is not permitted. Collecting rocks or plants is not allowed without written permission.

The Coastal Plain

27

The Roanoke River
From the Mountains to the Sea

In a cow-filled mountain meadow in southwestern Virginia, there flows a trickle of water called the North Fork. A few miles south, the South Fork rushes over waterfalls lined with thickets of hemlock and rhododendron. The North Fork and the South Fork join just west of Roanoke, Virginia, to form the Roanoke River, which is also known as the Staunton River in some parts of Virginia. The shallow river bubbles over rocks as it winds its way through the city. Later, other rivers join it, including the Dan and the Hyco. The Roanoke enters North Carolina in Warren County, runs through the city of Roanoke Rapids, and then grows even larger as it meanders its way to the Albemarle Sound. Over its 400-mile length, the river changes from a small mountain stream to a rocky Piedmont river to a broad river surrounded by swamps in the Coastal Plain.

All told, the Roanoke River drains about 8,900 square miles in Virginia and North Carolina (Figure 27-2). Rain that falls in this area, which is called a drainage basin, flows over the ground into streams that eventually join the Roanoke River. Of course, some rain that falls in the basin evaporates, gets absorbed by plants, or is lapped up by animals. And a large portion of rainwater soaks into the ground and moves as groundwater, much of which also ends up in the Roanoke. (Most Carolina rivers are supplied by both rainfall and groundwater, which is why they don't usually dry up completely during a drought.) The river grows ever larger on its way to the sea as more and more tributaries add water to it. The average stream flow of the Roanoke River near Roanoke, Virginia, is about 250 cubic feet per second (cfs) while downstream at Roanoke Rapids, North Carolina, it's about 5,000 cfs. Just before entering the Albemarle Sound, it's about 8,000 cfs. At any point in a mature stream, the amount of water is typically in inverse proportion to its average velocity at that point. As streams age, they develop graded streambeds, which simply means that the streambed gets less and less steep from start to finish. So the water starts out fast and gradu-

FIGURE 27-1. Route 45 bridge crossing (from top) the Cashie, Middle, and Roanoke rivers. Photograph courtesy of The Nature Conservancy.

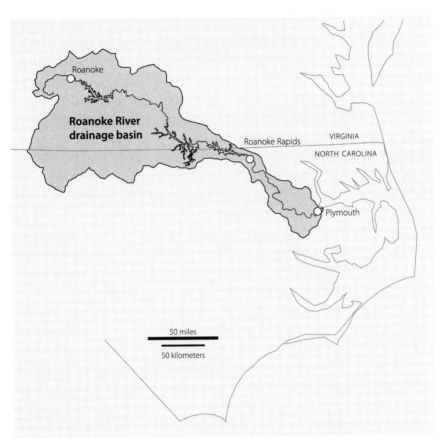

FIGURE 27-2. The Roanoke River drainage basin.

ally moves slower and slower. At the same time, the volume of water in the stream increases as tributaries add water.

In the past half century, large dams built for flood control and electric generation have affected both the sediment transport and the water flow of the river. Before it reaches the Coastal Plain, the river is dammed eight times. The John H. Kerr Dam, just above the North Carolina border a little west of I-85, was built in 1952 by the Army Corps of Engineers for flood-control purposes. In 1940 a huge flood caused the Roanoke to rise 30 feet above flood stage at Roanoke Rapids, which corresponded to a flow of 261,000 cfs, more than 50 times the average flow. The reservoir created by the dam, Kerr Lake, covers 50,000 acres and is heavily used for water recreation. There are two dams closer to Roanoke Rapids, both operated by Dominion Power to generate electricity. The two reservoirs formed by these dams are Lake Gaston and Roanoke Rapids Lake. Because the primary purpose of the dams is to generate electricity, and because electricity cannot be stored, the water flow downstream of the dams varies according to the demand for electricity. At peak demand during the daytime, the flow can reach 10,000 cfs, whereas at night during low demand, it drops to 3,000 cfs.

We know that rivers carry sediment, but what happens to this sediment when a river is dammed? Upstream of the dam, the reservoir is a still body of water. When the river enters the lake, the velocity drops to zero, and the sediment that was destined to be carried downstream settles out. All reservoirs eventually "silt up," although it takes decades for large reservoirs like Kerr Lake to do so. Downstream of the dam, the water is clearer than it would be if there were no dam. This can cause problems for organisms that rely on nutrients that are carried by the rivers; it can also starve downstream areas of sediment, contributing to erosion problems.

At Roanoke Rapids and at Weldon, the river goes over its last falls and rapids before entering the Coastal Plain. Here the story is similar to that of Landsford Canal on the Catawba River in South Carolina (see Chapter 22). The narrow river and rock outcroppings made it possible for Native Americans and settlers to cross the river here. The same rocks prohibited boats from the Coastal Plain from getting to or around Roanoke Rapids, so in the early 1800s a system of canals was built to bypass the rapids. Locks in the canals raised and lowered boats 44 feet. The canals were used less and less after railroads came to the area in the mid-1800s. Today you can visit the Roanoke Canal Museum in Roanoke Rapids or take a hike along the canal trail between Roanoke Rapids and Weldon.

At Weldon, the Roanoke leaves rapids behind and becomes a wide river that will become even wider as it approaches the Albemarle Sound. An access point maintained by the North Carolina Wildlife Resources Commission at Weldon is a good place to observe the Roanoke's metamorphosis from Piedmont river to Coastal Plain river. From this vantage point you can compare the rocky nature of the river upstream to the broad, smooth river downstream.

As the Roanoke enters the sediments of the Coastal Plain, there are no longer any igneous or metamorphic rocks to stand in its way and affect its course. You might think that would mean that the river would straighten up and flow to the sea in the most direct way possible. In fact, rivers tend to meander, even in the absence of hard-rock obstacles. On any slight bend in a river, the water on the outside of the bend moves faster than water in the middle, and the water on the inside of the bend moves slower. The fast water picks up more sediment while the slow water drops sediment, so the river erodes sediments on the outside of a bend and deposits sediments on the inside of a bend. The eroded bluffs on the outside bend are called cut banks, and the sediments that build up on the inside bend are called point bars. Over time, point bars and cut banks migrate, with the result that small bends in the river become amplified. When a bend gets loopy enough, a flood can cause the river to take a shortcut and cut off the bend altogether, leaving behind still water in the abandoned bend called an oxbow lake. A wonderful example of a meandering river is the Mississippi from St. Louis to New Orleans. A road atlas will show you many oxbow lakes along the river where it forms the border between Mississippi and Louisiana. You can see where the river has changed course over the years by looking for places where the state line and the river no longer coincide, leaving a small loop of one state stranded on the other state's side of the river.

Although there are no more hard-rock rapids in the river after Weldon, there are still some interesting soft (sedimentary) rocks ahead. At Fort Branch, in Martin County just east of Hamilton, 70-foot bluffs tower above the south side of the river (Figure 27-3). During the Civil War, Confederate soldiers at Fort Branch shot cannons at Union gunboats coming up the Roanoke. It's hard to see the face of the cliffs while you are at Fort Branch; the best vantage point is from a boat on the river. The layers of variegated shades of brown and yellow have been called Rainbow Banks for as long as anyone around here can remember. These sediments from the Pliocene epoch are about 2 million years old; they were deposited during a warm period when sea level was about 270 feet higher than it is today. (This is the same rise in sea level that gave us the Orangeburg scarp mentioned in Chapter 5.) The clays and sands are rich in fossils, but collecting fossils from the cliff tops is hazardous and should not be attempted. Looking across the river, you can see how flat the opposite shore is. The sediments that make up these bluffs likely existed there as well, but they have already been eroded by the river in its outward movement; you're standing on the cut bank of a meandering river.

These are the last bluffs on the river. From here to the Albemarle Sound, the Roanoke becomes even wider and meanders all the more over its flat floodplain. In places, the river and its floodplain are 3 to 5 miles wide. Extensive swamps lie inside every bend. These swamps are typically lined

FIGURE 27-3. A view of the Roanoke River from the 70-foot-high bluffs at Fort Branch.

with fine clay particles deposited by floods; the clay contributes to the poor drainage. Thousands of years of meandering have left behind countless sandy ridges and swales in the swamps. Bald cypresses (*Taxodium distichum*), tupelo gums (*Nyssa aquatica*), and Spanish moss (*Tillandsia usneoides*) thrive here. In Devil's Gut, the swamp in the bend of the river between Williamston and Jamesville, there are old-growth cypress trees that are 400 to 500 years old—and a few that may be more than 1,000 years old. These behemoths are 4 to 6 feet in diameter and more than 100 feet tall. From the air, their crowns look like broccoli florets above the forest.

Periodic flooding creates levees along the riverbanks. Sediment-filled, fast-flowing floodwaters slow down when they rise out of their channels and spread over their floodplains. This decrease in velocity dumps sediment along the edges of the channel, thereby forming the levees. In places, the levees can be an obstacle for water trying to join the river, leading to the development of ponds called backwaters—for example, where Conoho Creek empties into the river near Williamston. This backwater is ringed by Spanish moss–draped cypress and tupelo gum trees.

More than 80,000 acres of the lower Roanoke River floodplain are under conservation management by a variety of governmental and private organizations, including the U.S. Fish and Wildlife Service, the North Carolina Wildlife Resources Commission, and The Nature Conservancy. The area is the largest unfragmented forested wetlands in the eastern United States and is teeming with birds and other wildlife, including black bear, white-tailed deer, bobcat, and otter.

One of the best ways to experience the lower Roanoke is to get out on the river in a boat. Downstream from Williamston, a nonprofit organization called the Roanoke River Partners has built 11 camping platforms along the river and several of its tributaries. These platforms allow canoeists and kayakers to explore the isolated and wild inner reaches of the Roanoke River and its floodplains, which are generally too swampy to be accessible by car or by foot.

Just before the river empties into the Albemarle Sound, it is joined by the Cashie River. The Cashie River is called a black-water river because it has the transparent tea color typical of rivers that originate in the sandy Coastal Plain. Most of the sand is too coarse to be picked up by the slow-moving river, so the water remains clear, and the tea color comes from tannic acid that is leached out of the soil. The Roanoke, on the other hand, is a brown-water river; it gets its muddy look from suspended clays picked up as it

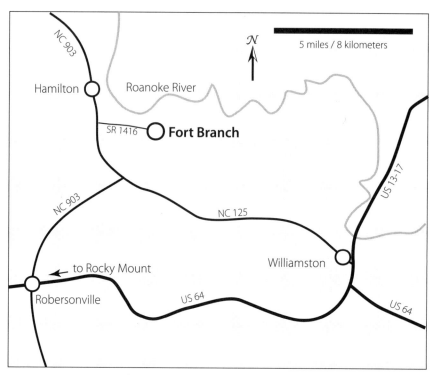

FIGURE 27-4. Location of Fort Branch.

travels through the Piedmont. Where the Cashie joins the Roanoke, the Roanoke is flowing in two channels separated by an island; the north channel is called the Middle River. A bridge on NC 45 crosses over the Cashie, the Middle, and the Roanoke just before they enter the Albemarle Sound, offering a spectacular view (Figure 27-1).

Looking at the mighty river as it dumps 8,000 cubic feet of water per second into the Albemarle Sound, it may be hard to believe that it started as a trickle in a mountain meadow hundreds of miles away. It becomes a little easier to believe when you consider that the river you're looking at contains a large part of the rain that fell not just in that mountain pasture but in almost 9,000 square miles of Virginia and North Carolina as well. The Roanoke also contains sediment from all over its drainage basin, which it deposits in the sound. Thus, the river continues the work that rivers have been doing for eons: eroding the land, transporting sediment to the sea-floor, and returning water to the sea.

Location and Access

Fort Branch is privately owned; it is open on weekends from April until early November. To get there, travel south about a mile from Hamilton, in Martin County, on NC 903. Turn left on Fort Branch Road (State Road 1416). Fort Branch is a couple of miles down the road on the left.

To drive over the three rivers on the NC 45 bridge, take 45 north from US 64 near Plymouth in Washington County. There is a website for the Roanoke River Partners where you can learn more about reserving camping platforms along the lower Roanoke: <http:/www.roanokeriverpartners .org/>.

Recommended Reading

Lynch, Ida Phillips. *North Carolina Afield: A Guide to Nature Conservancy Projects in North Carolina*. Durham: North Carolina Chapter of The Nature Conservancy, 2002.

Lynch, Ida Phillips, and J. Merrill Lynch. "Lower Roanoke River Floodplain: Swamps and Wetlands." In *Exploring North Carolina's Natural Areas: Parks, Nature Preserves, and Hiking Trails*, edited by Dirk Frankenberg. Chapel Hill: University of North Carolina Press, 2000.

28

Sugarloaf Mountain in Sand Hills State Forest
Sand and Longleaf

>> CHESTERFIELD COUNTY, SOUTH CAROLINA

From the top of Sugarloaf Mountain, in Sand Hills State Forest, there is a magnificent view in all directions of undulating pine-covered hills. Even though Sugarloaf is only 513 feet above sea level, and only 100 feet higher than the surrounding land, that's plenty high in this part of the world to produce a scenic overlook. The pines you are gazing at are growing in ancient beach and river sands, reworked by wind into sand dunes called the Sandhills. The Sandhills hug the border between the Coastal Plain and the Piedmont in South Carolina and in southern North Carolina, traversing South Carolina's Aiken, Lexington, Richland, Kershaw, and Chesterfield counties, and continuing into North Carolina's Richmond, Montgomery, Moore, and Harnett counties (Figure 28-2).

Why is there a "mountain" in the midst of all this sand? The rock outcrops along the trail up Sugarloaf and at the top of Sugarloaf provide clues. Take a close look at the texture. In some cases, the rock is made of coarse sand (hence its name: sandstone); in other places, it contains pebbles as well (conglomerate) (Figure 28-3). The variation in grain size is due to the variation in the energy of the rivers that deposited the sediments. Fast-flowing, more energetic streams that could carry heavier sediments deposited the pebbles; more gently flowing streams deposited the sand. Both the sandstone and the conglomerate are fairly well cemented—that is, the sediments are held together securely enough that it's not easy to knock off a piece of the rock. This makes the sandstone and conglomerate more resistant to erosion than the surrounding sediments (mostly unconsolidated sand), and that's why the rocks form a mountain. What holds the grains together is a dark reddish-brown matrix of iron oxide, essentially rust. The iron oxide was deposited by iron-bearing groundwater that percolated through the sediments. It's likely that this iron-cemented sandstone and conglomerate once covered a much larger area, but most of it has eroded away. Sugar-

FIGURE 28-1. The view out over the Coastal Plain from the top of Sugarloaf Mountain.

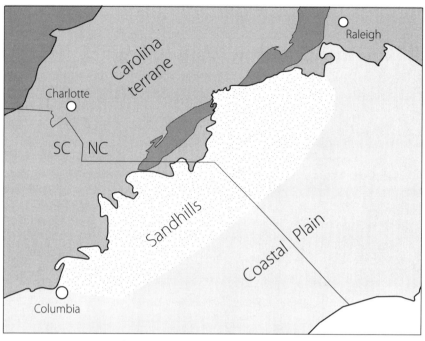

FIGURE 28-2. Location of the Sandhills within the Coastal Plain of the Carolinas.

loaf Mountain remains as a monadnock—an erosional remnant—in a sea of sand.

The sand in most of the Sandhills has its origins in the Cretaceous: it dates from between 86 and 84 million years ago. During the Cretaceous, sea level was as much as 800 feet higher than it is today, flooding most of the Coastal Plain and the Piedmont. Rivers carried rocks out of the Appalachians, broke them into pieces, and then deposited them as sediments into the sea. The sands and clays that had come from the mountains formed a broad, flat delta in the ocean, much like the Mississippi delta. Years later, sea level fell and these sands were exposed to the air. Winds shaped them into ever-shifting sand dunes. Eventually, as sea level continued to drop, vegetation took hold, and the dunes became the stationary Sandhills we know today.

Some geologists have speculated that the conglomerate making up Sugarloaf Mountain and some other high areas in the Coastal Plain may actually be much younger, as young as 10 million years old. There is evidence that the Appalachians underwent an as-yet-unexplained minor uplift, rejuvenating the topography and rivers, leading to a pulse of conglomerate deposition along the coast. No one has dated the sediments on top of Sugarloaf

FIGURE 28-3. A boulder of iron-cemented conglomerate along the trail up to Sugarloaf.

Mountain, so we cannot be certain of their age, but in any case most of the sand in the Sandhills is Cretaceous in origin.

As you're hiking, you'll probably notice the bright green "pom-poms" that look like bunches of grass growing along the trail. These are young long-leaf pine trees (*Pinus palustris*). No other pine tree begins life looking like this. For the first several years after germinating, a longleaf pine exists in a "grass stage," all the while sending down a long taproot. When its taproot is big enough, the tree suddenly develops a trunk and shoots up at a rate of 3 to 5 feet per year. Sending down that long taproot first helps the longleaf to survive in the hot and sandy soils of the Sandhills, where moisture from a rainstorm quickly drains away.

You can identify mature longleaf pines by their long needles, which are 12 to 18 inches in length, and their large cones, which can be almost 12 inches long. They may reach only 50 or 60 feet in height in the Sandhills, but in richer soils they can grow to more than 100 feet.

Although many people associate them with the Sandhills, these pines are not naturally restricted to sandy soils. Longleaf pine forests used to cover a significant part of the Carolinas and other southeastern states. They remain in the hot, dry Sandhills because these areas were not cleared for agriculture.

When Europeans first arrived in America, longleaf forests covered more than half of the Atlantic Coastal Plain and the Gulf Coastal Plain from Virginia to Florida and from Florida to eastern Texas (not including the Mississippi delta). There were an estimated 60 million acres of pure longleaf forest and an additional 30 million acres of forest that was a mixture of longleaf, other pines, and hardwood.

Here's how William Bartram, a naturalist who published a book on his travels in the Carolinas, Georgia, and Florida in 1791, described the longleaf forests: "We find ourselves on the entrance of a vast plain, generally level, which extends west sixty or seventy miles. . . . This plain is mostly a forest of the great long-leaved pine, the earth covered with grass, interspersed with an infinite variety of herbaceous plants, and embellished with extensive savannas, always green, sparkling with ponds of water" (*Travels of William Bartram*, ed. Mark Van Doren [New York: Dover, 1955], 51–52).

Of those original 90 million acres of longleaf, today there are less than 3 million acres left, and perhaps only 12,000 acres of old growth.

To early settlers, the longleaf forest was an inexhaustible source of naval stores—tar, pitch, rosin, turpentine, and lumber for masts and planks. As early as 1700, when the English explorer John Lawson made his famous journey through the Carolinas, settlers were producing tar, pitch, rosin, and turpentine from longleaf, and they continued to do so for more than a century. From the mid-1700s to the mid-1800s, North Carolina led the world in naval-store production.

Tar and pitch were obtained by slowly burning longleaf pine logs in clay-lined tar kilns, which were scattered everywhere in the forests. Turpentine and rosin were extracted from liquid resin collected from living trees. Resin is the sticky liquid that pine trees exude to cover wounds in their bark. Turpentiners chopped "pockets" in the base of trees, and then chipped grooves above the pocket to cause resin to flow down into the pocket. Turpentine was distilled from the resin, and what was left over was called rosin. Trees could survive the turpentiners' treatment, but they were left more vulnerable to disease, hurricanes, and forest fires.

In those days, wildfires frequently burned through longleaf forests. Mature longleaf pines are protected from fire by their thick bark. In fact, long-leaf forests need fire. Fire clears out underbrush to provide the bare ground that longleaf seeds require in order to sprout. It also prevents hardwoods from taking hold and taking over. Regular fires gave the virgin longleaf forests an open, parklike feel that was commented on by many early travelers. The lack of undergrowth meant that most fires were small and burned low to the ground. Fires were set by lightning, by Native Americans, and by some early "piney woods" settlers.

Centuries of naval-store production and clear-cutting followed by de-cades of fire suppression have reduced the original longleaf forest by nearly 98 percent. In many places, the longleaf forest has been supplanted by lob-lolly pines (*Pinus taeda*) and slash pines (*Pinus elliotii*), both of which are intolerant of fire.

At Sand Hills State Forest, rangers have been working to restore the longleaf by clear-cutting loblolly and slash pine, replanting longleaf, and setting controlled burns. Sales of timber and pine straw generate income for the self-supporting state forest. Sand Hills State Forest has a healthy population of red-cockaded woodpeckers (*Picoides borealis*), an endan-gered bird that nests in cavities that it excavates in living, mature longleaf pine trees.

In North Carolina, a good place to see the Sandhills and longleaf pine trees is Weymouth Woods Sandhills Nature Preserve in Southern Pines. This land was donated to the North Carolina Division of Parks and Rec-reation in 1963 by Mrs. James Boyd. Her father-in-law bought the land in 1903 to save it from logging. Near the Weymouth Center, one can see old-growth longleaf trees that are 400 to 500 years old. The Weymouth Center is located in the Boyds' former house; it is a couple of miles down the road from the visitor center at Weymouth Woods Sandhills Nature Preserve.

In 1932 B. W. Wells wrote, "Like a fine old aristocracy destroyed by war, the original longleaf pine forest of our sandhills has been completely cut and burned until the entire scene has so changed that no person of the ris-ing generation may now gain any real idea of the majesty and glory of the original forest. . . . The complete destruction of this forest constitutes one of the major social crimes of American history" (B. W. Wells, *The Natu-ral Gardens of North Carolina* [Chapel Hill: University of North Carolina Press, 1932], 114–16).

While the majestic, glorious original forest may be gone, fragments of it survive. Because the shifting soils of the Sandhills were not suitable for ag-

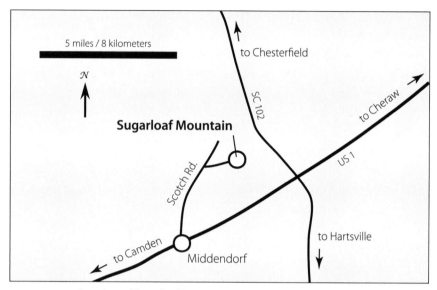

FIGURE 28-4. Location of Sugarloaf Mountain.

riculture, longleaf pines still stand here. The geology of the Carolina Sandhills created the last safe haven for the once-mighty longleaf forest.

Location and Access

Sugarloaf Mountain is in Sand Hills State Forest, which is off US 1 about 60
or 70 miles northeast of Columbia. Because of all the sand, the area is very
hot in the summer. A small daily fee is charged for horse riders and bicycle
riders. Camping requires a permit.

Recommended Reading

Bartram, William. *Travels of William Bartram*. Edited by Mark Van Doren. New
York: Dover Publications, 1955.
Earley, Lawrence S. *Looking for Longleaf: The Fall and Rise of an American Forest*.
Chapel Hill: University of North Carolina Press, 2004.
Wells, B. W. *The Natural Gardens of North Carolina*. Chapel Hill: University of
North Carolina Press, 1932. (A revised edition was published by UNC Press in
2002.)

29

Cliffs of the Neuse State Park
Under the Sea

>> WAYNE COUNTY, NORTH CAROLINA

There is only one place where you will find 90-foot cliffs in the Carolina Coastal Plain, and that's at Cliffs of the Neuse State Park. Although the presence of the cliffs is remarkable, the real story here is in the sediments that make up the cliffs. At Flanner Beach (see Chapter 32), the sediments tell of a recent warm period in the earth's history and the 20-foot rise in sea level that resulted from the warmer temperatures. At the Cliffs of the Neuse, the sediments tell a more dramatic story about a time when the earth was so warm that all the glaciers and the ice caps melted and sea level was 800 feet higher than it is today. A comparable rise in sea level today would put the shoreline in the western Piedmont.

The environs of the Cliffs of the Neuse also have a rich human history, no doubt in part because of the allure of the cliffs. When Europeans first arrived, Tuscarora Indians lived in the area and gathered at the cliffs for ceremonies and hunting. The Neuse was a major transportation artery for both native people and early settlers. During the Civil War, the Confederate navy built an ironclad ship—the css *Neuse*—in nearby Seven Springs (which was then called Whitehall). The ship was launched in the river, but soon ran aground and was destroyed to prevent its capture. (Its remains are on display in Kinston.) In the early 1900s vacationers flocked to Seven Springs to drink the local mineral water and to enjoy riverboat excursions to the cliffs. Moonshiners operated stills along Still Creek. Since 1945, the area has been a state park.

At the top of the cliffs, there is an observation deck overlooking the Neuse River. From the wooden railing, you can see the cliffs below, which are made of sand, silt, and shale (clay-rich, finely laminated sedimentary rock). For a better view, take the trail to the north (to your left as you face the river). It leads down the side of the cliffs to the river. As you walk down the trail, notice the array of plant types. Because the park contains such a

FIGURE 29-1. The view upstream from Cliffs of the Neuse.

variety of elevations and habitats, you will find plants that normally live west of here—such as galax (*Galax aphylla*)—as well as plants that normally live east of here—such as Spanish moss (*Tillandsia usneoides*). You will see longleaf pine and turkey oak (typical of the Sandhills), oak and hickory forests (typical of the Piedmont), and cypress and live oak (typical of Coastal Plain swamps).

If the water in the Neuse is low enough, you can walk along the river's edge to the bottom of the cliffs. Please stay off the cliffs themselves—the beauty of the cliffs will quickly be destroyed if people scramble up the crumbly sediments.

Notice the different materials that make up the cliff face (Figure 29-2). Some of the layers have steep, almost vertical faces while others form angled slopes. This tells you something about the makeup of the different layers: shale has more cohesion than loose sand, so the shale layers have

FIGURE 29-2. Interbedded sand and shale layers in an ancient delta now exposed at Cliffs of the Neuse.

steeper faces than the sandy layers. After a rain, you will notice springs seeping from the cliff at various places. These springs occur because rainwater percolates down through the porous sand until it hits impermeable shale. The water then travels laterally until it drips out of the cliff at the top of a shale layer.

You'll see rounded quartz pebbles scattered around. They are weathering out from a pebbly sand layer that tops the cliffs here and is much younger than the underlying sand and shale. The pebbles were carried and deposited by an ancient river and are likely the same age as the cobble deposit that you can see on the cliff tops at Raven Rock (see Chapter 24). In some cases, the pebbles have created miniature towers by protecting a column of sand beneath them from the erosional power of rain.

(After seeing the Cliffs of the Neuse, you may be struck by the similarity of the "sedimentary rock" in the wall of the North Carolina Underground exhibit in the North Carolina Museum of Natural Sciences in Raleigh. The artificial strata were modeled to mimic the sand and shale layers in the cliff face.)

There are fossils in the cliffs, although they are few and far between and not easy to find amid all the sand. (Remember that collecting fossils, rocks, artifacts, or plants in a state park is prohibited.) The fossils are of sea creatures, so we know the layers were deposited in salt water. The interbedded sand and shale layers are typical of an environment where a river dumps its sediment into a sound or the ocean, forming a delta; the deepwater end of a delta commonly has interlayered sand and mud (which becomes shale). The fossils tell us that these layers were deposited between 85 and 75 million years ago, in the Cretaceous period.

So we know that during the Cretaceous this area was covered by the ocean. What would cause the ocean to move so far inland? Geologists have discovered that during that time, for some as-yet-unknown reason, the system of plate tectonics was operating more quickly. This increase in plate circulation caused an increase in volcanic eruptions (see Chapter 3 for more information on plate tectonics). Some of the largest volcanic eruptions that the earth has ever seen took place in the Cretaceous. Out in the western Pacific Ocean, there is a submerged volcanic plateau—the Ontong Plateau—which is made of 60,000,000 cubic kilometers of basalt that erupted between 120 and 90 million years ago. As a comparison, the 1980 eruption of Mount St. Helens produced 1 cubic kilometer. Carbon dioxide is a major component of volcanic gases, and the huge eruptions significantly raised the carbon dioxide content of the atmosphere, leading to greenhouse warming of the climate. The earth became warmer than at any other time in the past 600 million years. The polar ice caps and all the glaciers melted. With no water locked up in ice, sea level rose. In addition, warm water is less dense and therefore takes up more space than cold water. The increase in the rate of seafloor spreading caused the midocean ridge to broaden, which then displaced more ocean water. The combined effects of a heated-up climate and seafloor spreading raised sea level to about 800 feet higher than it is today. During this time, all of Florida was underwater, and there was a vast inland sea from Texas to central Canada.

In the Carolinas, rivers brought silt, sand, and gravel from the Blue Ridge and dumped them into the sea, mixed up with the shells of dead sea creatures. Larger sediments were deposited near the mouths of rivers, where the current was fastest, and smaller sediments were deposited farther out in the ocean, where the river water slowed and eventually dissipated. When the earth cooled again, glaciers and polar ice caps grew and sea level dropped. The sea left behind stacks of sediments as evidence of its presence. Most of the sediments either have eroded away or are buried beneath younger sediments. In the northern part of the Coastal Plain, Cretaceous sediments are exposed in some valleys where rivers, like the Tar River, have cut down

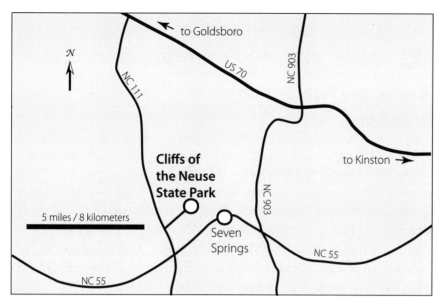

FIGURE 29-3. Location of Cliffs of the Neuse State Park.

through younger sediments. The best place to see a good thick stack of these sediments is right here at the Cliffs of the Neuse.

Look across the river from the observation deck: the topography is completely flat. That's because the river channel used to be located there and has already scoured the area flat. The cliffs you are standing on are on the outside of a bend in the river, where water flows faster than on the inside of the bend. Faster water erodes more sediment, so over time a river bend continues to migrate, eating into whatever rock or sediments it finds there. The river bend is migrating toward you, and into these cliffs, right now.

Although these cliffs have played a part in human history for several hundred years, they will last for only an instant in geologic time. The Neuse is destroying the cliffs and washing the sediments away. Many of them will be deposited in the ocean, where they will provide a record of today's sea level. But by the measure of a human lifetime, the cliffs will be here for a long, long time, telling the story of one of the greatest global warming events and sea-level rises the earth has ever experienced.

Location and Access

Cliffs of the Neuse State Park is 14 miles south of Goldsboro on NC 111.

30

Santee State Park
Mule-Eating Sinkholes

>> ORANGEBURG COUNTY, SOUTH CAROLINA

In 1841 and 1842 the English geologist Sir Charles Lyell traveled along the east coast of North America, making notes about the geology and the social customs of the New World. Although Lyell's predecessor, James Hutton, is often referred to as the father of modern geology, it was really Lyell's research and writing that laid the foundation for the science. In 1830 he published his book *Principles of Geology*, in which he elucidated and elaborated on the argument first proposed by Hutton—that the features we see on earth today are the result of earth processes that we also see today, such as erosion, earthquakes, volcanoes, and the deposition of sediments. Because erosion and deposition are very slow, it naturally followed that the earth must be much older than people thought. The notion that the earth's past can be interpreted by studying processes that operate today is known as uniformitarianism, and this new idea guided the intellectual thought not only of geologists but also of other prominent scientists in Lyell's day. Much of Charles Darwin's work during his voyage on the *Beagle* was clearly influenced by what he learned from Lyell. In fact, many of Darwin's ideas about evolution are an application of uniformitarianism to biology. Furthermore, the vast amount of time required for uniformitarianism meant there was enough time for evolutionary changes to have occurred.

Lyell's writings about his trip in North America were published in 1852. While in South Carolina, he wrote, "we slept at Wantoot, and then went by Eutaw to Vance's Ferry on the Santee river, then to Cave Hall, examining the tertiary white marl and limestone, and collecting the shells and corals contained in it" (Charles Lyell, *Travels in North America* [New York: J. Wiley, 1852], 139–40). He studied the fossils that he found in the limestone and determined the rock to be of Eocene age. He named it Santee limestone.

At Santee State Park, not too far from Eutaw, you can see Lyell's Santee

FIGURE 30-1. Sinkhole Pond.

limestone yourself. Go down Cleveland Road toward the pavilion; when you get to the edge of the lake, you will be able to spot the limestone in the bluffs along the shore of Lake Marion if the water level is not too high. (Lake Marion was not here when Lyell visited; it's a reservoir formed by a hydroelectric dam on the Santee River.) Look for fossils; these are the clues that Lyell studied 150 years ago to date this rock. There are fossils of mollusk shells and lacy fanlike structures, which were built by colonies of bryozoans. Outside the visitor center, you can see several boulders of fossil-filled Santee limestone that are from a quarry in Santee.

With our more refined geologic time scale, we now know that these rocks are about 40 million years old, meaning that they date from the Eocene epoch, as Lyell first determined. The Santee limestone was deposited in shallow ocean water during a time when sea level was about 500 feet higher than it is today and making a slow and irregular retreat from its maximum—800 feet higher than today—in the Cretaceous period (see Chapter 29, on the Cliffs of the Neuse). Limestone forms when the shells of microscopic and macroscopic sea creatures accumulate on the ocean floor. Shells are made of calcium carbonate, which reacts with acid. So if you put a drop of a weak acid on limestone, it will fizz. (Geologists use diluted hydrochloric acid. Vinegar may work, especially if you crush the stone a little bit first.)

Groundwater is naturally mildly acidic, so over time it dissolves calcium

FIGURE 30-2. A sinkhole at the trailhead of Sinkhole Pond Nature Trail.

carbonate out of limestone bedrock. Eventually large cavities can form in the rock. If the roof to one of these caves becomes too thin to support the weight of the overlying rock and soil, it will collapse, making a sinkhole.

Here's how Lyell described Santee sinkholes in his book: "Lime-sinks, or funnel-shaped cavities, are frequent in this country, arising from natural tunnels and cavities in subjacent limestone, through some of which subterranean rivers flow. An account was given me of a new hollow which opened about fifteen years ago, about two miles south of the Santee river, into which a mule drawing a plough sank suddenly. About a hundred yards from the same spot, I saw a large cavern sixty feet high at its entrance in the white limestone, from the mouth of which flowed a small stream" (Lyell, *Travels*, 140).

The Sinkhole Pond Nature Trail is the place to go to see some sinkholes for yourself. Right at the trail head, there is a small fenced-off sinkhole, about 20 feet deep (Figure 30-2). A little farther away is Sinkhole Pond—a depression with water in the lowest parts of it. Along the trail you will see a smaller, dry sinkhole within the larger depression. It is fenced off as well, although this small sinkhole has already expanded beyond the fence in places. If you listen you can hear water rushing under this sinkhole—that's one of those subterranean rivers Lyell wrote about.

Most people associate sinkholes with Florida. There are so many there

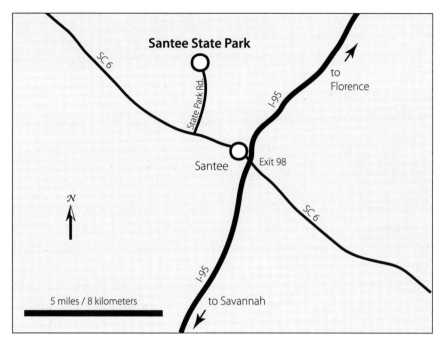

FIGURE 30-3. Location of Santee State Park.

because much of Florida is underlain by limestone, deposited during the many times that the state was covered by the ocean in the recent geologic past. The shallow water table in Florida results in a lot of thin-roofed caves that can easily collapse. If you want to see a sinkhole for yourself, but don't want to travel all the way to Florida, head for Santee State Park.

Location and Access

Santee State Park is off sc 6, a couple of miles northwest of Santee and I-95. The park offers camping, cabin rentals, fishing, and boating. South Carolina state parks charge a nominal admission fee.

Recommended Reading

Lyell, Charles. *Travels in North America, in the Years 1841–2: With Geological Observations on the United States, Canada, and Nova Scotia.* New York: J. Wiley, 1852.

31

Jones Lake State Park
The Mystery of the Carolina Bays

>> BLADEN COUNTY, NORTH CAROLINA

In the Coastal Plain of the Carolinas, there are thousands of oval-shaped depressions, all aligned northwest-southeast. Some are smaller than football fields; others are more than a mile long. Some contain water; most don't.

These depressions are called Carolina bays. Although they occur from Maryland to Georgia, they are most plentiful in North and South Carolina. Most bays are rimmed in sand, lined with peat, and home to dense thickets of the shrubby evergreen plants that give the Carolina bays their name: sweet bay (*Magnolia virginiana*), loblolly bay (*Gordonia lasianthus*), and red bay (*Persea borbonia*).

Jones Lake is a typical Carolina bay lake (Figure 31-1). When you go from the parking lot to the shore of the lake, you walk over the slightly raised sand rim that borders the bay. Notice how much less vegetation grows here than in the boggy areas right around the bay—only a few pine trees and small oaks grow in the sand.

There is a short nature trail that takes off north along the shore of the lake. It runs through thick tangles of sweet bay, loblolly bay, red bay, and fetterbush (*Lyonia lucida*). Bald cypresses (*Taxodium distichum*) grow along the water's edge. A short wooden boardwalk crosses a low area where, in times of excess rain, you will see water running out of Jones Lake. As you look out over the lake, the vegetation that crowds in on the bay from every direction clearly delineates its shore, and you can easily make out the elliptical shape.

What produced the curious collection of aligned pock marks that Jones Lake is a part of? An ancient meteorite shower? Nope. While this idea has been popular with the media and the public over the years, there is absolutely no evidence to support it. When meteorites hit the earth, they tend to make circular craters, not elliptical ones. Nor has anyone ever found

FIGURE 31-1. Cypress trees near the shore of Jones Lake.

meteorite fragments in and around the Carolina bays. Other hypotheses for the origin of the depressions have included fish spawning grounds and sinkholes. Today, most geologists agree that the depressions were formed when receding seas left puddles and ponds behind on the shore. Prevailing winds that blew from the southwest and the northeast created currents that scoured the southeast and northwest ends of the lakes, depositing sand from the lake bottoms onto these shores. The sand is easily visible today at the edges of many of the lakes. Waves churned by the winds carved out thousands of elliptical pits of nearly identical shape and alignment all up and down the coast of the Carolinas. Similar lakes are being formed by this process today in Tierra del Fuego in southern Chile.

Not all bays are perfectly elliptical; some are nearly circular, while others are egg shaped. In general, the smaller the bay, the more circular its shape. This makes sense if you think about their origin. All of the bays likely began as puddles and ponds, which tend to be fairly circular. As the windblown currents acted on the lakes, they enlarged and became more elliptical.

According to this hypothesis, all Carolina bays started out filled with water. Today, many, in fact most, do not hold water, although they may be boggy. In North Carolina, most Carolina bays are filled with peat, which is partially decomposed vegetation. South Carolina bays often do not hold

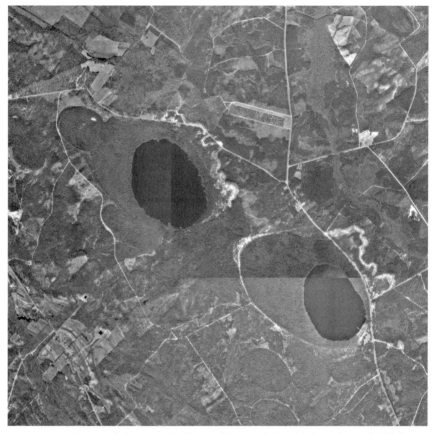

FIGURE 31-2. An aerial photograph of Jones (lower right) and Salters (upper left) lakes. Notice how the lakes fill only part of the bays, and that the other visible bays are completely filled with vegetation.

water either, but they are not filled with peat; they are typically underlain by a thick layer of clay (as much as 25 feet of it). Because of the difference in soil type, South Carolina bays support different—and much more varied—types of vegetation.

Peat forms when leaves and twigs pile up in an area of stagnant water where the lack of oxygen in the water prevents the organic matter from fully decomposing. Vegetative matter from the tangle of bay trees, vines, and briars around a Carolina bay accumulates in the water near the shore, forming peat. The living vegetation gradually moves out onto the peat, continuing to make more peat as it goes.

Over time, peat encroaches into the water until the entire bay is filled. In the aerial photo of Jones and Salters lakes (Figure 31-2), notice how peat and vegetation fill the northwest area of the original sand-rimmed shape. Standing water has been confined to the southeast part of the bays, and this water is quite shallow; both lakes are only about 10 feet deep at their deepest points.

The size of the lake that remains within a bay is likely related to the age of the bay. Bays that are mostly peat with little or no standing water probably have been around longer than bay lakes with little accumulated peat. Radiocarbon ages obtained from peat deposits in and around the bays shows that some of the bays may be as much as 30,000 years old, while others formed between 5,000 and 8,000 years ago, making these some of the most recent geologic features in the Carolinas. The range of ages of the bays also is evidence against an impact origin. It is highly unlikely that there would have been a meteorite shower here 30,000 years ago, and then another one in the same area 8,000 years ago.

The water in Jones and Salters lakes is typical of Carolina bay lakes—brown and transparent, like tea. The color comes from dissolved tannin, also called tannic acid, which is produced by decomposing vegetation. Water picks up tannin when it percolates through the peat. Tannin also makes the water quite acidic, in the range of pH 4.3–4.7. This pH value is similar to that of carbonated soda water, which gets its acidity from carbonic acid. The acidity limits the number of fish species that can live in Jones and Salters lakes; those present include yellow perch, chain pickerel, catfish, chub suckers, and blue-spotted sunfish.

Waterlogged, partially decomposed peat does not release many nutrients for plants to use. Carnivorous plants, like pitcher plants (*Sarracenia* spp.) and Venus flytraps (*Dionaea muscipula*), have evolved to survive in nutrient-poor peat bogs by catching and "digesting" insects. You may see some of these plants at Jones Lake, but remember that it is against the law to collect them.

A little bit southeast of Jones Lake State Park is another Carolina bay lake, one whose shores are commercially developed. It is called White Lake, and its waters are crystal clear. Why? If you look at an aerial photo of White Lake, you can see that the bay is filled nearly completely with water—there's not much peat (Figure 31-3). Perhaps White Lake is younger than Jones and Salters, and there hasn't been enough time to produce a lot of peat. Also, the only outlet from the lake is at the northwest end of the lake near the peat bog. During high water, the flow of the water is from the main body of the lake out through the peat-rich area, not the other

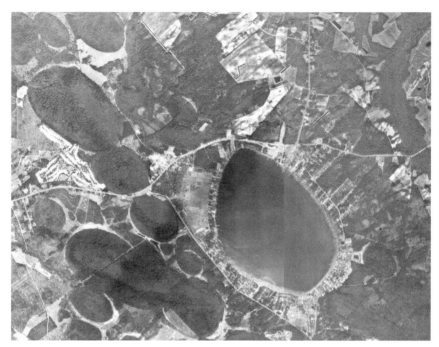

FIGURE 31-3. An aerial photograph of White Lake. Notice the many other Carolina bays, none of which contains standing water.

way around, as at Jones and Salters lakes. In addition, there is a clear-water spring at the bottom of White Lake providing a constant flow of clear water into the lake. This excess water pushes any of the tannin-stained water in the surrounding peat away from the lake. It's possible that the spring helps oxygenate the water, aiding decomposition of organic matter and inhibiting the formation of peat. Because there's less tannin in White Lake, its water is less acidic than Jones and Salters lakes, with the result that more species of fish live there.

Lake Waccamaw in Columbus County, North Carolina, is also a Carolina bay. One side of the bay is underlain by limestone, which acts as a chemical buffer. So although the water is lightly tea colored from peat, it is not as acidic as the water in most bays. Consequently, a much wider array of animal and plant species live in and around it, including several fishes and mussels found nowhere else in the world.

The park rangers at Jones Lake State Park have noticed that during prolonged droughts the water level in Jones and Salters lakes drops significantly and the water turns just as clear as White Lake. In order to think

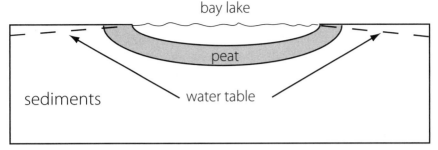

bay lake

peat

sediments   water table

FIGURE 31-4. The water table is near the surface around bay lakes.

of possible explanations, it's necessary to understand something about groundwater.

Groundwater is not made of streams flowing through tunnels in hard bedrock. Instead, it fills up all the tiny spaces in bedrock, much as water fills the holes in a sponge. In a sedimentary rock, the spaces are the pores between grains (sand grains, for instance). In igneous and metamorphic rock, the spaces are cracks. Generally, sedimentary rock can hold much more water than igneous or metamorphic rock. When rain hits the ground, it slowly percolates through the soil and down into the bedrock until it hits a totally impermeable layer—like clay or unfractured granite. This layer may be thousands of feet below the surface, or only a few feet. The rock or soil above the impermeable layer can be saturated with groundwater. The top of the saturated rock is called the water table. If you've ever dug a hole on the beach near the surf, you hit water quickly, so you know that the water table there is only a few inches below the surface. If you've paid someone to drill a well in your backyard, you know that the water table away from the shore is much deeper.

The water table in any area is not exactly flat; it tends to follow a muted version of the topography above—making it higher under hills and lower under valleys. Groundwater flows in the same general direction as the slope of the water table, but very slowly, typically less than a few feet per day.

Now we can get back to the question of why the water in Jones and Salters lakes clears up during a drought. Around the two lakes, the water table is very near the surface. In fact, during times of above-average rain, the water table is only a few inches below the surface. The water in the lakes, therefore, is kind of a porthole into the groundwater of the area (Figure 31-4).

During a drought the water table outside of the lake may drop below the lake level, and water in the lake will then flow out of the lake and into the

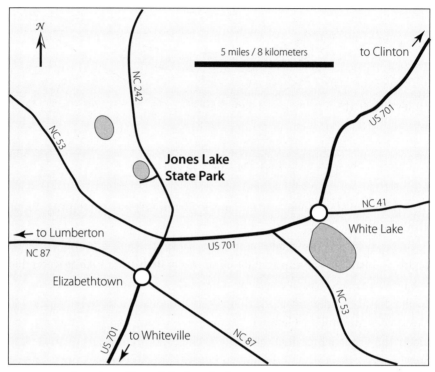

FIGURE 31-5. Location of Jones Lake State Park.

surrounding peat. This direction of water flow should reduce the amount of tannin in the water. During times of extra rain, the water level in a lake will be a little lower than the level of the water table outside the lake, thus "pushing" groundwater out of the peat and into the lake, which would increase the amount of tannin in the lake. Without more research, we can't be sure that the preceding explanation is complete and correct. Someone who wanted to solve this mystery decisively would need to drill a few water wells in the area to monitor changes in the groundwater height during periods of drought and abundant rain. Changes in the water table would reveal the direction of the groundwater flow, which in turn would shed light on what factors affect the concentration of tannin in the lake at different times.

The question of why the water in Jones and Salters lakes turns clear during a drought may not be quite as compelling as the question of why the Carolina bays exist in the first place. But it goes to show that there are unanswered questions all around us in the natural world. Almost anyone can come up with these kinds of questions and think of ways to begin answering them. All it takes is curiosity, close observation, and an open mind.

Location and Access

Jones Lake State Park is about 40 miles southeast of Fayetteville, off NC 242 a couple of miles north of the intersection of NC 53 and NC 242. Salters Lake, which is also in Jones Lake State Park, is accessible only by canoe. You need to register ahead of time with park staff in order to explore Salters.

Nearby Features

South of Jones Lake State Park on NC 53 is White Lake, a commercially developed bay lake. A little farther south of that is Singletary Lake State Park, which is available for group camping only; reservations are required.

32

Flanner Beach
The Rise and Fall of Sea Level

>> CRAVEN COUNTY, NORTH CAROLINA

Flanner Beach is not just another pretty river-front beach. In addition to soothing views of the Neuse River, it offers massive cypress stumps that are 125,000 years old and 20-foot bluffs that tell the story of a rapidly changing environment.

From the parking lot of the Neuse River Recreation Area, walk down to the river via a set of wooden steps. There are bluffs to both the right and left that preserve layers of sediment (Plate 12). If you look closely, you will see interesting differences from layer to layer. Downstream of the steps, the bottom layer of the bluffs is dark bluish gray and muddy with old stumps encased in it. In fact, you're walking on this layer as you walk along the shore, although the river has deposited a thin veneer of sand over the mud. You can see the stumps sticking up out of the sand in many places on the beach (Figure 32-1). The next layer up is made of clay-rich sand and silt that contains lots of clam shells and marine snail shells. Above this, you can see thin layers of sand interspersed with the darker colored clay-rich sand.

Upstream of the stairs (to the northwest), the bluffs are higher and contain more sand. At the top, 20 feet high, the layers are almost pure sand.

To understand the story these bluffs are telling, you have to know a little bit about different depositional environments. Water in different environments deposits different kinds of sediments. Streams deposit pebbles, sand, silt, clay, and shells from freshwater animals like mussels and snails. The sediments can be made of lots of different mineral and rock types, depending on what kind of bedrock the stream flows over. Size depends on the velocity of the current: fast-moving streams deposit coarse sediments; slow-moving streams deposit finer sediments. Water in a sound deposits clay, silt, shells from marine animals, and, occasionally, sand that is washed in by the ocean during storms. Ocean waves washing up on beaches deposit almost exclusively sand, usually mixed with shell fragments.

FIGURE 32-1. A 125,000-year-old cypress stump at Flanner Beach.

The bluffs at Flanner Beach contain other clues as well. The stumps in that bottom layer are cypress stumps. Cypress trees grow in fresh water, not salt water. The principle of superposition tells us that young sediments are deposited on top of old sediments; that means the layers get progressively younger from bottom to top. Knowing all this, the layers begin to speak to us.

The bottom layer, filled with clay and cypress stumps, represents an ancient freshwater river environment, much like the environment you see here today, although the fine grain size of the sediment indicates more of a swampy area rather than the shore of a river. The next layer is rich in clay, too, but it is filled with the shells of marine organisms. The marine shells tell us this layer was deposited by salt water; the mud tells us that it was a sound rather than an ocean-pounded beach. Furthermore, the fact that it is above the bottom layer means that the water that deposited it was higher than the water that deposited the layer with the stumps. That means sea level was rising. As it rose, the freshwater river was flooded with salt water and gradually changed into a sound. Still higher, we see more sand. In fact, the bluffs on the upstream side of the steps are topped with about 10 feet of sand that is just like the sand you'd see on an ocean beach. That tells us that sea level continued to rise until this area became the seashore. Because the bluffs are 20 feet high here, we know that at the time that sand was deposited, sea level was at least 20 feet higher than it is today. (The elevation of the river here today is probably about 1 or 2 feet above present-day sea level.)

Because the bottom layer of the bluffs is now exposed as the shore here, we know that after sea level rose, it fell again, and the Neuse River has cut down through these bluffs.

Sea level is almost always either rising or falling. That's because the earth's climate is almost always changing. The earth's orbit changes periodically, sometimes becoming more elliptical, sometimes less. The tilt of the earth's axis also has a periodic wiggle. These changes affect both the amount of solar radiation that hits the globe and the angle at which it hits. Moving continents affect global climate because they change ocean circulation patterns and snowfall patterns. When the earth warms, glaciers and polar ice sheets melt, flooding the oceans and causing sea level to rise. When the earth cools, water at the poles and at high altitudes freezes, causing sea level to fall.

Right now, the earth's climate is warming after an ice age that peaked about 18,000 years ago. That's why when you look at a map of the Carolina coast, you see a lot of "drowned" river valleys. As sea level rises, water floods river valleys near the coast. More recently, humans have begun to contribute to global warming by burning coal, oil, and other fossil fuels that release carbon dioxide and greenhouse gases (gases that trap the sun's heat in our atmosphere).

When sea level rises or falls, beaches move in response. In North Carolina, our beaches are on barrier islands, which are nothing more than long piles of sand (see Chapter 34, on Oregon Inlet). When sea level rises, barrier islands migrate landward. The primary mechanism by which barrier islands migrate landward is called "overwash." During storms, waves wash over a barrier island, depositing sand on the sound side. Over time, more and more sand is moved from the ocean side of the island to the sound side of the island, and the result is that the island moves toward the mainland. Because sea level is rising, the shoreline of the mainland is also moving inland.

The rates at which the barrier islands move and the rates at which the mainland shoreline move may be quite different, depending on the slope of the mainland. In North Carolina along the Pamlico Sound, the mainland rises very gradually. The shoreline has moved inland much more rapidly than the barrier islands of the Outer Banks have migrated. That's why these islands are stranded so far offshore. South Carolina has a steeper coast than North Carolina, so the shoreline isn't moving inland as fast, and the barrier islands have actually run up onto the mainland.

The picture for how barrier islands respond when sea level falls isn't as clear. They may become stranded, or they may migrate seaward when the tide carries sand out of the sounds through inlets.

Over the last 1.5 million years, since the beginning of the ice ages, barrier islands have formed and marched landward and perhaps back seaward many times in response to changing sea level. As they move, they sometimes leave sediment behind, as at Flanner Beach, providing a record of their migration.

The fossils at Flanner Beach are not the kinds that provide highly precise ages, but we know from other parts of the world with good age data that the last time there was a 20-foot rise in sea level was 125,000 years ago. The prominent Suffolk scarp (Figure 32-2) marks the shoreline created by this rise in sea level. Evidence from other parts of the world shows that the sea-level rise may have been unusually rapid, perhaps occurring within just a few decades. According to one proposed explanation, it was caused by the collapse and melting of the West Antarctic ice sheet, one of the major glaciers of Antarctica.

So our story at Flanner Beach is this: As sea level rose, salt water flooded an ancient cypress swamp, killing the cypress trees and depositing mud and marine shells. The barrier islands migrated inland and eventually covered the sediments that had been deposited in the sound. After all these sediments were laid down, the climate cooled. Glaciers and the ice caps grew again; sea level dropped; and the old sediments were left high and dry, to be scoured by wind and rain and eventually washed into rivers. A falling sea level doesn't leave a nice stack of clue-filled layers like this behind; instead it exposes old sediments to erosion. These bluffs are just leftovers—what wasn't eroded away when sea level fell.

Also included in the "leftovers" are the stumps, which are all that remain of the cypress trees that lived here 125,000 years ago when salt water began

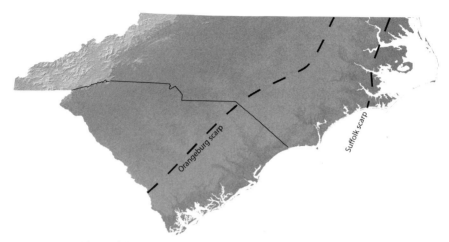

FIGURE 32-2. The Suffolk scarp is a 125,000-year-old shoreline; the Orangeburg scarp is a 2-million-year-old shore line.

encroaching. Although they haven't rotted or been "petrified" (undergone mineral replacement), they have been partially transformed to lignite, a very low-grade form of coal.

Look for the ancient cypress stumps not just in the bottom of the bluffs, but exposed on the beach southeast (downstream) of the wooden stairs. There are some modern cypress stumps here and there at Flanner Beach, but you can recognize the ancient ones by their enormous size (commonly 4 or 5 feet in diameter, some up to 8 feet) and by the fact that they are encased in the blue-gray clay.

Since the time that these cypress trees were alive, the earth has been going in and out of ice ages, with sea level falling and rising. It's interesting to note that today some of the ice shelves associated with the West Antarctic ice sheet are starting to break apart and melt. If the ice sheet continues to melt, there will be another 20-foot rise in sea level. Almost certainly within the next thousand years, Flanner Beach will once again be a true ocean beach, marked by a line of barrier islands.

Location and Access

Flanner Beach is part of the Croatan National Forest's Neuse River Recreation Area, which is near where the Neuse empties into the Pamlico Sound. Flanner Beach is accessible off US 70 between New Bern and Havelock.

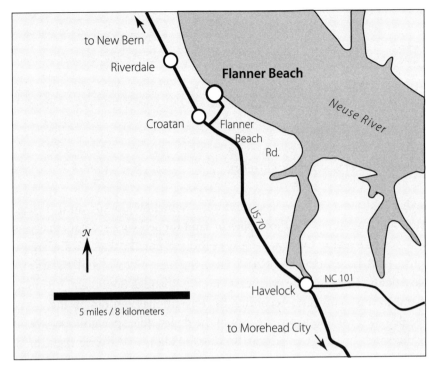

FIGURE 32-3. Location of Flanner Beach.

Unfortunately, while this book was in production, the Croatan Ranger District placed tons of boulders along the banks at Flanner Beach. These boulders completely block the view of the lower layers.

Recommended Reading

Carter, J. G., P. E. Gallagher, R. Enos Valone, and T. J. Rossbach. *Fossil Collecting in North Carolina.* Bulletin 89. Raleigh: North Carolina Geological Survey, 1988.

Pilkey, Orrin H., Jr., William J. Neal, Orrin H. Pilkey, Sr., and Stanley R. Riggs. *From Currituck to Calabash: Living with North Carolina's Barrier Islands.* 2d ed. Durham: Duke University Press, 1980.

Pilkey, Orrin H., Tracy Monegan Rice, and William J. Neal. *How to Read a North Carolina Beach: Bubble Holes, Barking Sands, and Rippled Runnels.* Chapel Hill: University of North Carolina Press, 2004.

Riggs, Stanley R., and Dorothea V. Ames. *Drowning the North Carolina Coast.* Raleigh: North Carolina Sea Grant, 2003.

33

Jockey's Ridge State Park
A Mountain of Sand

>> DARE COUNTY, NORTH CAROLINA

Saying that Jockey's Ridge is a sand dune somehow doesn't do it justice. After all, sand dunes are those piles of sand topped with sea oats that you walk across to get to the beach. Jockey's Ridge is not like that. It's the largest active sand dune on the East Coast. From the top, you can see all the way to the Atlantic Ocean to the northeast and the Roanoke Sound and Roanoke Island to the southwest. According to conventional wisdom, in the 1700s people raced wild ponies at the foot of the dune while spectators sat above in the sand. In 1903 the Wright Brothers made their historic flight on a similar, but smaller, sand dune a few miles north—Kill Devil Hill.

Jockey's Ridge is in fact a special kind of dune: it is unvegetated, steep, tall, and isolated (in the sense of not being part of an unbroken line of dunes along the coast). Dunes that have all four of these characteristics are called medaños. To get a medaño, you need regular winds blowing in opposing directions, and you need a huge supply of sand. At Jockey's Ridge, winds blow from the southwest from March through August and from the northeast from September through February. These opposing winds build up all the available sand into a tall, steep pile. From year to year the net migration of sand back and forth is low, but the sand is active enough to prevent vegetation from taking hold. Because the winter winds tend to be stronger, Jockey's Ridge is migrating 1 to 6 feet per year to the southwest. Jockey's Ridge State Park encompasses not only Jockey's Ridge itself but also many other sand dunes, which together cover 400 acres. Many smaller dunes in the park are vegetated—with sea oats (*Uniola paniculata*), American beach-grass (*Ammophila breviligulata*), and even loblolly pines (*Pinus taeda*).

Where does all this sand come from? In general, the coast north of Cape Lookout has a much thicker accumulation of young sediments and sand than does the coast to the south. This is because of a feature known as the Cape Fear Arch (see Chapter 35, on Carolina Beach State Park). The arch

FIGURE 33-1. Jockey's Ridge.

brings hard rocks closer to the surface south of Cape Fear, so that area has a relatively thin veneer of sand on top of older, better-cemented rocks. North of Cape Lookout, the flank of the arch plunges down, and a thick pile of young sediment fills the deep basin: this is the source of sand for Jockey's Ridge.

After you've climbed to the top of Jockey's Ridge and run to the bottom, take time to go exploring. Keep your eyes open, and you will see all kinds of beautiful and intriguing patterns in the sand.

First, take a look at the sand itself. It's a little bit different than the sand you make castles with on the beach—there are no shell fragments. Dunes are made entirely of small sand-size grains (mostly quartz), with no shells. That's because everything that's in a sand dune has been blown by the wind, and the wind doesn't normally pick up shells. If you examine the sand closely, perhaps with a magnifying glass or a hand lens, you'll see that individual grains are rounded and frosted. They have all been sand blasted by each other, so sharp corners have worn off and shiny surfaces have become cloudy. The grains are all nearly the same size because smaller particles tend to blow away rather than accumulate, and larger particles are too big to be picked up by the wind.

The wind rearranges loose sand into a large variety of interesting designs, most of which are informative as well as beautiful. Ripples or ripple marks are one example: they look like miniature fields of sand dunes. Most ripples form perpendicular to the wind, with their steep sides on the leeward side. (Water can also shape sand this way; Carolina beaches usually have plenty of ripple marks.)

Sometimes you may see new ripples forming at an angle to older ripples that were formed when the wind direction was different. Sometimes ripples appear to be striped, with dark grains in the troughs and lighter grains on the peaks. The dark grains are dense minerals, usually ilmenite (iron-titanium oxide) and magnetite (iron oxide). It is because they are denser than quartz that they tend to settle in the troughs. If you have a magnet, you can use it to pick up the magnetite particles.

"Wind shadows" are another interesting pattern in the sand that can tell you which way the wind is (or has been) blowing. A pebble, a small pile of wet sand, or even an especially large quartz grain creates a wind break, keeping sand grains behind it from being blown away (Figure 33-2). The combination of a small clump of wet sand and an old leaf or pine needle can create a fantastic wind-sculpted shape.

Wind shadows are clues to how dunes originate. In a place with plenty of sand and wind, sand will tend to accumulate behind any windbreak, no matter how small; if the wind direction is consistent, more and more sand will pile up on the leeward side. Thus a dune is born, growing larger as it catches more sand. Although we will never know exactly what obstacle gave birth to Jockey's Ridge, once the dune began, it would have served as its own wind shadow.

On a windy day, you can see sand blowing off the top of the dune and tumbling down the lee side. The sand sliding down the lee side builds up in thin layers, inclined at the angle of repose of dry sand (between 30 and 35 degrees). The layers may be differentiated from each other by slightly different sizes of grains or by darker-colored grains. Later, when the wind shifts, more layers may pile up on top of these, but in a different direction. The pattern made by these inclined layers is called cross-bedding (see Figure 2-1). Cross-beds are created and destroyed as winds shift. When dunes become deeply buried and the sand is cemented together into sandstone, cross-beds are often preserved, giving geologists a clue to the origin of the rock (Figure 33-3). Cross-beds are commonly preserved in sandstone and quartzite (metamorphosed sandstone). Pilot Mountain is a good place to see cross-beds in quartzite, although the cross-beds there were made by water rather than wind (see Figure 18-3). The best place to look for cross-

FIGURE 33-2. Wind shadows. The wind was blowing from right to left.

beds at Jockey's Ridge is among the smaller dunes, where you'll occasionally find an eroded bank that exposes these angled layers.

The tops of old cross-beds that have been covered and are now being exhumed by wind can display beautiful swirling patterns (Figure 33-4). Those that were made of both quartz sand and dark, dense minerals make especially interesting designs. Erosion presents a flat surface that is essentially a cross-section through a three-dimensional framework of inclined cross-beds.

Jockey's Ridge may seem an inhospitable place for animals, but if you look, you will find animal tracks in the sand, including those of many insects, lizards, spadefoot toads, and gray foxes. Look for deer tracks around the moist pockets in the park called blowouts. A blowout occurs when a regular swirl of wind scours all the sand out of a particular area. If the wind reaches the water table, a pond will be the result (Figure 33-5). If the bottom of a blowout is moist but there is no standing water, it can become a pocket of vegetation.

Don't be fooled by tracks that on close inspection turn out to be strangely irregular. Follow these tracks to see if you can find what made them—in-

FIGURE 33-3. A thin veneer of loose rippled sand migrating across old cross-beds.

stead of an insect, it may well be a dried leaf, skipping and twirling along. Notice also that living plants make tracks. Grasses and shrubs blown by the wind often inscribe arcs around their bases.

If you're very lucky, you may find a fulgurite, a fragile, tubelike piece of once-molten glass formed when lightning strikes the dune and melts sand grains together. Jockey's Ridge is the highest point around, so it is frequently struck by lightning. There are several fulgurites on display in the visitor center. Because this is a state park, if you do find a fulgurite, leave it where it is.

The impetus for making this area a state park came in 1973 when development threatened the big dune. Citizens joined together to convince the state to purchase the land. In 1975 the legislature agreed to do so and created Jockey's Ridge State Park. It's hard to draw boundaries around wind-blown sand, however. In the 1980s the state had to purchase a miniature golf facility and a hamburger shop that were being covered by wind-blown sand. In 1994 sand was moving onto Soundside Road and threatening several homes, so the park hired contractors to move about 15,000 cubic yards of sand from the southern end of the park to the northern end. Park rang-

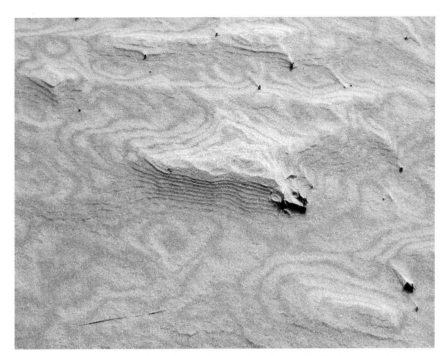

FIGURE 33-4. Patterns like these form when wind erodes gently dipping cross-beds.

ers regularly collect old Christmas trees and lash them to sand fences near the borders of the park to create artificial dunes that will help keep sand in the park.

As you wander around, notice which areas are hard-packed sand and which areas are covered with loose sand. This will give you clues to how the sand is moving now. The hard-packed areas are where sand is being eroded, exposing compacted sediments below, and the areas of loose sand are where sand is being deposited.

In recent years, there has been a lot of concern that Jockey's Ridge may be losing sand. In 1996 scientists funded by the Natural Heritage Trust Fund used maps from 1950, 1974, and 1995 to try to quantify loss and movement of sand in the park. They found that the elevation of the peak of Jockey's Ridge was 138 feet in 1950 and 87.5 feet in 1995—a loss of about 50 feet. A dune on the east side of the park went from 73 feet to 58.2 feet in the same time period—a loss of about 15 feet. A dune on the south side of the park remained about 50 feet high the whole time.

Using a computer analysis of topographic maps, the scientists also looked at the volume of sand in the entire park from 1974 to 1995. They found that

FIGURE 33-5. A water-filled blowout at Jockey's Ridge.

it went from 282.8 million cubic feet to 279.7 million cubic feet. That's a difference of 3.2 million cubic feet of sand, which at first blush sounds like a lot. Consider, however, that the difference is equal to only 1 percent of the total amount of sand. Put another way: it's as if a 3-inch layer of sand had been removed from the entire park. But the error in the mapping could have easily exceeded 3 inches, so it's not possible to say for sure whether sand is being lost.

The scientists did discover that the dunes were moving southwest, primarily through movement of sand from the crests to the bases of the dunes. They concluded that while the dunes were moving and changing shape, the park was probably not losing sand. Only time will tell whether the dunes will continue to lose height and migrate slowly southwest in the coming years, or begin to change in another way.

Location and Access

Jockey's Ridge State Park is in Nags Head off the US 158 bypass. If it's sunny, expect the park to be hotter than surrounding areas. The sand gets extremely hot and radiates heat. Wear shoes to protect your feet from hot

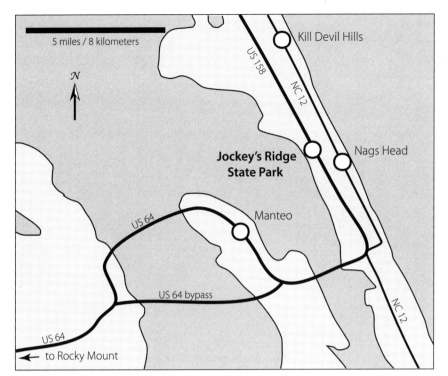

FIGURE 33-6. Location of Jockey's Ridge State Park.

sand. Jockey's Ridge is frequently struck by lightning, so leave the park quickly if a storm approaches. Hang gliding is regulated by the park rangers; lessons are available. Sandboarding is allowed in designated areas for part of the year. Camping is not allowed.

Nearby Features

Nags Head Woods, owned by The Nature Conservancy, is on US 158 not far north of Jockey's Ridge. Turn off the highway at Ocean Acres Drive. It's not often you see such a beautiful, diverse, and mature maritime forest on a barrier island. It thrives in a pocket that is relatively protected from the ocean's salt spray by Jockey's Ridge to the south and another medaño—Run Hill—to the north.

You can get to Run Hill by taking West Airfield Road off US 158, north of Nags Head Woods. Clamber to the top and walk about a quarter mile to the sound side of the dune, where you will have a tranquil view of the

FIGURE 33-7. Run Hill, north of Nags Head Woods, showing migration of the dune over the forest.

sound and of Nags Head Woods. As you look to the west, you can see Run Hill sliding into the forest, covering trees as it goes (Figure 33-7).

From the top of Run Hill, you can see another medaño to the north—Kill Devil Hill, where the Wright brothers monument is. It is technically no longer a medaño because it has been completely covered with grass in order to stabilize it for the monument.

34

Oregon Inlet
The Fickle Nature of Barrier Islands and Inlets

>> DARE COUNTY, NORTH CAROLINA

In 1963 the 2.5-mile-long Herbert C. Bonner Bridge officially opened in Dare County. The bridge, named in honor of a North Carolina legislator, spans Oregon Inlet. Since then, the bridge has stayed put, but the inlet has not.

Inlets are not carved in stone; they are scooped out of sand. That's why they move back and forth, and open and close—thwarting commercial fishing operations, stranding beach communities, and threatening buildings and roads.

Oregon Inlet and Hatteras Inlet both opened on September 7, 1846, as a result of a hurricane. Inlets frequently open immediately after a hurricane or nor'easter when water in the overfull sound bursts through a barrier island to the ocean. Oregon Inlet was named for the *Oregon*, a side-wheeler steamship that was the first vessel to pass through the new inlet. All inlets change as sands shift, but many at least stay approximately in the same place from year to year. Oregon, however, has been moving south fairly rapidly ever since its birth; Bodie Island Lighthouse, which was built in 1872 to mark the inlet, is now about 2 miles away from it. From Oregon Inlet, you can see the lighthouse far to the north.

The inlet has continued its migration since the Bonner Bridge was built (Figure 34-1). Bodie Island creeps farther and farther south, and now it extends nearly a mile underneath the bridge. The underpinnings of the southern end of the bridge have been threatened by the movement of the inlet. A wall of large rocks (called a "terminal groin") has halted, for now, the erosion of the northern tip of Pea Island, where the southern end of the bridge is anchored (Figure 34-2). Because the tip of Bodie Island is still moving southward, the inlet is narrowing and must be constantly dredged to keep it open.

For several decades, citizens and politicians argued about whether the U.S. Army Corps of Engineers should construct a pair of mile-long jetties

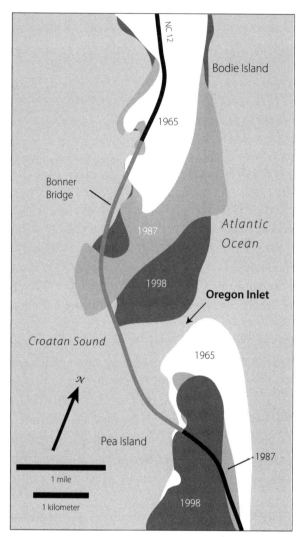

FIGURE 34-1. Changes in the shape and location of Oregon
Inlet from 1965 to 1998.

to stabilize Oregon Inlet. Proponents of the jetties said that they would
protect commercial fishing interests and the bridge. Opponents said that
the jetties would set off a sequence of unintended consequences, including
trapping sand that was moving southward in the longshore current. You've
experienced a longshore current if you've ever been swimming in the ocean
and noticed after a while that you have drifted down the beach away from
where you left your beach towel. The longshore current is a result of waves

FIGURE 34-2. The terminal groin at the south side of Oregon Inlet.

approaching the beach at an angle, not straight on, which causes a net flow of water—and sand—parallel to the shoreline. The jetties would thus prevent sand from the inlets from reaching the Pea Island National Wildlife Refuge and the Cape Hatteras National Seashore farther south. That essentially made the jetties against federal law, because they would be starving a national wildlife refuge and a national seashore of sand. For now, the rock wall and the dredgers keep the inlet open.

From Cape Lookout to the Virginia border, there are currently four inlets: Drum, Ocracoke, Hatteras, and Oregon (Figure 34-3). Ocracoke Inlet is the only one of the four that has existed since mapmakers arrived in the 1500s. Drum Inlet opened in a storm in the 1930s. It sanded over in 1971. In the late 1970s the Army Corps of Engineers opened a new inlet about 2 miles south of where Drum Inlet had been. It, too, sanded over. In 1997 the corps opened it again. In 1999 Hurricane Dennis created an inlet near where the original Drum Inlet had been. This 1999 inlet has not been in the news much because it is on a remote part of the Cape Lookout National Seashore where there are no permanent residents.

In 2003 Hurricane Isabel made an inlet just northeast of Hatteras Village that was 1,700 feet wide and 30 feet deep. As a result, residents of Hatteras were stranded for six weeks while the Army Corps of Engineers filled the inlet with sand and rebuilt NC 12. Once the infilling began, it took about two weeks to close the inlet; the work was hampered by the fact that tidal currents swept out much of the sand that was dumped in.

It's not really a surprise when inlets open, close, or move. Geologically speaking, there's always something going on at the beach. On a small, daily scale, waves tumble shells, sand, and even bits of broken glass in the surf like a giant rock polisher. Tides come and go, obliterating sand castles and filling holes left by beachgoers. Wind rearranges the dunes. Not as frequently, but still regularly, storm waves eat away at the dunes, either carrying sand offshore or washing it to the back side of the island (often covering a road in the process).

On an even larger scale, our barrier islands are on the move. Barrier islands are thin strips of sand that line most of North Carolina's coast. The current generation of barrier islands developed about 18,000 years ago, following the peak of the last ice age, when glaciers melted and sea level rose. As the ocean rose, seawater flooded the river valleys along the coast, and waves eroded a tremendous amount of sand and other sediment from the land. The sand formed spits on the headlands jutting out between drowned river valleys. The spits, which ran parallel to the shore, were eventually surrounded by water as sea level continued to rise. They had become barrier islands.

The sand originally came from the Blue Ridge and the Piedmont. Ancient rivers eroded those areas and carried away bits and pieces of rock, which broke apart into minerals. Weak minerals disintegrated into tiny, silt-sized pieces or weathered into clay. Durable minerals, such as quartz, broke apart into grains of sand, which the rivers deposited on the Coastal Plain and in the ocean. Today most Carolina rivers dump their sediment in the still waters of the Albemarle and Pamlico sounds rather than in the ocean. The few rivers that do make it to the ocean have much less sediment than ancient rivers because of dams upstream that trap the sediment (see Chapter 27, on the Roanoke River).

Carolina beach sand contains shell fragments as well as mineral grains. Many of the shells that you find on North Carolina beaches are actually shells of animals that lived in the sound. The dark gray and black shells commonly seen on the ocean-side beach can be hundreds or even thousands of years old and are from sound-dwelling oysters. The reason that shells from sound-dwelling creatures are now on the ocean side of the barrier islands is that the islands are migrating toward the mainland, and as they do so, they are running over old sound-side deposits.

At present, sea level is continuing to rise, at a rate of about 1 foot per century, as a result of both natural post–ice age warming and global warm-

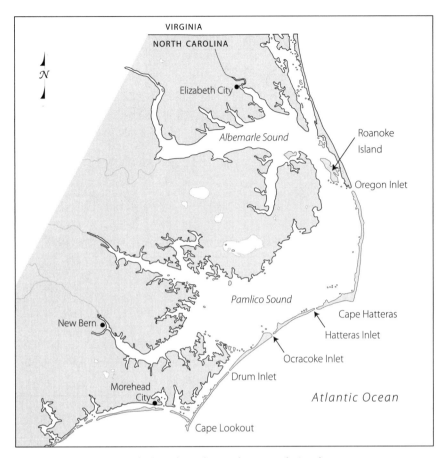

FIGURE 34-3. Locations of inlets along the northern North Carolina coast.

ing due to human production of greenhouse gases, and it is this rise in sea level that causes barrier islands to migrate. During storms, waves bring sand up and over an island in a process called overwash. This increases the island's elevation and adds sand to the sound side of the island. (Overwash also plays an important role in supporting creatures that reproduce in the sound; overwash sand quickly becomes colonized by marsh grasses to provide salt marsh habitat.) Sand also comes into the sound via inlets. This sand forms tidal inlets in the sound that can gradually add to and widen the island on the sound side. Over time, as the sea rises, these processes remove sand from the seaward side of an island and add sand to the back, resulting in landward migration.

Mainland shorelines also change as sea level rises. If the mainland shore-

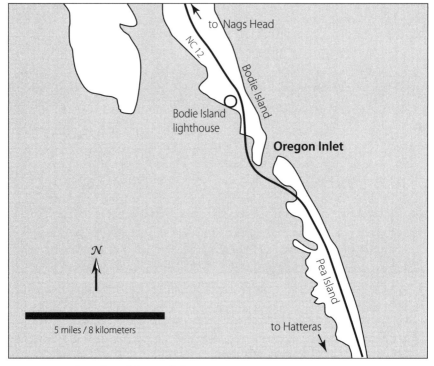

FIGURE 34-4. Location of Oregon Inlet.

line is not moving back as fast as a barrier island is migrating, the island can eventually run up onto the mainland. This is the case on the northern South Carolina shores and the southern North Carolina shores.

Today, most North Carolina barrier islands are not just moving; they are also getting narrower. This may stem in part from human interference with natural sand movement. By building dams on rivers and jetties in the ocean, we may simply be starving the barrier islands. Rising sea level is surely also playing a role, especially given that barrier islands worldwide appear to be narrowing. The narrowing of the islands will facilitate landward migration because overwash has a shorter distance to travel.

Carolinians love the beach. We love it so much that we've built houses, roads, bridges, and more on the sand. But shorelines move, and beach houses topple into the sea. The shifting sands that have created the beautiful barrier islands and beaches will continue to shift, creating problems for people who live or own property on the beaches. Over the long run, it is no more possible to fight the ocean and win than it is to build a sandcastle that can withstand the incoming tide.

Location and Access

Bonner Bridge is on NC 12. There is a parking lot on the Pea Island side of Bonner Bridge.

Nearby Features

Pea Island National Wildlife Refuge is on the south side of Oregon Inlet. There are nature trails and observation platforms for viewing the many birds that live on Pea Island or stop there while migrating.

Recommended Reading

Pilkey, Orrin H., Jr., William J. Neal, Orrin H. Pilkey, Sr., and Stanley R. Riggs. *From Currituck to Calabash: Living with North Carolina's Barrier Islands.* 2d ed. Durham: Duke University Press, 1980.

Pilkey, Orrin H., Tracy Monegan Rice, and William J. Neal. *How to Read a North Carolina Beach: Bubble Holes, Barking Sands, and Rippled Runnels.* Chapel Hill: University of North Carolina Press, 2004.

35

Carolina Beach State Park
Sugarloaf, Shells, and Sinkholes

Imagine a state park at the beach and you might imagine all sand. Carolina Beach State Park, however, packs a lot of variety in its 761 acres. Yes, there is sand, but you will also find limestone sinkholes, an outcrop of a rock made almost entirely of shells, an ancient sand dune, and numerous different ecosystems. The rare Venus flytrap (*Dionaea muscipula*) also lives in Carolina Beach State Park.

Carolina Beach is located just north of Cape Fear, where the Cape Fear River empties into the ocean. Carolina Beach, on the east bank of the river, is on an island that used to be a peninsula; in 1929 a connector was cut through the island to link the Cape Fear River and Masonboro Sound. The connector, called Snow's Cut, is part of the Intracoastal Waterway, a narrow inland waterway that runs from Boston, Massachusetts, to Key West, Florida, and from Apalachee Bay in northwest Florida to Brownsville, Texas, on the Rio Grande.

Snow's Cut is a good place to see an outcrop of a rock called coquina, a sedimentary rock made primarily of fossil shells. The outcrop is most easily seen from a boat on the river, but you can visit the outcrop on land via unofficial trails from Carolina Beach State Park. Another place nearby to look for coquina is along the seashore at Fort Fisher State Historic Site, opposite the visitor center (Figure 35-2). (Don't confuse the riprap blocks of gray granite put there to slow erosion with the native blocks of brown shelly coquina. The granite, by the way, is about 300 million years old and was quarried from the Sims pluton mentioned in Chapter 25.) There is also a small coquina outcrop at Kure Beach, north of Fort Fisher.

Carolina Beach State Park is underlain by the coquina, which formed when shells of marine creatures accumulated along the shore from about 70,000 to 50,000 years ago, during the Pleistocene epoch. By looking at the kinds of mollusks in the coquina, we can tell that the climate at this location

FIGURE 35-1. Carolina Beach State Park.

more than 50,000 years ago was essentially identical to the climate today. The earth was coming out of an ice age, and the warming climate was melting polar ice and causing sea level to climb. The coquina beds are slightly higher than modern-day sea level so we know that they were deposited at a time when sea level was about 5 or 6 feet higher than it is today.

The coquina bedrock has made for some interesting topography in the park. Shells are made of calcium carbonate, which dissolves in weak acid. Groundwater is usually mildly acidic because it combines with carbon dioxide in the atmosphere and soil to form carbonic acid; so it leaches calcium carbonate out of coquina. If enough cavities form in the rock, a portion of the bedrock can collapse, opening up a sinkhole on the surface. Florida has many sinkholes because much of the state is underlain by limestone, which is high in calcium carbonate. At Carolina Beach State Park, you can see three sinkholes along the Sugarloaf Trail: Grass Pond, Lily Pond, and Cypress Pond. Not fed by any streams, these ponds are dependent on rainfall for their water. In other parts of the world, dissolving limestone can form caves, such as Mammoth Cave in Kentucky.

Offshore outcrops of the coquina, which would withstand the ocean's erosive powers more firmly than loose sand, may be partly responsible

FIGURE 35-2. Coquina boulders at Fort Fisher State Historic Site.

for the shape of North Carolina's three distinctive capes: Cape Fear, Cape Lookout, and Cape Hatteras. But no one knows for sure. It may be that circulating ocean currents have carved out the spaces between the capes. There are also some large-scale subsurface structures in the Coastal Plain that may play a role. Underneath the sediments of the Coastal Plain are the same kinds of hard rocks you find in the Piedmont, and they are folded into broad, gentle arches and basins. You can't see the arches and basins on the surface because they are filled in and covered with a thick layer of sediments. The spine of a broad fold in the crust called the Cape Fear Arch runs northwest-southeast, roughly along the boundary between the two Carolinas. To the northeast of the Cape Fear Arch is a basin called the Albemarle Embayment. To the southwest of the Cape Fear Arch is the Charleston Embayment (Figure 35-3).

To decipher subsurface geology, we rely primarily on data collected while drilling wells for water, oil, or other purposes. For instance, the upward arching of the metamorphic basement rocks beneath Cape Fear is clearly illustrated by the fact that a geothermal exploratory well drilled there penetrated only 1,550 feet of sediment before hitting older metamorphic rocks,

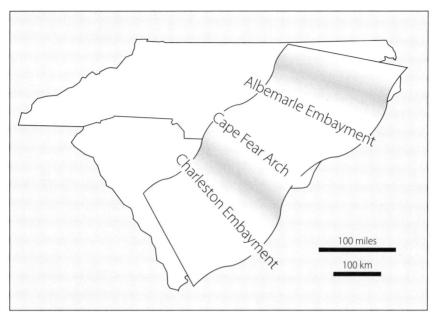

FIGURE 35-3. The subsurface arch and embayments in the Carolinas.

whereas one drilled on Cape Hatteras, down the flank of the arch, encountered 9,878 feet of sediment before hitting metamorphic rocks.

Some of the sediments on top of the metamorphic rocks have been folded along with the metamorphic rocks; sediments deposited more recently have not. By noting the ages of the sediments that are folded and the ages of the sediments that are not, we can tell that these arches were active up until about 5 million years ago, although some minor arching may be taking place today. The origin of the arches is not clear, although the infrequent—but sometimes damaging—earthquakes in the coastal Carolinas may be a result of the same kinds of stress that were responsible for the arches (see Chapter 36, on the Charleston earthquake of 1886).

On the Sugarloaf Trail, there is also an ancient sand dune, now covered with vegetation, for which the trail is named. You can clamber to the top and enjoy a view from 55 feet above sea level. This dune appeared on early maps of the area and was apparently used as a landmark by riverboat captains on the Cape Fear. The area around and including Sugarloaf has a long and rich human history, beginning with Indians who lived along the Cape Fear. They spoke a language related to that of the Sioux Indians. Because of clashes with other Indian tribes and with Europeans, the Cape Fear In-

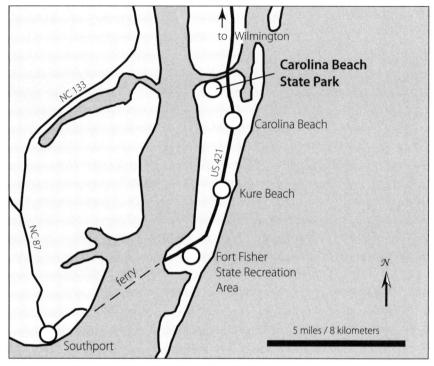

FIGURE 35-4. Location of Carolina Beach State Park.

dians left this area by 1725. The first known European to see Cape Fear was Giovanni da Verrazzano, who was exploring for France in 1524. Brunswick was founded in 1726, and Wilmington (which was called Newton) was founded in 1733. Settlers made the area an important port for collecting agricultural products, timber, and naval stores from inland and shipping them overseas. Brunswick was devastated during the Revolutionary War and never really recovered. During the Civil War, 5,000 Confederate troops camped at Sugarloaf during the siege of Wilmington.

Venus flytraps grow in the park along the edges of pocosins. (A pocosin is a type of swamp in the southeastern United States that is usually wooded or shrubby.) A good place to look for the plants is along the Fly Trap Nature Trail, from spring until late fall. The only place on earth where Venus flytraps live is within a 75-mile radius of Wilmington, North Carolina. Flies and other insects are attracted to the plants' red-lined "traps," which snap shut when the insects land. The plant "digests" the insect over the course of a few days. Carnivorous plants have evolved to live in places with poor soil; insects provide minerals and other nutrients that are not otherwise available. Other carnivorous plants that live at Carolina Beach State Park include sundews (*Drosera* spp.), butterwort (*Pinguicula* spp.), bladderworts (*Utricularia* spp.), and pitcher plants (*Sarracenia* spp.).

The park contains an unusual diversity of plants, including almost three dozen that are designated as rare by the North Carolina Natural Heritage Program. The variety of plants is a result of the variety of habitats, from longleaf pine forests to pocosins to brackish marshes. If you're spending time at the shore and begin to crave a change in botanical and geological scenery, Carolina Beach State Park is a great place to find it.

Location and Access

Take US 421 south from Wilmington about 15 miles to get to Carolina Beach State Park.

Recommended Reading

Carter, J. G., P. E. Gallagher, R. Enos Valone, and T. J. Rossbach. *Fossil Collecting in North Carolina*. Bulletin 89. Raleigh: North Carolina Geological Survey, 1988.

36

Colonial Dorchester State Historic Site
The Charleston Earthquake of 1886

>> DORCHESTER COUNTY, SOUTH CAROLINA

Shortly before 10:00 at night on August 31, 1886, an earthquake hit Charleston, South Carolina. Distraught citizens rushed out into the streets as church bells clanged and buildings crumbled. About 15,000 chimneys fell, and the vast majority of the brick buildings in the city were damaged. Fewer frame buildings were damaged because they tended to sway instead of cracking. While the exact death toll is unknown, it has been estimated at 100 people. Some Charlestonians camped in public squares for weeks, afraid or unable to return to their houses.

The earthquake, which consisted of two main shocks about 8 minutes apart, was felt all the way from New York to Cuba, and from Bermuda to the Mississippi River. Most towns within 200 miles of Charleston experienced some degree of damage. Three hundred chimneys fell 75 miles away in Savannah, Georgia.

Church bells rang in Charlotte, where a reporter wrote, "People . . . were seen to stagger, and the steady rocking of the buildings was heard in all directions accompanied by a faint jingle of glass" ("A Great Shock: The Whole Country in the Grasp of an Earthquake," *News and Observer*, September 1, 1886, 1). A report from Chapel Hill said, "Throughout the town women cried, neighbors ran to each other's houses, folks in bed were shaken up, looking glasses quivered, crockery rattled and philosophers were confounded." In Asheville, well to the west, there was also shock: "Houses were violently shaken and the inhabitants all left them and went into the streets. . . . Much alarm was caused, but no damage was done in the town or the surrounding country" ("The Old North State Sustains No Injury: Dispatches from Many Points Tell What the Quake Did," *News and Observer*, September 2, 1886, 1).

If you've ever taken a tour of Charleston, your guide no doubt pointed

FIGURE 36-1. Damage from the 1886 Charleston earthquake; photograph taken at the corner of East Bay and Cumberland streets. Courtesy of South Caroliniana Library, University of South Carolina, Columbia.

out evidence of the catastrophic earthquake: many of the old houses in the Battery on the harbor have earthquake bolts on their exteriors, which were installed after the quake to prevent any further movement of the walls. If you haven't been to Charleston, you may never have heard of the event, even though it was the most destructive earthquake to hit the eastern United States in recorded history. Three quakes in 1811 and 1812 in New Madrid, Missouri, were more powerful, but they did not cause as much damage because that area was so sparsely populated.

The epicenter of the Charleston earthquake is thought to have been near Summerville, about 20 miles northwest of Charleston. Mr. Thomas Turner, who was president of the Charleston Gas-Light Company, was at his summer home in Summerville during the earthquake, and this is how he described it:

> I had been out in the garden and admired the beauty of the
> evening, and was entering the door of the Hall when, without any
> rumble or premonitory symtoms [sic], just as I was stepping in at the
> door, for a single instant the floor seemed to sink from under me,
> I seized the door jambs to steady myself, when the floor seemed to

go down in front of me at an angle of about 25 to 30 degrees. It was so sudden and unexpected, that I was thrown forward into the Hall about ten feet—and as quickly thrown backward, ere I could fall onto the piazza, and again thrown forward into the house. At this moment I observed my Sister-in-law crawling on all fours, she having been thrown from her room on the S.W. . . . We endeavored to leave the house, amidst the crush of falling chimneys and plaster—but at every attempt we made to reach the door, we were hurled backward and forward and from side to side, as if we had been in the gangway of an ocean steamer in a heavy cross sea. (Kenneth E. Peters and Robert B. Herrmann, eds., *First-Hand Observations of the Charleston Earth-quake of August 31, 1886, and Other Earthquake Materials*, Bulletin 41 [Columbia: South Carolina Geological Survey, 1986], 106)

Colonial Dorchester State Historic Site near Summerville is a good place to see some of the effects of the earthquake. Dorchester was established on the Ashley River in 1697 by Congregationalists from Massachusetts. The fort there was constructed in 1775. The walls of the fort are made of "tabby"—a mix of oyster shells and lime. Not many years after the fort was completed, the inhabitants abandoned the town and moved most of the buildings to Summerville to escape the mosquitoes. When the 1886 earthquake occurred, all that remained in Dorchester was the fort and the tower of the Parish Church of St. George's. Today, you can visit the site and see evidence of the quake in both the church tower and the walls of the fort. You can also observe archaeologists at an active dig site working to uncover artifacts of the colonial town.

The brick church tower has X-shaped cracks on both the north and the south sides (Figure 36-2). These kinds of cracks are characteristic of earthquake damage. As the tower swayed one way, one leg of the X formed; when it swayed back the other way, the other leg of the X formed. The direction of the movement here was approximately east-west.

The church tower was repaired after the earthquake, so the photograph does not convey the full extent of the damage. One person who visited the church tower soon after the quake wrote, "From its summit large blocks of brick and mortar—as much as 15 or 20 cubic feet in each block—were dislodged and hurled in four directions. One large mass struck the ground 35 feet from the base of the tower on the northeast side, and in its descent stripped branches and bark from a tree with which it came in contact"

FIGURE 36-2. The cracked church tower at Colonial Dorchester.

(C. E. Dutton, "The Charleston Earthquake of August 31, 1886," *U.S. Geological Survey Ninth Annual Report, 1887-1888* [Washington, D.C.: Government Printing Office, 1889], 297).

The fort's walls contain many cracks that were generated by movement during the earthquake (Figure 36-3). Cutting the southern wall of the fort is a large crack where the wall has been offset about 4 inches. On line with this crack is another crack in the northern wall that some geologists have interpreted as a continuation of the south wall crack. If they are connected, that may indicate the trace of an actual fault through the fort. It is also possible that the cracks do not correspond to an actual fault surface but

FIGURE 36-3. A crack in the tabby wall at Fort Dorchester.

are simply the result of the brittle walls' cracking and shifting during the quake. In either case, these fractures can tell us something about the directions that the land was moving during the quake.

Geologists think the 1886 earthquake was caused by movement along the Woodstock fault and a branch of the Woodstock fault called the Sawmill Branch fault. The Charleston area has probably been hit by at least several large earthquakes over the past 5,000 years as movement has taken place along these and other faults. The topography of the land surrounding the Ashley River at Dorchester indicates a history of uplift due to earthquakes: notice how broad the river and its floodplain are both upstream and downstream of Fort Dorchester. But right at the fort the river incises a channel through a bluff. This bluff is part of a broad ridge that was probably lifted up by a series of earthquakes.

The magnitude of the 1886 earthquake has been estimated to have been between 6.9 and 7.3 on the Richter scale. The Richter scale was developed in 1935 and is based on measurements taken from seismograph records. There were no seismometers around in 1886, so the Richter magnitude of the Charleston quake is an estimate based on the amount of damage that occurred. Each successive whole number on the Richter scale corresponds to 10 times the ground shaking represented by the previous number. Each successive whole number also represents an earthquake that releases 33 times more energy than one represented by the previous number. Recent earthquakes with magnitudes similar to that of the 1886 Charleston earthquake were the 1989 Loma Prieta earthquake in San Francisco with a magnitude of 7.1 and the 1994 Northridge earthquake in southern California with a magnitude of 6.7.

Perhaps surprisingly, an earthquake of similar magnitude in California would not be felt as far away as the Charleston quake was. Crust on the East Coast is older, colder (more brittle), and less broken up by faults than crust on the West Coast, so it transmits shocks more efficiently.

It's interesting to compare the Charleston quake to the Sumatra-Andaman quake of December 26, 2004. That quake had a magnitude of 9.0, meaning that the amplitude of the ground shaking was 100 times more than that of the Charleston quake. The amount of energy released in a single 9.0 quake is so huge that it would take more than 1,000 Charleston quakes to release the same amount of energy.

Should Charleston be bracing for another big earthquake? Seven seismic stations in the Charleston-Summerville area take measurements constantly; smaller earthquakes occur in the region frequently. One of the largest of these took place in August 1992; it had a magnitude of 4.1—not intense enough to cause any significant damage. Prior to the 1886 quake, no one knew that this area was capable of generating large earthquakes because none had been recorded. We don't know how often earthquakes of the 1886 magnitude recur, although they are probably rare because this

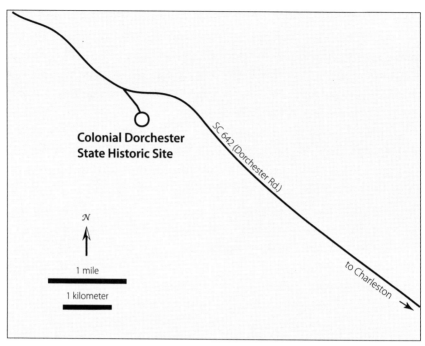

FIGURE 36-4. Location of Colonial Dorchester State Historic Site.

is not an active plate boundary. The fact that small earthquakes pop off frequently shows that the crust is being actively stressed. Almost certainly Charleston will be hit by another big quake—but no one knows when.

Location and Access

Colonial Dorchester State Historic Site is about 20 miles northwest of Charleston on SC 642. There is a nominal admission fee.

GLOSSARY

Acadian orogeny: The tectonic collision and mountain-building event that occurred when a rifted-off fragment (or several fragments) of Gondwana hit Laurentia. The Acadian orogeny is well defined and identified in the northern Appalachians, where it has been dated to 420 to 370 million years ago. The evidence for it in the Carolinas is not as solid. (See Chapter 5.)

accretionary wedge: Ocean floor sediments and pieces of oceanic crust that are scraped off the subducting plate by the overriding plate at a convergent plate boundary.

Alleghanian orogeny: The collision between Gondwana and Laurentia that began about 330 million years ago; it pushed up the Appalachian mountains and was part of the formation of the supercontinent Pangea.

amphibole: A mineral group with the chemical formula $X_{0-1}Y_2Z_5(Si,Al)_8O_{22}(OH,F)_2$, where X is sodium or potassium, Y is some combination of calcium, sodium, magnesium, iron, manganese, and lithium, and Z is some combination of iron, magnesium, manganese, aluminum, and titanium.

amphibolite: A dark metamorphic rock made mainly of amphibole and plagioclase feldspar, with little or no quartz.

andalusite: A mineral, Al_2SiO_5, which forms under low pressure and elevated temperature. Kyanite and sillimanite are polymorphs of andalusite.

andesite: A fine-grained volcanic igneous rock intermediate in composition between rhyolite and basalt.

angle of repose: The maximum angle at which loose sediments of a particular size and shape can maintain a stable slope. The angle of repose of sand is usually between 30 and 35 degrees.

anticline: A structural feature in which layers of rock are folded into an arch.

anticlinorium: A series of anticlines and synclines whose overall shape is that of an anticline.

argillite: A fine-grained, hard, weakly metamorphosed sedimentary rock similar to slate but not as fissile.

augen gneiss: A metamorphic rock, gneiss, in which certain groups of minerals, commonly feldspar, appear as large lens-shaped or blocky crystals or aggregates of crystals in the surrounding matrix.

avoirdupois ounce: 28.41 grams. *See also* troy ounce.

banding: Light and dark layers in a metamorphic rock; caused by segregation of minerals during metamorphism.

barrier island: A long, narrow island of sand semiparallel to the coastline; may be quite near the coast (e.g., Bogue Banks, North Carolina) or many miles offshore (e.g., the Outer Banks, North Carolina). Barrier islands typically form off tectonically quiet coastlines where the slope of the continental shelf and coast are relatively gentle.

basalt: An extrusive igneous rock rich in pyroxene and calcium feldspar. Because it cooled quickly on the surface of the earth, its mineral grains are mostly too small to be seen with the naked eye.

bauxite: A rock rich in aluminum hydroxide minerals; the principal ore of aluminum; forms in tropical regions.

bay lake: A Carolina bay containing standing water.

bedding: Layers of sedimentary rock that can be distinguished from one another by grain type, size, or other visual characteristics.

bedrock: The solid mass of rock that underlies soil or unconsolidated sediments.

beryl: A mineral, $Be_3Al_2Si_6O_{18}$. If trace amounts of chromium are present, making it green, the mineral is called emerald.

beryllium: A metallic element having the chemical symbol Be.

biogenic: Refers to sediment or rock formed by the processes or remains of living organisms. Coal and limestone are biogenic rocks.

biotite: A black variety of mica that is rich in iron and magnesium.

bladed: Refers to a mineral with a long, narrow, flat shape.

Blue Ridge: A part of the Appalachians that extends from Virginia to Georgia characterized by high elevations and metamorphic and igneous rocks; also the name of the Carolinas' mountainous physiographic province.

Blue Ridge escarpment: The abrupt change in elevation that marks the topographic boundary between the Piedmont and the Blue Ridge.

boudins: The "sausage link" shapes that result when metamorphic deformation causes a sedimentary or metamorphic layer to stretch out, thin, and break into separate elongated shapes.

boulder: A loose rock (sediment particle) greater than 256 mm (a little more than 10 inches) in diameter.

breccia: A sedimentary rock composed of angular particles larger than sand (larger than 2 mm in diameter); often the particles are in a finer-grained matrix. *See also* conglomerate *and* volcanic breccia.

calcite: A mineral, calcium carbonate ($CaCO_3$).

carat: The unit of weight used for gemstones; one carat is 200 mg.

Carolina bay: An oval-shaped depression of almost any size, typically lined with peat or clay, whose long axis is oriented northwest-southeast; it may or may not contain water. Carolina bays are found on the Atlantic Coastal Plain and are particularly numerous in North and South Carolina.

cemented: Refers to sedimentary rocks in which the particles are held together by mineral precipitates.

chlorite: A greenish mineral that typically occurs in flakes or sheets like mica.

clastic: Made of sedimentary particles. *See* clasts.

clasts: Sedimentary particles formed by the physical breakdown of larger rocks and minerals.

clay: A sediment particle less than 1/256 mm in diameter; also refers to a mass of clay-sized particles, and to a mineral group characterized by sheetlike crystals with abundant water within the crystals.

coal: A combustible rock made primarily of carbon from plant remains.

Coastal Plain: The easternmost physiographic province of the Carolinas; it is underlain by sediments and sedimentary rocks.

cobbles: Sedimentary particles between 64 and 256 mm (or between about 2.5 and 10 inches) in diameter.

conglomerate: A sedimentary rock consisting of rounded particles larger than sand (larger than 2 mm in diameter); it often consists of large particles in a fine-grained matrix. *See also* breccia.

contact metamorphism: Metamorphism that occurs as the result of proximity to hot magma.

continent: One of the earth's major landmasses that is at higher elevation than the ocean floor and typically arises abruptly from the ocean floor.

continental crust: Crust typically found in continents; rich in silicate minerals and more buoyant (less dense) and thicker (20–40 miles) than oceanic crust (3–6 miles).

continental divide: A topographic feature that separates two or more large drainage basins. Rain that falls on one side of the divide drains to a different side of the continent (and ultimately a different ocean or other body of water) than rain that falls on the other side.

continental shelf: The edge of a continent that is beneath the ocean. The ocean remains relatively shallow over the shelf; where the shelf ends, there is a drop-off to the deep ocean.

convergent plate boundary: A zone where two plates are coming together. If the leading edge of one of the plates is oceanic crust, it will subduct under the continental crust. If the leading edges of both plates are continental, the plates collide, producing mountains. If both plates are oceanic, usually the older, and therefore colder and denser, plate will subduct.

coquina: A sedimentary rock that contains abundant macroscopic shells.

core: The center of the earth; a sphere composed mostly of iron with lesser amounts of nickel. The outer core is about 1,500 miles thick and is liquid; the inner core, with a radius of about 750 miles, is solid.

corundum: A mineral, Al_2O_3. Sapphire and ruby are varieties of corundum.

creek: Geologically speaking, all bodies of running water are streams, regardless of their size. In common usage, a "creek" usually signifies a small stream.

crenulations: Small folds that look like sharp wrinkles; folds whose wavelengths are a few millimeters.

cross-beds: Inclined sedimentary layering within the normal stratification; cross-beds typically form as a result of the migration of sand dunes and ripples. Differently inclined cross-beds indicate different directions of migration, related to changes in wind direction or stream flow.

crust: The thin (3–40 miles) outer layer of the earth.

crystallize: Solidify into a crystalline structure, as in minerals crystallizing out of magma.

cut bank: A steep, eroded stream bank along the outer arc of a bend in a stream.

dacite: An extrusive (fine-grained) igneous rock similar to rhyolite but with more plagioclase feldspar.

deposition: The laying down of sediments. Sediments such as sand or gravel can be deposited by wind, water, or ice.

depositional environment: The place in which sediments were deposited—a swamp or a desert, for example.

diabase: Rock of basaltic composition (rich in pyroxene and calcium feldspar) whose crystals are larger than basalt but smaller than gabbro; usually intruded into existing rock near the surface of the earth, where it cools quickly, but not as quickly as basalt.

dike: A relatively thin tabular igneous intrusion that cuts across preexisting rock layers. *See also* sill.

diorite: An igneous rock that is intermediate in composition between granite and gabbro, with visible crystals (meaning that the magma cooled slowly underground). It often has a salt-and-pepper appearance.

divergent plate boundary: A zone where two plates are pulling apart from one another, with new oceanic lithosphere being created at the boundary.

drainage basin: A region of land where rainfall flows into a particular river; also called a watershed. Rain that falls outside a particular drainage basin flows to a different river.

eclogite: A metamorphic rock formed under conditions of high pressure, made principally of garnet, quartz, and omphacite, which is a type of pyroxene.

eddy: A current of water moving in a different direction than the main current, often in a circular direction.

element: Any of more than 100 different kinds of matter that consist of atoms of only one kind. Elements cannot be broken down into simpler chemical forms; oxygen, carbon, and hydrogen are examples of elements.

emerald: A gemstone that is the green form of beryl. Trace amounts of chromium are responsible for the color.

environment of deposition. *See* depositional environment.

erosion: The wearing away of rocks or sediments by mechanical processes (such as wind, water, and ice) and/or chemical processes (such as the dissolving of limestone by groundwater and rainwater).

escarpment: A steep topographical break in elevation between highlands and lower elevations.

estuary: The part of a river that empties into the ocean and is close enough to the ocean to have tidal ebb and flow.

evaporites: Minerals that are soluble in water and are deposited by precipitation from evaporating salt water.

exfoliation: A type of weathering that occurs in massive rocks (typically intrusive igneous), whereby sheets or tabular blocks of rock parallel to the ground surface peel off.

extrusive: Refers to igneous rocks that cooled quickly at the surface of the earth.

Fall Zone (Fall Line): The boundary between the Piedmont and the Coastal Plain; often marked by falls and rapids as rivers leave the hard rocks of the Piedmont and enter the more easily eroded sediments of the Coastal Plain.

fault: A crack in rock or sediment along which movement has taken place.

fault scarp: A steep slope produced by motion along a fault.

felsic: A term applied to light-colored igneous rocks, which are rich in feldspar and quartz.

feldspar: The most common group of minerals in the earth's crust. Plagioclase feldspars contain calcium and sodium, ranging from anorthite ($CaAl_2Si_2O_8$) to albite ($NaAlSi_3O_8$) but most commonly with a composition intermediate between the two. Potassium feldspars ($KAlSi_3O_8$) include orthoclase, microcline, and sanidine.

fissile: Capable of being split into thin layers.

fold: A structure in which rock layers have been bent.

foliation: Thin layers distinguished by color or texture that form as a result of pressure during metamorphism.

fool's gold: Common name for pyrite, a mineral made of iron and sulfur (FeS_2). It is typically brass yellow with cubic crystals.

fossil: The ancient remains of a plant or animal or the trace of a plant or animal (such as a footprint or a burrow) preserved in the earth's crust. Commonly, the remains have been completely replaced by minerals, which preserve the shape of the original material.

fresh: Refers to a clean, unweathered surface of rock. *See also* weathered.

fulgurite: A tubelike structure formed when lightning strikes loose sand (as in a dune) and fuses the grains together.

gabbro: Igneous rock of basaltic composition (rich in pyroxene and calcium feldspar) but with visible crystals (meaning that the magma cooled slowly underground); typically dark.

garnet: A mineral formed most commonly by metamorphism, with crystals that are typically dark red dodecahedrons.

gem: A mineral that humans value for rarity and beauty. Diamonds, rubies, sapphires, and emeralds are precious gemstones.

geology: The scientific study of the earth, including its history and its processes. Some of the major divisions of geology are structural geology (the study of structures such as faults and folds and their tectonic origins), paleontology (the study of ancient life), hydrology (the study of surface and groundwater movement), paleoclimatology (the study of past climate changes), seismology (the study of earthquakes), geochemistry (the study of the chemical properties and processes of the earth), and geomorphology (the study of landforms).

geothermal: Refers to heat from inside the earth.

glacier: Essentially, a river of ice; a mass of ice that originates on land with definite borders and direction of movement, formed by compaction of snow.

global warming: The theory that earth's climate is warming because of the increase of certain gases, principally carbon dioxide, in the atmosphere. Most of these gases are produced when humans burn fossil fuels.

gneiss: A coarse-grained metamorphic rock that commonly has alternating bands composed of light minerals (quartz and feldspar) and dark minerals. Pronounced "nice."

Gondwana: An ancient continent made up of parts of present-day Africa and South America; rifted apart in the Cretaceous.

Gondwanan terranes: Exotic terranes that originated on the margin of the ancient continent Gondwana, rifted off, and were accreted onto other continents. In the Carolinas, these are an amalgamation of named subterranes, separated by faults, found to the east of the Piedmont terrane. They all contain metamorphic bedrock, but they differ in type of bedrock and in degree of metamorphism. The Gondwanan terranes collided with ancestral North America between 450 and 350 million years ago.

grains: A term that can be used to refer to mineral crystals (as in igneous or metamorphic rocks) or sedimentary particles.

granite: An intrusive igneous rock with visible crystals and rich in quartz and feldspar; usually has a light or pinkish color.

granite dome: A rounded mountain of massive granite exposed at the earth's surface.

greenhouse effect: The ability of earth's atmosphere to trap the sun's heat, making earth's climate warm enough to support human life.

greenhouse gases: Gases that trap the sun's heat. The most abundant greenhouse gas is carbon dioxide, which occurs naturally and is also released into the environment when humans burn fossil fuels and wood.

Grenville orogeny: A mountain-building continental collision that took place between 1,200 and 900 million years ago, resulting in the formation of the supercontinent Rodinia.

groin: A structure built out into the ocean perpendicular to the shore to trap sand; often built in groups.

groundwater: Water that is trapped in the pores and cracks of sediment and bedrock below the water table.

grus: Weathered particles of granite.

gypsum: A mineral, $CaSO_4$-$2H_2O$, that forms when salt water evaporates.

halite: A mineral, $NaCl$, also called sodium chloride or rock salt, that forms when salt water evaporates.

hematite: A mineral, Fe_2O_3; the principal ore of iron.

hypothesis: An unproven idea that appears to explain the available evidence. *See also* theory.

Iapetus Ocean: The ocean that separated the ancient continents of Laurentia and Gondwana.

ice age: A period of time during which the earth's climate is relatively cold and there are many glaciers.

igneous rock: A type of rock formed by the cooling of molten rock. Intrusive igneous rocks cool underground and have visible crystals; extrusive igneous rocks cool at the surface and have small or microscopic crystals.

ilmenite: A mineral made of iron, titanium, and oxygen ($FeTiO_3$); a principal ore of titanium.

impermeable: Refers to a material through which water cannot flow.

intrusive: A term applied to igneous rocks that solidify slowly from molten rock underground.

jetty: A long structure built out into the ocean to stabilize an inlet.

joint: A crack in a rock along which little or no movement has taken place.

kyanite: A mineral found in metamorphic rocks made of aluminum, silicon, and oxygen (Al_2SiO_5). The metamorphic conditions under which it typically forms are high pressure and relatively moderate temperature. Andalusite and sillimanite are polymorphs of kyanite.

Laurentia: An ancient continent that consisted of large parts of present-day North America.

lava: Molten rock at the surface of the earth.

lee (leeward): Sheltered from the wind, or in the opposite direction as that from which the wind is blowing.

limestone: A sedimentary rock made mostly of calcium carbonate ($CaCO_3$); often made of macro- or microscopic shells of sea creatures.

lithosphere: The outer rigid layer of the earth, which includes the crust and the uppermost part of the mantle. The lithosphere is about 60 miles thick. Tectonic plates are made of lithosphere.

longshore current: An ocean current that runs near and more or less parallel to the shore; caused by waves striking a coastline at an oblique angle.

mafic: A term applied to typically dark-colored rocks that are low in silica and rich in iron-magnesium silicate minerals (dark-colored minerals such as olivine and pyroxene).

magma: Molten rock underground.

magnetite: A magnetic mineral made of iron and oxygen (Fe_3O_4); an important ore of iron.

mantle: The layer of the earth between the crust and the core.

massive: Refers to rock that has a homogeneous texture and no discernible layers.

medaño: A tall, isolated, unvegetated sand dune.

metabasalt: Basalt that has been slightly metamorphosed.

metamorphic rock: Rock that has been subjected to enough heat and pressure, usually because of deep burial, to change some or all of the minerals without melting them.

meteor: A meteoroid that has entered the earth's atmosphere, producing a fiery trail; popularly called a shooting star.

meteorite: A meteoroid that has survived the trip through the earth's atmosphere and hit the earth's surface.

meteoroid: A small solid particle traveling through space.

mica: A group of soft minerals that tend to occur in flakes or sheets; muscovite and biotite are examples.

midocean ridge: A zone where new oceanic lithosphere is being produced, forming a long "mountain range" under the ocean; a divergent plate boundary.

mineral: A naturally occurring material formed by geologic processes and having a definite chemical composition and characteristic crystal form, such as quartz, pyrite, and feldspar.

monadnock: An isolated mountain or hill, usually formed when weaker bedrock surrounding it is eroded away.

muscovite: A light-colored variety of the mineral group mica, with the formula $KAl_2(AlSi_3)O_{10}(OH)_2$.

noncomformity: A type of unconformity in which igneous or metamorphic rocks are overlain by younger sedimentary rocks.

nor'easter: A storm that occurs in the winter on the east coast of North America, in which the wind blows from the northeast.

normal fault: A fault that accommodates extension of the crust, in which one side slides down relative to the other side. Such faults are commonly found at divergent plate boundaries.

nucleation point: The site at which a crystal begins growing.

oceanic crust: Crust that underlies the oceans; chiefly basaltic.

orogeny: A regional mountain-building event caused by the collision of tectonic plates.

outcrop: An exposure of rock that is continuous with the bedrock; not loose rock.

overwash: The flow of the ocean over a barrier island to the sound, typically during a storm.

oxbow lake: A lake that begins as a loop in a meandering river. During a flood, the river cuts off the loop and leaves behind a standing body of water.

paleosol: An ancient soil layer.

Pangea: The supercontinent formed near the end of the Paleozoic era, about 300 million years ago, when all the world's continents were clustered together.

pebble: A loose rock (sediment particle) between 2 and 64 mm (or between about one-sixteenth of an inch and 2.5 inches) in diameter.

phyllite: A fine-grained, foliated metamorphic rock that has a characteristic sheen because of the parallel orientation of small mica crystals.

Piedmont: A physiographic province characterized by gently rolling hills that stretches from New Jersey to Alabama. In the Carolinas, it is bounded on the east by the Coastal Plain and on the west by the Blue Ridge.

Piedmont terrane: The crustal fragment, now part of the Carolinas, that collided with Laurentia 460 million years ago in the Taconic orogeny. Its borders do not coincide with the Piedmont physiographic province.

placer mining: Mining among loose sediment, usually in or near streambeds.

plate: A large piece of the earth's lithosphere that moves as a unit.

plate tectonics: The body of knowledge that describes how the earth's lithospheric plates move, collide, pull apart, and scrape past one another.

pluton: A massive body of igneous rock that solidified from molten rock underground.

pocosin: A shrubby bog, often elevated slightly from surrounding land; usually contains peat.

point bar: Sediment deposited on the inside of a bend in a river.

polymorphs: Minerals that have the same chemical composition but different crystal structure because of differences in the environment of formation. Graphite and diamond are polymorphs. Kyanite, andalusite, and sillimanite are also polymorphs.

pothole: A hole with smooth circular walls worn into a rock by sediments swirled around by eddies in a stream.

principle of superposition: The geologic principle stating that in undisturbed sedimentary strata the oldest layers are on the bottom and the youngest are on the top.

pyrite: A shiny brass-yellow mineral that often occurs in cubic crystals; made of iron and sulfur (FeS_2); often called fool's gold.

pyrophyllite: A soft mineral rich in aluminum ($Al_2Si_4O_{10}(OH)_2$).

pyroxene: A group of minerals with the following formula: $XYSi_2O_6$, where X is usually magnesium, iron, calcium, or sodium and Y is usually magnesium, iron, or aluminum.

quartz: One of the most common minerals on earth (SiO_2). Small amounts of various impurities create varieties such as rose quartz, amethyst, smoky quartz, and rutilated quartz.

quartz veins: Fractures in rock that are filled with milky white quartz. Quartz veins form when hot silica-rich water moves through cracks; as the water cools, quartz is deposited.

quartzite: A metamorphic rock made chiefly of quartz; metamorphosed sandstone.

radioactivity: The property that some elements have of spontaneously changing ("decaying") to other elements by emitting particles from their nuclei.

radiocarbon dating: Using radiocarbon (the isotope ^{14}C) to calculate the age of a rock or other material that contains carbon. Using conventional techniques, radiocarbon can be used to date materials that are up to 30,000 years old. *See also* radiometric dating.

radiometric dating: The technique of calculating the age of a rock by knowing the decay rate of radioactive elements in the rock and measuring and comparing the amount of radioactive material that has already decayed and the amount that has not yet decayed.

relief: The difference in elevation between the lowest points and the highest points in a particular area. A mountainous region is an area of high relief. A plateau is an area of low relief, even though it may be at a high elevation.

rhyolite: An extrusive igneous rock with the same composition as granite, but having crystals that are too small to be seen with the naked eye. Rhyolite tends to be a fairly uniform light gray; it is rich in quartz and feldspar.

rift: To tear apart, as in a continent rifting in two.

rift basin: A deep valley, bounded on one or both sides by faults, that forms when a continent rifts. Rift basins form perpendicular to the forces pulling the continent apart. After rifting is complete, there are rift basins along the edges of both continents, semiparallel to the coasts.

ripple marks: A semiregular wrinkled texture formed in sediments by the movement of wind or water.

river: Geologists use the word "stream" to apply to all moving bodies of water, regardless of size. In common usage, "river" refers to a large or major stream.

river basin: The region that is drained by a particular river and its tributaries. *See also* drainage basin.

rock: An aggregation of mineral matter; usually composed of minerals or rock fragments, and usually consolidated although sometimes only weakly (a poorly cemented sandstone, for example). The three major divisions of rock are sedimentary, igneous, and metamorphic.

Rodinia: An ancient supercontinent formed by the assemblage of many of the earth's continents mostly in the southern hemisphere from about 1,200 to 900 million years ago.

ruby: A variety of the mineral corundum, Al_2O_3. Trace amounts of chromium give ruby its red color. *See also* sapphire.

sand: Sediment particles that are between 1/16 and 2 mm in diameter. In common usage, "sand" often refers to quartz particles, but the term may be used for any particle of any composition in this size range.

sand dune: A pile of loose sand whose shape and movement is controlled by wind.

Sandhills: An inland area of mostly unconsolidated sand in the western part of the Coastal Plain in southern North Carolina and northern South Carolina.

sapphire: A variety of the mineral corundum, Al_2O_3. Trace amounts of impurities, probably iron or titanium, give sapphire its blue or yellow color. *See also* ruby.

scarp: A steep slope formed by erosion or a fault.

schist: A medium- to coarse-grained metamorphic rock rich in mica, whose semiparallel orientation gives the rock a layered appearance.

seafloor spreading: A divergent plate boundary under the ocean where plates are moving away from each other and basaltic magma is welling up; typically forms midocean ridges.

sedimentary rocks: Rocks made of sediments (bits and pieces of rocks, minerals, or organic materials such as shells) or rocks that precipitate out of solution (such as gypsum).

sediments: Loose particles of varying sizes including bits and pieces of rocks and minerals and organic matter such as shells.

sericite: A fine-grained variety of white or silver mica.

shale: A fissile sedimentary rock made of very fine grains (clay or silt).

shear zone: The area surrounding and including a fault, which can be recognized by the crushed or finely layered appearance of the rock.

silica: Silicon dioxide, SiO_2. Quartz and opal are two of the many forms of silica.

silicate minerals: Minerals containing silicon and oxygen in the form of SiO$_4$ tetrahedron-shaped molecules.

silicon: An element; after oxygen, the second most common element in the earth's crust.

sill: A layer of magma intruded between or parallel to preexisting rock layers in the crust. *See also* dike.

sillimanite: A mineral, Al$_2$SiO$_5$. Andalusite and kyanite are polymorphs of sillimanite.

silt: Sedimentary particles with diameters in the range of 1/16–1/256 mm.

sinkhole: A depression in the ground formed when limestone bedrock has been dissolved away by rain and groundwater (both of which are naturally slightly acidic) to the point that the land's surface collapses.

slate: A fine-grained metamorphic rock that tends to break along horizontal planes due to the parallel arrangement of platy (sheetlike) minerals. Slate is used for landscaping flagstones and roof shingles.

sorted: The degree to which sediments are deposited in groups of similar size. Well-sorted sediments are all nearly the same size.

stratum (plural: strata): A visually distinct layer of rock. The term is usually used with reference to sedimentary rocks.

stream: A body of moving water of any size, whether a backyard creek or the Mississippi River.

strike-slip fault: A crack in the earth's crust along which blocks of earth have moved horizontally. Such a fault is commonly found at transform plate boundaries.

subduction: The process of one plate sinking under another plate. Usually oceanic crust, which is dense, is subducted under continental crust, which is buoyant.

syncline: A structure in which rock layers are folded more or less into a U shape.

Taconic orogeny: The collision about 460 million years ago between the crustal fragment referred to as the Piedmont terrane and the ancient continent Laurentia.

tannin: Tannic acid; astringent chemicals found in plants that, in areas of sandy soils, give natural bodies of water a tea-colored tint.

tectonic: Refers to forces in the earth that cause plates and smaller blocks of crust to move; also refers to the structures that result from these movements.

terrane: A crustal block that preserves a distinct geologic history that is different from adjoining blocks, which are separated by faults. In the Carolinas, the word is typically used for pieces of crust that may have originated on other continents and were accreted during collisions. Exotic terranes originated on other continents; suspect terranes are of unknown origins.

texture: Often used by geologists to describe the visual characteristics of a rock, such as the size and size range of grains, whether there are layers of any type present, and whether there is variation of these attributes throughout the rock.

theory: A comprehensive and widely accepted explanation that is supported by a considerable body of evidence and has repeatedly been confirmed by observation and experimentation; e.g., the theory of gravity, the theory of evolution.

thrust fault: A fault that results from crustal shortening (as in a continental collision). The fracture is typically low angle, sometimes almost horizontal, and one block of rock has moved up and over another. Thrust faults are commonly found at convergent plate boundaries.

topography: The contour and shape of the land.

transform plate boundary: A boundary between two plates that are moving horizontally past one another.

Triassic basin: A rift basin that formed when Pangea rifted during the Triassic. Triassic basins are found all along the east coast of North America and the west coast of Africa. *See also* rift basin.

troy ounce: 31.103 grams. *See also* avoirdupois ounce.

ultramafic: Refers to rocks containing iron-magnesium silicates with even less silica than mafic rocks. Much of the earth's mantle is made of ultramafic rocks.

unconformity: A surface, usually caused by erosion, between rock layers of different ages, signifying a gap in time.

viscosity: The internal properties of a liquid that affect how slowly or quickly it flows. High-viscosity fluids flow more slowly than low-viscosity fluids.

volatiles: The parts of magma that readily vaporize, such as water and carbon dioxide.

volcanic breccia: A rock composed of angular ejecta (rocks ejected from a volcano) in a fine-grained matrix of volcanic ash and fragments.

volcano: A place in the earth's crust where molten magma erupts as lava, gas, and ash; also refers to the mountain, usually made of cooled lava and ash, that is present there.

water table: The surface below which the ground is saturated with water. In soils, sediments, and sedimentary rocks, fractures and pore spaces between the sediments are filled with water; in nonporous (metamorphic and igneous) rock, fractures in the rock are filled with water.

weathered: Refers to a rock surface that has been exposed to the elements for long enough that it has a different texture and/or color than a fresh surface. Changes may be caused by chemical weathering of minerals (e.g., feldspar to clay), oxidation and rust staining, plant and lichen growth, and dirt.

weathering: The process by which rocks are broken into sediments; may be chemical (e.g., the effect of acidic groundwater) or mechanical (e.g., the impact of wind).

ADDITIONAL RESOURCES

Maps

Dantzler, John, and John Clark. *Hiking South Carolina.* Helena, Mont.: Falcon, 1998.
De Hart, Allen. *Hiking South Carolina Trails.* Old Saybrook, Conn.: Globe Pequot Press, 1998.
———. *North Carolina Hiking Trails.* 3d ed. Boston: Appalachian Mountain Club Books, 1996.
The United States Geological Survey publishes topographic maps. Call 1-800-USA-MAPS (1-800-872-6277) or log onto <http://store.usgs.gov>. Most outdoor stores also carry the maps.

Rock, Mineral, and Fossil Books

Carter, J. G., P. E. Gallagher, R. Enos Valone, and T. J. Rossbach. *Fossil Collecting in North Carolina.* Bulletin 89. Raleigh: North Carolina Geological Survey, 1988.
Chesterman, Charles W. *The Audubon Society Field Guide to North American Rocks and Minerals.* New York: Alfred A. Knopf, 1978.
Pough, Frederick H. *Rocks and Minerals.* Peterson Field Guides. Boston: Houghton Mifflin, 1988.
Streeter, Michael. *A Rockhounding Guide to North Carolina's Blue Ridge Mountains.* Almond, N.C.: Milestone Press, 2003.

Other Books of Interest

Bartram, William. *Travels of William Bartram.* Edited by Mark Van Doren. New York: Dover Publications, 1955. (Originally published as *Travels through North & South Carolina, Georgia, East & West Florida* in 1791.)
Beyers, Fred. *North Carolina, the Years before Man: A Geologic History.* Durham: Carolina Academic Press, 1991.
Biggs, Walter C., Jr., and James F. Parnell. *State Parks of North Carolina.* Winston-Salem: John F. Blair, 1989.
Carpenter, P. Albert, III. *Gold in North Carolina.* Information Circular 29. Raleigh: North Carolina Geological Survey, 1993.
———, ed. *A Geologic Guide to North Carolina's State Parks.* North Carolina Geological Survey Bulletin 91. Raleigh: North Carolina Geological Survey, 1989.
Daniel, I. Randolph, Jr. *Hardaway Revisited: Early Archaic Settlement in the Southeast.* Tuscaloosa: University of Alabama Press, 1998.

Earley, Lawrence S. *Looking for Longleaf: The Fall and Rise of an American Forest*. Chapel Hill: University of North Carolina Press, 2004.

Frankenberg, Dirk. *The Nature of North Carolina's Southern Coast: Barrier Islands, Coastal Waters, and Wetlands*. Chapel Hill: University of North Carolina Press, 1997.

———. *The Nature of the Outer Banks*. Chapel Hill: University of North Carolina Press, 1995.

———, ed. *Exploring North Carolina's Natural Areas: Parks, Nature Preserves, and Hiking Trails*. Chapel Hill: University of North Carolina Press, 2000.

Gohdes, Clarence. *Scuppernong: North Carolina's Grape and Its Wines*. Durham: Duke University Press, 1982. (Contains information about Medoc Vineyards.)

Horton, J. W., and V. A. Zullo, eds. *The Geology of the Carolinas*. Knoxville: University of Tennessee Press, 1991. (Very technical; not for a general audience.)

Jones, H. G., ed. *Sketches in North Carolina, USA, 1872 to 1878: Vineyard Scenes by Mortimer O. Heath*. Raleigh: Division of Archives and History, 2001. (Contains sketches and watercolors of Medoc Vineyards.)

Knapp, Richard F., and Brent D. Glass. *Gold Mining in North Carolina: A Bicentennial History*. Raleigh: Division of Archives and History, 1999.

Lawson, John. *A New Voyage to Carolina*. Chapel Hill: University of North Carolina Press, 1967. (Originally published in 1709.)

Lennon, G., W. J. Neal, D. M. Bush, O. H. Pilkey, M. Stutz, and J. Bullock. *Living with the South Carolina Coast*. Durham: Duke University Press, 1996.

Lyell, Charles. *Travels in North America, in the Years 1841–2: With Geological Observations on the United States, Canada, and Nova Scotia*. New York: J. Wiley, 1852.

Lynch, Ida Phillips. *North Carolina Afield: A Guide to Nature Conservancy Projects in North Carolina*. Durham: North Carolina Chapter of The Nature Conservancy, 2002.

Murphy, Carolyn Hanna. *Carolina Rocks! The Geology of South Carolina*. Orangeburg, S.C.: Sandlapper Publishing, 1995.

Orr, Douglas M., Jr., and Alfred W. Stuart, eds. *The North Carolina Atlas: Portrait for a New Century*. Chapel Hill: University of North Carolina Press, 2000.

Peters, K. E., and R. H. Herrmann, eds. *First-Hand Observations of the Charleston Earthquake of August 31, 1886, and Other Earthquake Materials*. Bulletin 41. Columbia: South Carolina Geological Survey, 1986.

Pilkey, Orrin H., Jr., William J. Neal, Orrin H. Pilkey, Sr., and Stanley R. Riggs. *From Currituck to Calabash: Living with North Carolina's Barrier Islands*. 2d ed. Durham: Duke University Press, 1980.

Pilkey, Orrin H., Tracy Monegan Rice, and William J. Neal. *How to Read a North Carolina Beach: Bubble Holes, Barking Sands, and Rippled Runnels*. Chapel Hill: University of North Carolina Press, 2004.

Riggs, Stanley R., and Dorothea V. Ames. *Drowning the North Carolina Coast*. Raleigh: North Carolina Sea Grant, 2003.

Schwarzkopf, S. Kent. *A History of Mt. Mitchell and the Black Mountains: Exploration, Development, and Preservation*. Raleigh: Division of Archives and History, North Carolina Department of Cultural Resources, 1985.

Silver, Timothy. *Mount Mitchell and the Black Mountains: An Environmental History of the Highest Peaks in Eastern America*. Chapel Hill: University of North Carolina Press, 2003.

Visvanathan, T. R. *Earthquakes in South Carolina: 1698–1975*. Bulletin 40. Columbia: South Carolina Geological Survey, 1980.

Ward, Trawick H., and R. P. Stephen Davis, Jr. *Time before History: The Archaeology of North Carolina*. Chapel Hill: University of North Carolina Press, 1999.

Wells, B. W. *The Natural Gardens of North Carolina*. Chapel Hill: University of North Carolina Press, 1932. (A revised edition was published by UNC Press in 2002.)

Wooten, Richard M., Mark W. Carter, and Carl E. Merschat. *Geology of Gorges State Park, Transylvania County, North Carolina*. Information Circular 31. Raleigh: North Carolina Geological Survey, 2003.

INDEX

Page numbers in italics refer to illustrations. Locators beginning with "Pl." refer to color plates.

quartzite, 13, 138, *139*, 240; in sand dunes, 240–41, *242*, *243*; in sandstone, *10*, 240–41; in Triassic sediments, 160

Crowders Mountain, N.C., 83, 121, 154

Crowders Mountain State Park, N.C., *46*, 121–26

Crust: composition of, 19; response to continental collisions, 21, 37, 52–53, 72, 77, 83, 187, 192; response to continental rifting, 42, 71, 84, 104; types and density, 19, 43. *See also* Continental crust; Oceanic crust; Plates

Crystals: nucleation of, 98, 113; origins of, 6–7

Cut banks, 203

Cypress: ancient stumps at Flanner Beach, 232, 233, *233*, 235–36; in Carolina bays, 224, 225; old-growth, 205

Dacite, 143

Dams: on Cape Fear River, 180; negative effects of, 202, 250, 252; on Roanoke River, 201–2; on Yadkin River, 148

Dan River, 137, 199

Dan River basin, 40, 158, *159*

Darwin, Charles, 220

Deep River basin, 40, 158, *159*, 160–61

Deltas, *217*, 218

Deposition: environment of, 8–9, 232; in present-day Carolinas, 5

Devil's Gut, N.C., 205

Devonian period, 25, 27, *28*

Diabase: described, 40, 156, 158–59, 194; near Forty Acre Rock, 194; at Museum of Life and Science, 156–59, *157*; origins of, 40, 156–58, 194; at Penny's Bend, 159–60, *161*; structures of, 40, 158, 194

Diamonds, 175, 176. *See also* Gems

Dikes, 40, 158, 194

Dinosaurs: Carolina fossil displays of, 170; in Carolinas, 2; extinction of, 27. *See also* Fossils

Diorite: described, *11*, 12, 164; at Landsford Canal, 164–65, *165*, *166*, *167*; origins of, 164

Divergent plate boundaries: active today, 20, 40, 157–58; Carolinas' occupation of, 31; crustal response to, 20; described, 20, *21*;

faults associated with, 15; and igneous rock formation, 10, 12. *See also* Continental rifting; Midocean ridges; Rift basins

Dorchester, Colonial, S.C., *46*, 260–66

Drainage basin: defined, 199; of Roanoke River, 199, *201*, 206

Dredging, 247, 249

Drum Inlet, N.C., 249, *251*

Dunes. *See* Sand dunes

DuPont State Forest, N.C., *46*, 56–61

Durham subbasin, 40, 158, *159*

Earth: age of, 30; population of, 3

Earthquakes: Alaskan (1964), 21; in California, 265; potential for in Carolinas, 17, 265–66; causes of, 20, 21, 22; Charleston (1886), 31, 260–66; Chilean (1960), 21; measuring, 265; most powerful worldwide, 20, 21, 265; and subsurface arches, 257; Sumatra-Andaman (2004), 21, 265

Eastern Continental Divide, 4, 140

Eclogite, 24–25

Emeralds: on display, 170, 176, Pl. 10, Pl. 11; largest Carolina, 176; origins of, 89, 175, 176. *See also* Gems

Emerald Village, N.C., 89

Eno River, 151, 159–60, *161*, 163

Environment of deposition, 8–9, 232

Eocene epoch, *28*, 220

Erosion: as agent of geologic change, 1, 3, 5; causes of, 1; dams contributing to, 202; differential, 121, 124; mountains resistant to, 4, 83, 94, 123–24, 136, 144, 152; in present-day Carolinas, 5; and retreat of Blue Ridge escarpment, 42, 104; in soil-covered areas, 94–95; of tectonic windows, 72, *73*, 79; uncovering metamorphic rocks through, 14, 132. *See also* Weathering

Erwin, N.C., 4, 180

Escarpments. *See* Blue Ridge escarpment

Estuaries, 5

Eurasian plate, 20, *20*, 22

Evaporites, 7–8, 9

Exfoliation: described, 92, 115, 191; at Forty Acre Rock, 191; at South Mountains State Park, 115, *116*; at Stone Mountain, 92, *92*

Garnets: as clue to metamorphic rock, 12, 13, Pl. 2, Pl. 3; in eclogite, 24; as semiprecious gem, 176

Gems: as clues to metamorphic rock, 12; defined, 175; on display, 170, 176, Pl. 10, Pl. 11; North Carolina known for, 175; origins of, 175–76; precious, 175–76; semiprecious, 176; tourist mining attractions for, 89, 176. *See also* Diamonds; Emeralds; Garnets; Rubies; Sapphires

Geochronology, 29

Geologic change, 1

Geologic time: relating to human terms, 29–30; scale, *28*; ways of measuring, 27–29. *See also* Carolinas' geologic time line

Geology. *See* Carolinas' geology

Geothermal wells, 256–57

Gibbes, Mount, N.C., 81, *87*

Glaciation: in Carolinas, 2, 35; global, 2, 35; and sea level changes, 41, 218, 234

Glaciers: melting of, 218, 234, 235, 236; sediment transport by, 8

Glassy Mountain, S.C., 4

Global Positioning System (GPS), 23

Global tectonics, 19, 22–23. *See also* Plate tectonics

Global warming: during Cretaceous period, 41–42, 104–5, 218; during Rodinia rifting, 35; predictions for, 236; present-day, 234, 250–51

Gneiss: Blowing Rock, 74; at Caesars Head and Table Rock, 105–8, *106*, *107*; at Chimney Rock, 49–52, *50*, *53*, *53*, 54; described, 49, 57, 62–64, 82, 105; granitic, 51–52, 57, 105–6; heterogeneous, 62; at Mount Mitchell, 82; at Raven Rock, 180–82, *181*; Toxaway, 109, 110; at Whiteside Mountain, 62–64, *65*; at Woodall Shoals, 98, 100

Gold: density of, 128–29; discovery of in California, 131; discovery and mining of in Carolinas, 127–31, 133, Pl. 7, Pl. 8; fool's, 132, 188; hydrothermal deposits of, 132; origins of, 125, 131–32; and Reed Gold Mine, *128*, 131, 133–34

Gold Hill, N.C., 130, 132

Gondwana: ancient terranes comprising, *34*; collision with Laurentia, 39; modern continents comprising, 24, 35, 52; origins of Carolina terrane in, 23–24

Gondwanan terranes: Charlotte terrane originating in, 124, 154, 165; geologic maps of, Pl. 4, Pl. 5; movements of, 36–39, *37*, *38*; origins of, 36

Gorges State Park, N.C., 109–10

GPS (Global Positioning System), 23

Grains: coarse, 49; in igneous rocks, 10–12, *11*, 156, 190; in metamorphic rocks, 13, 62, 99; in sedimentary rocks, 7–9, 70; windblown, 9, 239. *See also* Sediments

Grandfather Mountain, N.C.: conglomerate at, 33, 68–73, *71*; Elisha Mitchell's visit to, 85; field trip, *46*, 68–74, *69*; tectonic window at, 72–73, *73*, 79

Granite: Caesars Head, 57, 105–6; Castalia, 188, 193; composition of, 90; described, 106, 190; erosive forces on, 94–95, 144, 191–92; Forty Acre Rock, 190–93, *191*, *193*; Liberty Hill, 188, 193; at Medoc Mountain, 186–88, *187*, 193; metamorphosed, 62–65, 75, 76, 77, *78*, 105–6, 119; Mount Airy, 39, 95–96, 187, 192; origins of, 11–12, 34, 39, 51–52, 57, 105, 187–88, 192–93; Pageland, 192–93; Rolesville, 187, 193; Sims, 188, 193, 254; soil formation from, 90–91, 192; Stone Mountain, 39, 90–95, *92*, 187–88, 192; Table Rock, 57, 105–6; Toluca, 119; Whiteside, 62–65; xenoliths in, 193, *193*

Grassy Creek, N.C., 56

Grassy Creek Falls, N.C., 60

Great Rift Valley, Africa, 2, 20

Great Salt Lake, Utah, 9

Greenhouse warming. *See* Global warming

Grenville orogeny: described, 33; on geologic time scale, *28*; and Rodinia reconstruction, 33, *34*; and Toxaway gneiss, 109, 110

Groundwater, 229–30, 255

Grus, 90–91

Gypsum, 7

Haile Mine, 130, 133

Halite, 7–8

Hanging Rock, N.C., 83, 136

Hanging Rock State Park, N.C., 137, 139, 142
Hardaway archaeological site, 145
Harney Peak, S.D., 81
Hatteras, N.C., 249
Hatteras Inlet, N.C., 247, 249, *251*
Henderson gneiss, 49–52, *50*, 53, *53*, 54
Henry's Knob, S.C., 125
Hess, Harry, 19
Hiddenite, N.C., 176
Hiddenite (mineral), 176
High Falls, N.C., 56, 57, 59, *59*
High Shoals Falls, N.C., 113, *114*, 115–17
Himalayas, 21, 22, 27
Hooker Falls, N.C., 56–57, *57*
Horne Creek Living Historical Farm, N.C., 142
Hyco River, 199
Hydrothermal activity, 124, 125, 131–32, 154

Iapetus Ocean: origins of, 35; sand in
    Carolina rocks, 35, 76–77, 137; Taconic ac-
    cretionary wedge origins in, 35–36, 52, *66*,
    84, 99–100
Ice ages: in Carolinas' geologic history, 2, 41,
    236, 255; climate changes since last one,
    234, 250–51; and plant distribution, 139
Igneous rocks: geologic processes revealed in,
    17; grain size characteristics of, 10–12, *11*,
    156, 190; mineral clues in, 11–12; nucleation
    of crystals in, 113; origins of, 6–7, 10–11,
    66, 158, 164, 194; plutonic, 11; volcanic, 11.
    See also Andesite; Basalt; Dacite; Diabase;
    Diorite; Gabbro; Granite; Rhyolite
Ilmenite, 138, 240
Indian-Australian plate, *20*, 22
Indians. *See* Native inhabitants
Inland seas, 218
Inlets, 247–49, *248*, *249*, 251, *251*
Intracoastal Waterway, 254
Irian Jaya, Papua New Guinea, 2
Iron oxide, 208
Isacks, Bryan, 19, 22–23

Jacob Fork River, 115, 117
Jetties, 247–48, 252
Jockey's Ridge State Park, N.C., *46*, 138,
    238–46, *239*

Joints: as a plane of rock weakness, 56–57, 68,
    71, 95, 117; at Caesars Head, 108; defined,
    108; at DuPont State Forest, 56–57; at
    Grandfather Mountain, 68, *71*; at High
    Shoals Falls, 117, *118*; origins of, 117
Jonesboro normal fault, 158
Jones Lake, N.C., 224, *225*, 226–30, *226*
Jones Lake State Park, N.C., *46*, 224–31

Kerr Lake, N.C., 201, 202
Kill Devil Hill, N.C., 238, 246
Kings Mountain, N.C., 126
Kings Mountain belt, 124
Kings Mountain National Military Park, S.C.,
    126
Kings Mountain State Park, S.C., 126
Kuhn, Thomas, 23
Kure Beach, N.C., 254
Kyanite, 9; commercial uses for, 125; composi-
    tion of, 13, 124, 153–54, 175; at Crowders
    Mountain, 121–24, *123*; described, 82, *123*,
    125; erosion resistance of, 83, 84, 94, 123,
    153; at Mount Mitchell, 82–85, *83*; origins
    of, 13, 123, 124, 154, 175

Lake Gaston, N.C., 202
Lake Marion, S.C., 221
Lake Waccamaw, N.C., 228
Lamont Geological Observatory, 19
Landsford Canal State Park, S.C., *46*,
    164–69
Landslides, 115, 151–52, Pl. 9
Laurentia: colliding with Gondwana, 39;
    Gondwanan terranes colliding with, 36–39,
    38; Piedmont terrane colliding with, 35–36,
    37, 64–65, *66*, 99; as proto–North America,
    35, 52, 84; Western Blue Ridge rocks origi-
    nating in, Pl. 4
Lava, 10. *See also* Magma
Layering. *See* Foliation
Levees, 205
Lévi-Strauss, Claude, xiv
Liberty Hill granite, 188, 193
Lignite, 236
Limestone: cave formations in, 255; clues to
    origins of, 9; depositional environment of,

Pegmatite: described, 66, 89, 175; at Emerald Village, 89; and gemstone formation, 89, 175; nucleation of crystals in, 98, 113; origins of, 66, 89, 98; at South Mountains State Park, 113–15; at Whiteside Mountain, 66; at Woodall Shoals, 98

Penny's Bend, N.C., 159–60, *161*, 163

Peregrine falcons, 66–67

Peri-Gondwanan terranes. *See* Gondwanan terranes

Phyllite, 62, 152

Physiographic provinces of Carolinas, 3–5, Pl. 1

Piedmont: ancient Appalachians in, 84; Fall Zone boundary of, 4, 178, Pl. 1; physiographic province of, 3–4; sea level fluctuations in, 2, 210; as source of Carolina beach sand, 250; topography of, 139–40

Piedmont terrane: on Carolina geologic map, Pl. 4; origins of, 35–36, *37*, 99; sillimanite abundance in, 154; subduction flip under, 64–65, *66*, 105. *See also* Taconic orogeny

Pig Pen Bluff, N.C., 83

Pilot Mountain, N.C.: elevation of, 137; erosion resistance of, 83, 136; as monadnock, 4; quartzite at, 35, 79, 136–38, *137*, *139*, 140; tectonic window at, 79, 140–41

Pilot Mountain State Park, N.C., *46*, 135–42

Pinnacle, The, N.C., 121, 125

Placer mining, 127–28, *129*

Plate boundaries: Carolinas' presence at, 31; crustal activity at, *21*; geologic processes at, 19–22, 31, 32; metamorphism at, 12; molten rock production at, 10; relative motion at, 20; types of, 20, *21*. *See also* Convergent plate boundaries; Divergent plate boundaries; Transform plate boundaries

Plates: changing shapes of, 31; crust types in, 19; defined, 19; earth's major, *20*; measuring movement of, 3, 23; velocity of, 27. *See also* *individual plate names*

Plate tectonics: and climate changes, 218, 234; developing and proving theory of, 19–23; driving mechanism of, 25; as engine of geologic change, 1; mechanics of, 19–22; and metamorphic rock formation, 7, 12

Pleistocene epoch, *28*, 254–55

Pliocene epoch, *28*, 203

Plutonic igneous rocks, 11

Plutons: Caesars Head, 57, 105–6; Castalia, 188, 193; defined, 57; Forty Acre Rock, 190–93, *191*, *193*; Liberty Hill, 188, 193; Medoc Mountain, 186–88, *187*, 193; Mount Airy, 39, 95–96, 187, 192; Pageland, 192–93; Rolesville, 187, 193; Sims, 188, 193, 254; Stone Mountain, 39, 90–95, *92*, 187–88, 192; Table Rock, 57, 105–6; Toluca, 119; Whiteside, 62–65

Pocosins, 258

Point bars, 203

Polymorphs, 154

Poor Mountain Formation, 51, 52–53, *52*

Potholes: in DuPont State Forest, 59; origins of, 59, 91; at South Mountains State Park, 117; at Stone Mountain, 91; at Woodall Shoals, 98–99

Principle of superposition, 15, 27–28, 233

Pumpelly's Rule, 99

Pyrite, 132, 188

Pyrophyllite, 153, *153*

Pyroxene, 175

Quarries: Morrow Mountain prehistoric, 143–45, *146*, 147, 148, 149; at Museum of Life and Science, 156, *157*, 158; at Occoneechee Mountain, 151, 153, Pl. 9

Quartz: as common mineral in rocks, 9, 85, Pl. 2; composition of, 84–85, 124; erosion resistance of, 56, 83, 94, 123, 144; origins of, 123, 124, 175, 182; in pegmatite, 113; ratios in gneiss and schist, 82; sand formation from, 250; semiprecious, 176; veins of, 123, 130, 131, 182, Pl. 8

Quartzite: cross-bed formations in, 13, 138, *139*, 240; described, 13, 152; erosion resistance of, 94, 136, 144; kyanite, 123, *123*; at Linville Falls, 76–79, *76*, *77*, *78*; at Occoneechee Mountain, 152, *152*; origins of, 76, 137–38, 182; at Pilot Mountain, 136–38, *137*, *139*, 140, 141; at Raven Rock, 180, 182; streaks in, 78, 138

Radiometric dating, 28–29

Rainbow Banks, 203

Raleigh, N.C., 4, 39

Rapids: on Catawba River, 165, 168; at Fall
Zone, 178

Rauisuchian, 161, *162*

Raven Cliff Falls, S.C., 108

Raven Rock State Park, N.C., *46*, 178–84, *179*

Ravens, 139

Red Sea, 20, *20*, 157–58

Reed Gold Mine, N.C., *46*, 127–34, Pl. 7

Reservoirs, 201–2

Rhyolite: described, 143, 144; Morrow Mountain, 143–47, *145*, *146*, 149; origins of, 11–12,
147

Richter scale, 265

Ridgeway Mine, 133

Rift basins: Grandfather Mountain conglomerate originating in, 33, 72–73; and ocean
formation, 156–58; origins of, 33, 71–72,
156–58; present-day openings of, 20, 71,
157–58; and salt dome formation, 9. *See
also* Triassic basins

Rift-flank uplift, 42, 104–5

Ring of Fire, 19

Ripple marks, 239–40, *242*

Rivers: as agents of geologic change, 1, 3, 5,
40–41, 206; bend dynamics in, 202–3,
219; blackwater, 205; brownwater, 205–6;
cobbles deposited by ancient, 182–83, 217;
and depositional environments, 8–9, 70,
202, 232; elevation loss in, 166; impedi-
ments to sediment transport by, 201–2,
250, 252; velocity dictating sediment size
in, 3, 70, 203, 205, 218, 232; water sources
for, 199. *See also specific river names*

Roan Mountain, N.C., 32, 85

Roanoke Rapids, N.C., 4, 180, 199, 201, 202

Roanoke Rapids Lake, N.C., 202

Roanoke River, *200*, *204*; dams on, 201–2;
drainage basin of, 199, *201*, 206; field trip,
46, 199–207; floodplain of, 203–6

Roanoke River Partners, 205, 207

Rocks: dating, 28–29; heat affecting density of, 104; main types of, 6; oldest in
Carolinas, 32, 74; oldest on earth, 30. *See*

also Igneous rocks; Metamorphic rocks;
Sedimentary rocks

Rockslides, 115, *116*, 117

Rocky Mount, N.C., 4, 180

Rodinia: assembly of (Grenville orogeny),
2, *28*, 33; reconstruction from geologic
record, 33, *34*; rifting of, 2, 33–35, 71

Rolesville granite, 187, 193

Round Top, N.C., 51

Rubies, 170, 175–76. *See also* Gems

Run Hill, N.C., 245–46, *246*

Rust, 208

Rutile, Pl. 10

Salt domes, 8, 9

Salters Lake, N.C., 226–31, *226*

San Andreas fault, 22

Sand: from ancient delta, *217*; angle of repose
of, 240; cross-bed patterns in, 138, *242*,
243; from Iapetus Ocean in Carolina geology, 35, 76–77, 137; mixture on Carolina
beaches, 250; origins of, 250; quartzite formation from, 76, 137–38, 182; in Sandhills,
210–11

Sand dunes: ancient Sugarloaf, 257–58; composition of, 239; lightning strikes at, 242,
245; and medaño formation, 238, 245–46;
migration of, 242–44, *246*; origins of, 240;
underlying Sandhills, 210; windblown patterns at, 239–41, *241*, *242*, *243*, 244. *See also*
Barrier islands; Beaches

Sandhills: elevation of, 4; location of, 208, *210*;
and longleaf pine habitat, 211–14; origins
of, 210–11. *See also* Coastal Plain

Sand Hills State Forest, S.C., 208, 213, 214

Sandstone: cross-bedding in, 9, *10*, 240–41;
depositional environment of, 8; dirty, 115;
origins of, 6, 7; at Sugarloaf Mountain, 208;
Triassic, 160. *See also* Quartzite

Sanford subbasin, 40, 158, *159*, 160

Santee limestone, 220–22

Santee State Park, S.C., *46*, 220–23

Sapphires, 175–76. *See also* Gems

Satellite navigation, 3, 23

Sauratown Mountains, N.C., 136–37, 138, 139,
140

Submarine mountain ranges. *See* Midocean ridges

Subsurface arches, 255–57, *257*

Suffolk scarp, 42, 235, *236*

Sugarloaf Mountain, S.C., *46*, 208–14

Sugarloaf Mountain thrust fault, 51–53

Sugarloaf sand dune, 257–58

Sumatra, 84

Sumatra-Andaman earthquake (2004), *20*, 21, 265

Summerville, S.C., 261, 262

Sumter National Forest, S.C., 97, 101

Supercontinents. *See* Pangea; Rodinia

Superposition, principle of, 15, 27–28, 233

Suspect terranes, 36. *See also* Piedmont terrane

Swamps: ancient at Flanner Beach, 235–36; pocosins, 258; of Roanoke River basin, 203–5

Sykes, Lynn, 19, 22–23

Tabby, 262, *264*

Table Rock Mountain, N.C., 79

Table Rock Plutonic Suite, 57, 105–6

Table Rock State Park, S.C., 105–9; granitic gneiss at, 57, 105–6, *106*, *107*

Taconic orogeny: described, 35–36; and formation of Woodall Shoals, 99–100; on geologic time scale, *28*; and kyanite formation, 84–85; and subduction flip under Piedmont terrane, 64–65, *66*, 105

Tallulah Falls Formation, 109–10

Tannin, 205, 227, 230

Tar River, 218

Tater Top, N.C., 145

Tectonic plates. *See* Plates; Plate tectonics

Tectonic windows: described, 72, 79; Grandfather Mountain, 72–73, *73*, 79; Sauratown Mountain, 79, 140–41

Terminal groins, 247, *249*

Terranes: defined, 23; early belt terminology for, 32; exotic, 24, 154, 182; geologic map of, Pl. 4; suspect, 36. *See also* Carolina terrane; Charlotte terrane; Gondwanan terranes

Thrust faults, 15, *16*; at Chimney Rock, 51–53; crustal movement in, 15, *16*, 37, 53, 72, 77; at

Grandfather Mountain, 72–73, *73*; Linville Falls, 72–73, *73*, 75, 77–80, *78*; numerous in Carolina mountains, 79–80; possible Acadian, 38; at Sauratown Mountains, 140–41. *See also* Faults

Timor, 2

Toluca granite, 119

Tourmaline, Pl. 11

Town Creek Indian Mound State Historic Site, N.C., 150

Toxaway gneiss, 109, 110

Transform plate boundaries: described, *21*, 22; faults associated with, 15

Traversodonts, 161–62

Triassic basins: Carolina locations of, 40, 158, *159*, Pl. 4; fossils found in, 160–62, *162*; halite casts found in, 7–8; and igneous rock formation, 158, 194; origins of, 40, 156–58, 194; sediment deposition in, 33, 40, 71–72, 160–61; valleys as markers for, 158. *See also* Rift basins

Triassic Period, *28*, 40, 156–58, *162*

Trilobites, 24, *25*

Triple Falls, N.C., 56, 57–59, *58*

Tristes Tropiques (Lévi-Strauss), xiv

Trupe, Chuck, 24, 78

Unconformity, 15

Uniformitarianism, 220

University of North Carolina, Chapel Hill, 24, 29, 68, 85, 87, 160–61

Uwharrie meteorite, 170, 172, *172*

Uwharrie Mountains, N.C., 4, 145, 149

Uwharrie River, 148

Valle Crucis, N.C., 35

Valleys: as clue to faults, 16; as clue to Triassic basins, 158

Venus flytraps, 227, 254, 258–59

Volcanic breccia, 147

Volcanic igneous rocks, 11

Volcanism, bimodal, 34

Volcanoes: in accretionary wedge, 64–65, *66*; in Cretaceous period, 218; and hydrothermal gold deposits, 132; and igneous rock formation, 6, 11; as mountain-building

events, 121; origins of, 20, 21, *21*; in Pacific
Ocean, 19, 218; in Piedmont terrane, 65,
66, 105

Wadati, Kiyoo, 19
Wadesboro subbasin, 40, 158, *159*
Wateree River, 148, 165
Waterfalls: Bridal Veil Falls, N.C., 56, 59; in
Fall Zone, 178, 180; Grassy Creek Falls,
N.C., 60; High Falls, N.C., 56, 57, 59, *59*;
High Shoals Falls, N.C., 113, *114*, 115–17;
Hooker Falls, N.C., 56–57, *57*; Linville Falls,
N.C., 75–80, *76*, *78*; Northington Falls,
N.C., 180, 182; overhangs in, 60; Raven Cliff
Falls, S.C., 108; Smylie's Falls, N.C., 180;
Stone Mountain Falls, N.C., 92, *93*; Triple
Falls, N.C., 56, 57–59, *58*; Whitewater Falls,
N.C., 110, Pl. 6; Wintergreen Falls, N.C., 60
Water table, 229–30, *229*
Weathering: chemical, 85, 90, 91, 180, 191–92,
191; differential, 108; from flowing water, 91,
91; and formation of granite domes, 94–95;
mechanical (exfoliation), 92, *92*, 115, *116*,
191. *See also* Erosion
Weathering pits, 90, 91, 191–92, *191*
Weldon, N.C., 202, 203

Wells, B. W., 213
West Antarctic ice sheet, 235, 236
Weymouth Woods Sandhills Nature
Preserve, N.C., 213
White Lake, N.C., 227–28, *228*, 231
Whiteside Mountain, N.C.: field trip, *46*,
62–67, *63*; granitic gneiss at, 62–65, *65*
Whitewater Falls, N.C., 110, Pl. 6
Willard, Rod, 24
Wind: abrasion of grains by, 9, 239; dune
sculpting by, 238–42, *241*, *242*, *243*, *244*;
sediment sorting by, 8, 239
Wind shadows, 240, *241*
Wintergreen Falls, N.C., 60
Woodall Shoals, S.C., *46*, 97–101, *98*
Woodstock fault, 264–65
Wright brothers, xiii, 238
Wright Brothers Memorial, 96, 246

Xenoliths, 193, *193*

Yadkin River, 140, 148
Yellowstone National Park, 132
Yosemite National Park, 92, 115

Zircon, 30